The L&N Railroad
in the Civil War

ALSO BY DAN LEE

Kentuckian in Blue: A Biography of Major General Lovell Harrison Rousseau (McFarland, 2010)

The L&N Railroad in the Civil War

A Vital North-South Link and the Struggle to Control It

DAN LEE

McFarland & Company, Inc., Publishers
Jefferson, North Carolina, and London

LIBRARY OF CONGRESS CATALOGUING-IN-PUBLICATION DATA

Lee, Dan, 1954–
 The L&N Railroad in the Civil War : a vital north-south link and the struggle to control it / Dan Lee.
  p.   cm.
 Includes bibliographical references and index.

 ISBN 978-0-7864-6157-8
 softcover : 50# alkaline paper ∞

 1. United States — History — Civil War, 1861–1865 — Transportation. 2. Railroads and state — United States — History — 19th century. 3. Railroads — Military aspects — United States — History — 19th century. 4. United States. Army — Transportation — History — 19th century. 5. Confederate States of America. Army — Transportation. 6. Industrial mobilization — United States — History — 19th century. 7. Louisville and Nashville Railroad Company — History — 19th century. 8. United States — Politics and government, 1861–1865. 9. Confederate States of America — Politics and government. 10. Railroads — United States — History — 19th century. 11. Railroads — Confederate States of America — History. I. Title.
 E491.L48   2011
 973.7 — dc22   2010053628

BRITISH LIBRARY CATALOGUING DATA ARE AVAILABLE

© 2011 Dan Lee. All rights reserved

No part of this book may be reproduced or transmitted in any form or by any means, electronic or mechanical, including photocopying or recording, or by any information storage and retrieval system, without permission in writing from the publisher.

Front cover: The L&N locomotive *Quigley* (Louisville and Nashville Railroad Records, University of Louisville Archives and Records Center, Louisville, Kentucky)

Manufactured in the United States of America

McFarland & Company, Inc., Publishers
 Box 611, Jefferson, North Carolina 28640
  www.mcfarlandpub.com

To the memory of Joseph Leslie Lee

Table of Contents

Acknowledgments	ix
Preface	1
Introduction	5
1 — The Journey Begins, 1850–1860	11
2 — The End of Peace, 1860–1861	17
3 — The Federals Advance	27
4 — The First Drops of Blood Are Drawn	33
5 — The Stalemate Is Broken	42
6 — On to Nashville	53
7 — The Year of the Thunderbolt	60
8 — Confederate Kentucky?	76
9 — Destination Louisville	90
10 — Return of the Thunderbolt	103
11 — Guerrillas and the Great Raid	124
12 — A World without Morgan	138
13 — The Uneasy Interlude, 1864	147
14 — Hell Boils Over	163
15 — The Last Guerrilla	180
Afterword	189
Chapter Notes	193
Bibliography	199
Index	207

Acknowledgments

It is not an entirely original thought to say that a book is like a child. It is conceived, fretted over, brought to maturity, and then sent forth into a competitive world to succeed or fail. It cannot be snatched back. Its successes are a source of continuing pride; its mistakes are an embarrassment. And, if it takes a village to raise a child, the same might be said of the mighty tribe of contributors who help nurture a book to its full development.

From that group there are always a few who must be singled out for the generosity of their help. In the case of this book, the author wishes to thank Mr. Jim Holmberg, Ms. Sarah-Jane Poindexter, and Mr. Jacob Lee of the Filson Historical Society, Louisville, Kentucky. Also deserving of thanks is Ms. Carrie Daniels, University Archives and Records Center, University of Louisville.

Finally, the author wishes to thanks his wife, Linda Akins Lee, for her continual patience and computer expertise.

When I hear the iron horse make the hills echo with his snort like thunder, shaking the earth with his feet, and breathing fire and smoke from his nostrils ... it seems to me as if the earth had got a race now worthy to inhabit it. If all were as it seems, and men made the elements their servants for noble ends! If the cloud that hangs over the engine were the perspiration of heroic deeds, or as beneficent as that which floats over the farmer's fields, then the elements and Nature herself would cheerfully accompany men on their errands and be their escort.

— Henry David Thoreau in Walden

Preface

The story of the Louisville & Nashville Railroad during the Civil War has an unexpected resonance for the 21st century American. Consider this.

It was a time of terror. The suffering of the civilian population was considerable, but the military suffered more. The army was stretched almost to its limit, fighting in two theaters. The country was divided about how to proceed as the body count continued to grow, year after year.

More than ever before, the federal government relied upon private contractors to help prosecute the war. It was a controversial alliance, a calculated risk on the part of the government to entrust so much of national defense to private interests. The titans who led private industry were not accountable to the people and answered to no one but their stockholders. One corporation in particular had powerful friends in the government and seemed to receive especially lucrative considerations. It occupied the morally ambiguous middle ground between patriotism and profit.

Certainly, it sounds like a familiar description of modern America, but the year was 1864.

• • •

The L&N was a state-of-the-art transportation system that had the added attraction of being one of the very few American railroads that ran from north to south. As such, it was uniquely valuable to the federal government. James Guthrie, president of the L&N, quickly divined the fact and used it ruthlessly to pressure the government into concessions that were the envy of other railroads. Guthrie was a double-rectified capitalist whose faith was uncorrupted by the weakening influence of patriotism.

Money and power were Guthrie's Janus-faced idol, and the L&N directors were disciples in adoration.

There were those, like Governor Andrew Johnson, who considered Guthrie's wartime actions the equivalent of extortion. Certainly, the officers in the field recognized that the railroad and its grasping president were not serving the national interest to the extent that they might, if their loyalty were not divided between the dollar and military demands. They complained repeatedly to the Lincoln administration, but Guthrie was playing a brutally hard game, and he yielded no ground. Neither did the government force him to. Because of the value of the L&N to the military objectives in the West (and also, perhaps, because of the inside influence of Assistant Secretary of War Thomas A. Scott, who in civilian life was railroad executive) the government turned an indulgent eye to all but Guthrie's most egregious practices, and the L&N made greater net profits each year of the war.

Increasing profits was precisely the goal of Guthrie and company, and in truth, from the corporate point of view, it did not really matter if the North won the war or not. The L&N would endure. Guthrie seemed to prefer the Union, to a point, but in the spring of 1861, he happily traded with both sides until a circuit court judge enforced a government embargo. At the conclusion of the conflict, if the South successfully seceded, the L&N would profit greatly by being an international railroad, crossing the border between Federal Kentucky and Confederate Tennessee.

James Guthrie. Louisville & Nashville Railroad Records, University of Louisville Archives and Records Center, Louisville, Kentucky.

Yet, almost in spite of the profiteering leadership of Guthrie and his board of directors, the L&N did play a significant role in the ultimate Union victory. Recognizing its strategic importance, the

Confederates at first seized all of it that they could. The Federals responded with a vigorous push south along the L&N and wrenched it from Southern control. From that time on, with the main stem and its branches solidly within Union lines, the L&N pumped a continual stream of supplies to the advancing Federal armies. To the Rebels, the L&N presented an intolerable menace, and they devoted much effort and manpower to its destruction. Armies contended along its length, and when the armies were gone, partisan rangers and dreaded guerrillas like Ellis Harper, Sue Mundy, and Henry C. Magruder prowled the L&N, trying to cripple the ability of the North to supply first Buell, then Rosecrans, Sherman and Thomas. Thus, though it was a narrow corridor, the L&N became a trail marked with fire and blood. Fought over from end to end and often vandalized, the L&N endured and emerged at war's end poised to become one of the major corporations of the New South.

The war might arguably have ended much sooner if the L&N had performed at full capacity on behalf of the Union army in Tennessee and Georgia. Yet the outcome of the war might have been altogether different without the vital service it provided, though it was sluggish at times and came at a very high price.

The following is the history of the Louisville & Nashville Railroad and the men who fought to control it during the War Between the States.

Introduction

Late in the night of September 23, 1863, at the War Department in Washington, D.C., an extraordinary meeting took place among some high officials of the Lincoln administration. In the hot, yellow light of the hissing gas jets, Secretary of State Edwin M. Stanton could see through the tiny lenses of his eyeglasses the men he had invited to his office: President Lincoln, General-in-Chief Henry W. Halleck, Secretary of the Treasury Salmon P. Chase, Secretary of State William H. Seward, and various aides and advisors. There was a disaster brewing in the Western Theater, and it was the responsibility of these men to prevent it.

Major General William S. Rosecrans, having seen his army broken apart at Chickamauga on September 20, was now besieged with its battered remnants in Chattanooga. The Rebel general Braxton Bragg held Lookout Mountain and Missionary Ridge and was throwing shells from the heights down among the Yankees, but a quieter menace threatened the existence of the Army of the Cumberland. Bragg's Confederates controlled all of the supply lines into Chattanooga, save one fragile mountain trail, and the Federals were starving. Stanton's man on the scene, Charles A. Dana, estimated that Rosecrans' three corps would be finished before mid–October unless help could be hurried to them.

General Ambrose Burnside was in Knoxville with elements of the Army of the Ohio, but he showed a decided reluctance to leave his East Tennessee base, and even if he overcame his mulish resistance to helping Rosecrans, he could not be in Chattanooga in less than ten days. With General William T. Sherman, the prospect of quick help for Rosecrans was even more remote. Sherman was en route, marching east along the route of the Memphis & Charleston Railroad, but was still three hundred miles away.

To Stanton, it seemed that the only solution was a radical one: to detach the 11th and 12th Corps of Major General George Gordon Meade's Army of the Potomac and send them to Rosecrans by rail, a demanding trip of over 1,200 miles.

There were immediate objections. Lincoln pointed out that Meade could not attack General Lee with an army diminished by the loss of two corps. Stanton replied that he saw no sign that General Meade had any intentions of attacking Lee. Neither did he think that Lee, weakened after the battle at Gettysburg, would attack Meade. General Halleck objected that Meade's troops could not arrive at Chattanooga in less than forty days and probably more like sixty days. Stanton, though, had done his homework. He had been in communication with General Jeremiah T. Boyle, commander of the District of Kentucky, about the condition of the Louisville & Nashville Railroad, the central link in the plan. Boyle had confidently informed Stanton, "The Louisville and Nashville Railroad can transport 3000 men daily, using whole stock for the purpose. The company have [sic] 30 passenger cars, 200 box and rack cars, 125 flat cars; besides these, Adams Express has 20 cars." Satisfied with Boyle's answers, Stanton contended that the troop movement could be accomplished in five days.[1]

Five days! An astonished Lincoln weighed in again. Having been burdened for three years with generals who had the "slows," the president was skeptical of promises of quick maneuvers by the army. He said he doubted that the proposed force could even get to Washington in five days, much less Chattanooga. He offered to bet Stanton. Stanton refused the wager but held firm. He pointed out that confiscated bales of cotton were shipped north from Chattanooga by rail and arrived in five days' time; the same could be done with soldiers headed in the opposite direction.

The discussion dragged on. Chase and Seward were persuaded that Stanton's plan could be made to work. Finally, the others conceded that it was worth the effort. The meeting broke up in the wee hours of September 24. Within a half-hour Stanton was wiring instructions to General Meade in the field to get General Oliver O. Howard's 11th Corps and General Henry W. Slocum's 12th Corps in motion. Then Stanton telegraphed his operative in Chattanooga, Charles Dana, that troops would be in Nashville within a week "with orders to push on immediately wherever General Rosecrans' wants them." Stanton dispatched Assistant Secretary of War Thomas A. Scott to Louisville to observe and facilitate the troop movement.[2]

On the morning of September 27, the first troops left Washington,

D.C., and by the afternoon of September 28 two corps totaling 23,000 soldiers, all under the command of Major General Joseph Hooker, were on their way to the Western Theater.

It was a complicated movement. The Baltimore & Ohio Railroad carried the "Potomacs" from the capital city to Benwood, West Virginia, on the Ohio River. The Central Ohio took them on to Indianapolis. The next leg was on the Jeffersonville, Madison, & Indianapolis Railroad south to the Ohio River opposite Louisville. There was no railroad bridge at Louisville, and the men had to cross the Ohio River on pontoon bridges made of coal barges. From Louisville, the Northern boys took the L&N to Nashville, and finally, the Nashville & Chattanooga carried them to Bridgeport, Alabama, the railroad terminus closest to Chattanooga.

Aside from a few mishaps, including a couple of collisions between trains in the convoy, a derailment, and an unexpected bottleneck at Indianapolis, which cost several hours of time, the trip was uneventful and more uncomfortable than dangerous. The boys in the passenger cars were the lucky ones; the others rode in boxcars, struggling to keep their balance on hastily erected benches. The boxcars were stuffy and so crowded that a soldier of the 150th New York wryly observed that the "space in the car allowed nearly enough room for each man to breathe in, provided all did not breathe simultaneously." For those who had an interest in breathing, soldiers with axes knocked holes in the sides of the cars for ventilation.[3]

On September 30, the first of the troop trains chugged into Bridgeport. They had made the trip, as Stanton predicted, in less than a week. Within two days, 20,000 troopers had arrived, along with 60 artillery pieces, horses, ammunition, and baggage. Marching to Chattanooga, these men would help open the supply line (the "Cracker Line") that allowed the Army of the Cumberland to survive Bragg's siege and on November 24 would win the "Battle Above the Clouds" on Lookout Mountain to begin the breakout. General Hooker wired Stanton, "You may justly claim the merit of having saved Chattanooga."[4]

It was the railroads that had made it possible. Shelby Foote called this 1863 redeployment by rail "the swiftest of all the mass movements of troops in history." Certainly, it was one of the most efficient. In fact, it was accomplished with so little drama that it was, and has been, overlooked. One almost wishes that the event had been more difficult, so that in the tradition of those ever-inspiring sagas of hardships overcome and successes won, it would be recognized as the remarkable thing that it was. For something really had changed. Troops had moved by train before but nothing of this magnitude and speed. Distance was dissolved now that man had learned to use the railroad as a tool of war.[5]

• • •

War unleashes the mightiest of man's forces, and the side that can marshal the most of those forces is the side that wins. The basic three forces are those of the government, of the military, and of industry. The Civil War demonstrated the role each has to play. The Union had them all in sufficiency, if not in abundance. Conversely, the South had an inadequacy of each — a government that had to be birthed on the run, a military that was poorly armed with too few weapons and most of them imported because of the Confederacy's weak, almost nonexistent, industrial base. The South had tremendous spirit, but spirit was not enough.

The Southern point of view had always been that since cotton was such a beneficent king, there was no need to develop a system of manufactories, and since the Almighty had blessed the South with such a complete web of navigable rivers, there was no need to spend public funds to create a man-made transportation system.

It was not until late — too late — in the antebellum period that the South was caught up in the Northern and Midwestern fascination with railroads. Robert C. Black wrote that, in the late 1850s, "everywhere through Dixie the railroad mania ran at full tide. During the final antebellum year the forests of the Appalachians swarmed with surveyors and engineers as the states of the Atlantic seaboard strove to burst through their ancient mountain barriers." But then Black emphasized a pertinent fact: "The construction boom had not produced in the Southern States a *system* of iron rails."[6]

So it was that, at the beginning of the war, the North had more than double the number of miles of track than the South. Furthermore, the interstate tracks in the North tended to be uniform in gauge (the distance between the rails); the tracks in the South rarely were.

In both regions, the tracks generally ran east to west; few railroads ran north to south. Here was a unique business opportunity, and one that was seized upon by a group of prewar Kentucky investors who, with the state legislature as an ally, created the Louisville & Nashville Railroad Company in 1850. The timing was more fortunate that anyone could have realized. The L&N was conceived as a moneymaker, and it did make many men rich, but its value during the war, as the only major railroad west of the Appalachians that ran between and into the two warring sections, was greater than any calculation measured in dollars and cents. The Louisville historian Robert McDowell quoted Stewart Holbrook as saying in his *The Story of American Railroads*, "The L&N could be rated as a major factor in winning the war, as far as transportation was concerned." McDowell also quoted Robert S. Henry, whose opinion was even stronger than Holbrook's. In *The Story of the Confederacy*, Henry wrote, "The L&N itself was probably the most vital line in the entire nation."[7]

Henry made his evaluation of the L&N with the benefit of hindsight, years after the events of 1861–1865. But North or South, few men who lived through that time could have disagreed with Henry's choice of words. "Vital," Henry said, and vital it proved to be.

1

The Journey Begins, 1850–1860

When Confederate General Simon Bolivar Buckner moved into Bowling Green, Kentucky, with an occupying force on September 18, 1861, he was striking early one of the chords that would resonate through the entire war. What attracted him to the Warren County seat was not the rich farmland rolling away in all directions but rather the central position it occupied on the L&N Railroad. The plan was for Buckner's 4,500 men to hold this point and push north to cripple northern transportation and at the same time prevent any troop movements into the heart of Tennessee by way of the main stem.

Civil War generals were notoriously slow in giving up the Napoleonic tactics they had studied at the West Point. The traditional approach would doom scores of thousands of young men to die in ranked, frontal assaults because the generals could not seem to grasp the deadly innovation of the rifled musket. And it was not only the least able of the general officers who were guilty of this blunder but also the greatest. Robert E. Lee ordered frontal assaults, so did U.S. Grant, so did William T. Sherman.

And yet, somehow, the generals were uncharacteristically quick to realize the importance of railroads, and they fought to deprive the enemy of their use. Some 30 percent of Union forces were assigned to railroad defense. Every theater of war saw railroad destruction as a costly but necessary feature of the struggle, and some men's names became almost synonymous with the prybar and the bonfire.

General William T. Sherman's reputation as the Federal authority in railroad destruction has remained bright down the years. He perfected his technique between Atlanta and Savannah, but there were many others, North and South, who were accomplished in the tactical and strategic destruction of railroads. U.S. Grant doomed the defenders of Vicksburg when he cut their railroad supply line at Jackson, Mississippi. While fighting General Lee in Virginia in 1864, Grant once again focused on railroad destruction as an essential ingredient to victory and threw one raiding party after another toward the railroads that supplied Lee's besieged army at Petersburg. General Grant could not whip them, so he would starve them.

The B&O Railroad in West Virginia was under repeated attack by the partisan gangs led by John H. McNeill and John S. Mosby, and in 1864, the railroad between Montgomery, Alabama, and Atlanta, Georgia, was badly broken up by General Lovell Harrison Rousseau in one of the most successful behind-the-lines operations of the entire war. There were fewer railroad incidents west of the Mississippi because there were fewer railroads, but there were incidents even there. Both Bloody Bill Anderson and General Sterling Price made the Northern Missouri Railroad a special target in the fall of 1864.

The historian John E. Clark pointed out that during the years 1861 to 1865, "every major battle was fought within twenty miles of a railroad or a river port."[1]

Luckily for its citizens, there was no major battle at Bowling Green. General Buckner slipped into the Warren County seat without a fight and found himself in control of the southern half of one of the newest railroads in America.

The Kentucky General Assembly had chartered the Louisville & Nashville Railroad Company on March 5, 1850. The founding document was filled with conditions. Capital stock was initially set at $3,000,000. Shares sold for $100 apiece, and those counties through which the iron road passed could buy as many shares as they could afford, no limit. The president of the railroad and his board of directors could choose the route of the 66-foot-wide right of way, and for those farmers whose land was selected, the county sheriff and a panel of 12 men would "justly and impartially fix the damages which the owner or owners shall sustain by the use and occupation of the said property."[2]

The railroad would enjoy a 30-year monopoly, for the legislature agreed to grant no competing charters, and during these years the L&N would earn "$3^1/_2$ mills per mile for every one hundred pounds of goods, merchandise or property handled provided the distance was over twenty miles and under fifty miles." A moderate rate was also set for persons and livestock.[3]

1—The Journey Begins, 1850–1860

This was the Kentucky charter. A charter also had to be obtained from the legislature of Tennessee. Technically, it passed before the Kentucky charter by about a month, on February 9, 1850; but it was plain that while the Tennesseans were resigned to the inevitability of the railroad, they were not very enthusiastic about it. Concerned that their sister city on the Ohio River would dominate the railroad and by extension the broader economy, the Tennesseans wrote into their charter that construction must begin at both ends simultaneously. Further, the railroad was mandated to run through Gallatin and terminate on the north bank of the Cumberland River across from Nashville. The L&N would not be permitted to invade the city proper. Freight would be offloaded at Edgefield and packed into Nashville by horse-drawn vehicles. This restriction was later lifted.

These technicalities taken care of, surveyors took to the field immediately, south from Louisville and north from Nashville. However, the precise route had not yet been finalized. There were two good ones from which to choose, and it was decided that the choice would be based on which communities in the central reaches of the proposed line pledged the most subscriptions. They had to court the railroad. Local citizens would show their desire to have the L&N by the size of the bond issues they approved.

Louisville took the lead, naturally, and pledged $1,000,000 (increased through the years of construction to more than three times that amount). Hardin County pledged $300,000 and Hart County, $100,000. Warren County promised $300,000, and the city of Bowling Green (after a brief flirtation with the idea of constructing a separate line to Nashville) came through with $1,000,000. Simpson County pledged $100,000. In Tennessee, Sumner and Davidson Counties each put up $300,000, and Robertson County subscribed $200,000.

The route being set on the basis of this show of devotion, the L&N signed a contract in April 1853 with Morton, Seymour and Company, the construction firm that would actually build the railroad for an agreed upon rate of $35,000 per mile. The job was to be finished in 30 months.

By fall, tracks had been laid to Lebanon Junction. Primarily, the work was done by the Irish workers of Morton, Seymour and Company, but this was not entirely the case. Maury Klein wrote, "Much of the grading and other work had been let to farmers along the route, who took their pay in bonds." Not only was this an effective way to attract more laborers, but it conserved the L&N's supply of ready cash.[4]

Most of the L&N ran through gentle country, but just south of

Lebanon Junction, the construction crews faced the first of two serious obstacles along the Kentucky portion of the route, Muldraugh Hill. Slightly misnamed (and often misspelled), Muldraugh Hill was actually a 75-mile-long escarpment oriented northwest to southeast from West Point in Hardin County to Calvary in Marion County and directly athwart the surveyed route. There was no way around it. But going over it was no easy trick either. Muldraugh Hill loomed 500 feet above the valley of the Rolling Fork River, its sides deeply scored by gorges that would have to be conquered by trestlework. The engineers decided to ascend to within 150 feet of the summit and then tunnel through, requiring almost 2,000 feet of blasting and digging through solid limestone. This one short but steep section of railroad would consume over half a million dollars.

The tunnel was such a challenge that the construction crews laid a temporary line to bypass it. The tunnel would not be completed until 1860. Meanwhile, the crews pushed forward into Severns Valley and beyond. The optimistic two-and-a-half-year deadline was forgotten. The tracks reached Elizabethtown, only about 50 miles from Louisville, in June 1858. Beyond Walker's Station (which was renamed Glendale by an L&N construction engineer), an outbreak of cholera struck down scores of Irish workers, but the work did not slow down. The dead were buried in the cemetery of St. Ignatius Catholic Church, and the living shoved forward toward the Hart County line. A few miles beyond, the second great obstacle along the L&N was encountered, the deep valley of the Green River at Munfordville.

By this time, changes had occurred at the L&N. The construction firm of Morton, Seymour and Company was now out of the picture, replaced by Justin, Edsall, and Hawley, who would muscle the road through to completion. There were also changes in the management of the company. The first president, Leven L. Shreve, had been replaced by former governor John LaRue Helm of Elizabethtown. Helm was overseeing the completion of a branch line to Lebanon in Marion County and was watching with interest the short railroad being built from Bardstown in Nelson County to the main stem.* He was vigorously pushing forward a plan to run another branch from Bowling Green to Guthrie, in Logan County on the state line; there, the railroad would link up with a line to Clarksville, Tennessee, and the Clarksville railroad would connect with a third line

---

The Bardstown and Louisville Railroad was completed in 1860 and immediately came under the control of the L&N. In 1864, the B&L went into foreclosure and was bought by the L&N. From that time on, it was officially referred to as the Bardstown Branch. For convenience, it is called by that later name throughout this book.

that was being built north from Memphis. It was an imaginative, costly, and controversial expenditure of funds, but Helm was strong-willed and determined to see it through.

However, the Bowling Green link was a distant dream until the Green River could be crossed. This was the responsibility of another new official of the L&N, the German-born engineer Albert Fink. He had worked for the B&O Railroad until lured away in 1857 by President Helm. Helm must have been surprised when Fink first walked into his office, for the German stood six feet seven inches tall. His first job for the L&N was to design and build the company's Louisville depot. That was small stuff. Next, the big man turned his efforts to the Munfordville project; here he would really earn his salary. To cross the Green River, Fink used an iron truss of his own design to erect a five-span bridge, 1,800 feet long, supported on stone piers and soaring 115 feet high. By the time it was finished on July 1, 1859, it had cost $165,000, but it was a thing of beauty, the Golden Gate of its day. Even *Harper's Weekly* took note of it, saying that it merited "national pride and eulogy." Fink was rewarded with a promotion and a title to warm his Teutonic heart: chief engineer and superintendent of the Machinery and Road departments.[5]

Now the going was easy and the southbound crews raced forward. At the same time, other crews hurried north from Nashville through Edgefield and Gallatin. Just north of Gallatin, the Tennessee crews faced an engineering challenge of their own in chiseling two tunnels through hillsides of unstable slate. The southernmost tunnel (later affectionately called "Big South") was 945 feet long. About 400 feet north was a second tunnel ("Little South") that measured 600 feet in length. Beyond Gallatin and the twin tunnels were Mitchellville, then Franklin, and finally Bowling Green, which they reached on August 10, 1859. The city of Nashville threw a celebration, a barbeque attended by 10,000 people who ate the food, listened to the orators, and cheered wildly when a special train pulled in from Bowling Green.

Only details remained to be finished. The last rail was spiked down on October 18, 1859, and the 185-mile-long line was completed. It had cost $7,221,000, but it was already earning a profit by short trips between the towns along its length. In the fiscal year ending on the last day of June 1859, the railroad earned a net profit of $140,000. Not only were the cars filled with freight and paying passengers, but the management had signed a contract with the U.S. government to haul mail at a rate of $100 per mile per year.

All that remained to be done was a triumphal journey down the entire length of the shining road, from Louisville to Nashville. A special train with 200 dignitaries pulled from the Louisville depot on October 27, 1859. The flag-draped train made celebratory stops all along the way. When the train was within 20 miles of Nashville, it was met by another special train from the Tennessee capital. Together the two steamed into the city. There, according to Kinkaid Herr, "the excursionists were wined and dined to repletion, being formally welcomed by the mayor of the city and its council and later being entertained at the State Capitol." Recovering from the effects of too much rich food and too much champagne, the celebrants returned to Louisville on October 29. Two days later, regular service commenced on the L&N.[6]

On January 24, 1860, Louisville threw a banquet even greater than Nashville's to celebrate the completion of the L&N. Delegations of industrialists and legislators were invited from the host state, as well as Tennessee, Indiana, and Ohio. Seven hundred guests in all were ushered into Louisville's Masonic Temple at 9:00 P.M. to the "inspiring music of a fine band." Seated at long tables, they stuffed themselves on "baked pike, saddle of venison, young pig, turkey, ham, chicken, broiled squirrel, diamond-backed terrapin, quail on toast, prairie grouse, bear steak, relishes, cold side dishes, desserts, freezes, cakes, pyramids, fruit, coffee, and champagne."[7]

While digesting this flesh-heavy feast, the guests were treated to a series of speeches and toasts. The first, by Judge William F. Bullock, predicted that the nation would now reap a golden harvest, the fruit of forward vision and venture capital. His address ended, "May we now indulge in the inspiring hope that the Republic is safe, safe from the assaults of faction, safe from the inroads of bigotry, fanaticism and crime, safe in the love and confidence of virtuous, united, and enlightened people!"[8] The *Louisville Daily Journal* reported that the crowd responded with shouts of "Hear! Hear!" amid a "feu de jois of champagne corks [which] kept rattling like hail on a skylight."[9]

To the servants out in the kitchen, the shouts and the popping of the corks must have sounded like the distant clamor of a tiny battle.

2

The End of Peace, 1860–1861

By spring 1860, the L&N was sitting pretty. The main stem and its branch lines to Lebanon and Bardstown drew from one of the richest agricultural zones of the state, in terms of both crops and livestock, and skirted the edge of promising deposits of coal and iron. Hardwood forests along the route provided the material for crossties and fuel. Farmers who lived near the L&N supplemented their income by cutting stands of timber for the wood-burning locomotives.

The railroad owned 30 locomotives. Twenty-nine had been bought from northern manufactories, but with the completion of the company shops at Tenth and Kentucky Streets in Louisville, the L&N set its own mechanics to building a locomotive. The engine, completed in 1860, was the first locomotive built south of the Ohio River. The company also owned nearly 30 passenger and baggage cars and nearly 300 freight cars.

It was unlikely that repairs were going to constitute much of an immediate expense, for the L&N had been built from the first with a concern for quality. The wrought-iron rails were spiked down to 2,700 crossties per mile and rested upon a bed of heavy gravel ballast that was at least a foot thick. The tunnels were oversized, the fills were wider than normal and were at grade level, and all cuts were at least 18 feet wide and flanked by slopes that slanted gently back from the tracks, preventing them from caving in to cover the road and cause expensive delays.

Some time later, a correspondent for the *New York Times* made the entire trip from Louisville to Nashville and filed a report of his impressions of the L&N. He wrote, "There is, perhaps, no line of railroad in the whole Southern country more noted for its excellent construction than that of the Louisville and Nashville Railroad. It runs in a southwardly direction —

The L&N locomotive *Quigley*. Louisville & Nashville Railroad Records, University of Louisville Archives and Records Center, Louisville, Kentucky.

the distance to the latter city being one hundred and eighty five miles—over an excellent ballasted track, diversified with heavy grades, deep cuts, tunnels and bridges of various character—evincing, in its every detail, superior engineering."[1]

The relative safety of travel on the L&N was one of the advertising boasts of this well-promoted railroad. In addition, passengers were made aware of the many attractions to be seen along the L&N corridor. They included Muldraugh Hill, the Green River Bridge, and nearby Mammoth Cave. Broadsides also reminded travelers that neither Nashville nor Louisville must necessarily be the end of their journey. From Nashville, an easy transfer could hurry passengers on their way to Chattanooga or Atlanta. Connections at Louisville could send travelers on to Cincinnati or Chicago. The advertising campaign appears to have worked, for two passenger trains a day, Monday through Saturday (only one on Sunday) made the ten-hour trip between Louisville and the Tennessee capital. The railroad did not emphasize the speed of its trains, the fastest in the country. Perhaps the advertising department believed that the thought of rocketing across the face of the earth at 40 miles per hour would scare passengers away.

Passengers were important. Back in the stagecoach days, an estimated 7,000 people a year traveled between the two terminus cities. Now they would be rail passengers, and ticket receipts would generate a lot of income. But it was freight that paid the bills. Company accountants predicted that

2 — The End of Peace, 1860–1861

annual profits would exceed $300,000 a year from shipping freight and mail. Compared to this, the sale of passenger tickets would be mere icing.

The directors of the L&N seem to have been content to rest on their already considerable accomplishments, but President John LaRue Helm was not entirely satisfied. There was still one great project to be completed, the connection from Bowling Green to Guthrie and beyond to Clarksville and Memphis. It was a tremendous undertaking. When finished, the whole of the Memphis & Ohio Railroad would be 100 miles longer than the L&N itself and could scarcely be considered a branch in the same way as the Lebanon Branch or the Bardstown Branch. It would lie mainly in Tennessee and would be largely beyond the control of the L&N, yet vast amounts of L&N money were going into it, and completion was still at least a year away. President Helm saw the potential of gaining the trade of the lower Mississippi valley. What did a great outlay of capital matter now when the profits could potentially be so much greater? However, his ardent advocacy of the Memphis project cost him the support of his more conservative directors, who were very concerned about "exorbitant expenditures." They handed Helm a no-confidence vote in early 1860, and he tendered his resignation effective February 21.[2]

The man who followed Helm as president of the L&N was James Guthrie, a 68-year-old native of Nelson County, Kentucky. In his boyhood, he had taken cargoes of furs, whiskey, and tobacco to New Orleans aboard flatboats, but he quickly saw that this was not the way to riches. Back in Bardstown, he settled down to read law in the office of John Rowan, the wealthy owner of Federal Hill (said to be the inspiration for "My Old Kentucky Home"), and was admitted to the bar in 1817. He learned that the life of a Kentucky lawyer involved almost as much risk as that of a flatboatman when he was shot in a Bardstown street brawl by a fellow attorney. The wound incapacitated him for a time, and he never fully recovered from its effects. His attacker soon after left Bardstown and later committed suicide.

Governor John Adair appointed Guthrie commonwealth attorney in 1820, and the young lawyer relocated to Louisville, where he became a civic leader. He served on the Louisville Board of Trustees from 1824 to 1828 and was chairman of the board for part of that time. He championed paved streets, installation of a sewer system, the draining of putrid marshes and ponds, and a bounty of one cent for each rat killed. When the city was incorporated in February 1828, Guthrie represented the 1st Ward and was elected chairman, serving from 1828 to 1839. His advocacy of civic improvements continued. He called for inspectors for wells and cisterns, and better equipped, more professional police and fire departments. He insisted on the need for health inspectors to combat the spread of smallpox and cholera. He endorsed the purchase of the acreage that later became Cave Hill Cemetery. He was interested in improved ferry service across the Ohio River and was even more interested in the erection of an iron bridge. His leadership helped give impetus to the creation in 1837 of the Ohio Bridge Company, a combined effort of the Kentucky and Indiana legislatures. Guthrie was an innovative and energetic civic leader, but his interests were growing beyond Louisville's city limits.

The next natural step for a young man on the make was state politics. He was elected as a Democrat to the Kentucky legislature and served first as a representative, from 1827 to 1831, and then as a senator, from 1831 to 1841. His committee assignments in both houses were the same: judiciary, internal improvements, finance, and education. Internal improvements, especially as it touched upon transportation, was his special interest.

Guthrie attended the 1849-50 Kentucky Constitutional Convention, where he strongly advocated for a continuation of slavery and contrasted the labor situation in Kentucky and Massachusetts. In his view, Kentucky's slave-based labor was far more favorable. He did not believe in emancipation and neither did he believe in the American Colonization Society's goal of relocating freed blacks to Africa. Blacks were incapable of self-government, he argued. To Guthrie, slavery was a venerable institution with roots in the deep past, and it continued to be a superior and desirable arrangement for an enlightened society.

Anna Ruth Spiegel argued in her biographical study of Guthrie, "Public Career of James Guthrie (1792–1869)," that it was Guthrie's forceful leadership at the Kentucky Constitutional Convention that propelled him to national prominence. He moved to the national stage in 1853 when he was appointed secretary of the treasury by President Franklin Pierce. A foreshadowing of his near future as a railroad magnate was seen when he addressed, on behalf of the Pierce administration, a convention in Memphis, Tennessee, and advocated the construction of a transcontinental railroad.

Upon his return to Louisville in 1857, Guthrie became vice-president of the L&N and then, after the resignation of John L. Helm, its president. It was a position that combined his interests in finance, transportation, and the targeted use of tremendous power.

From boyhood, people had noted Guthrie's focus and determination,

2 — The End of Peace, 1860–1861

whether at his studies or at sports. He had little time for the niceties of society. Admired by some for his relentless drive and energy, Guthrie was nevertheless regarded as an unpleasant man, "uncouth" and eccentric, "of a domineering and arrogant personality, and wholly lacking in the usual social graces of a politician." He had a stingy slash of a mouth, thin-lipped and narrow. His nose was long and straight, separating eyes as unfeeling as lumps of coal, dark beneath the heavy bone of his brow. He was clean shaven, which only emphasized the sharpness of his cheekbones and the sunken cheeks below.[3]

Unprincipled and ruthless, coarse in his manners and ugly in his appearance, Guthrie had only one obvious virtue: he was a man of superior competence. It was this trait that had carried him to success in law, business, and politics.

• • •

The election of 1860 almost cost the L&N its third president before he took his place at the head of the corporate table, for he was put forward as a presidential candidate by the Democrats at their April 1860 convention in Charleston, South Carolina. Before a candidate was selected, however, a platform had to be approved. Delegates from the Deep South insisted on a language that promoted slavery as a positive good and supported its extension into the western territories. Northern Democrats proposed a platform that was more moderate in tone. This milder platform was the one that the convention narrowly adopted. The fire-eaters from the South stormed out.

The remaining delegates tried to nominate a candidate — tried, in fact, for two days. On the third ballot, James Guthrie of Kentucky received 42 votes out of the 202 required, and the momentum seemed to be with him. Kentucky's delegation was behind Guthrie, regarding him as a compromise between the sitting vice-president, John C. Breckinridge, and Senator Stephen A. Douglas. On the forty-second ballot, Guthrie gathered 66 votes. There he stalled. Fifteen more ballots followed, with no candidate ever receiving enough votes for the nomination. It was plain to the Democrats that there was no need to continue. They adjourned but planned to try again in two months in Baltimore. Until then, Guthrie returned to his duties in Louisville.

The Democrats came together in Baltimore in June. By then, the task before them was plainer to see, for the Republicans had met in Chicago and nominated the Illinois railroad lawyer Abraham Lincoln as their candidate.

The knowledge of their opponent did not unify the Democrats in Baltimore, however. Almost immediately, a fight broke out over what to do with those Southerners who had walked away in April, some of whom wanted to come back. It was agreed that some would be allowed into the new convention, but those from Alabama and Louisiana would not. Now a second walkout occurred. The absence of these adamant Southerners left the Baltimore Convention under the control of those who favored Stephen A. Douglas. In the balloting that followed, James Guthrie received only ten votes and withdrew his name from consideration. Douglas was selected as the candidate of the Northern faction of the party. At their own convention, the Southern Democrats nominated John C. Breckinridge.

There were two Democratic candidates (plus the candidate of the cobbled-together Constitutional Union Party, John Bell) to oppose Lincoln in the general election. A four-way race was a guarantee that Lincoln would win. When he did win in November (not by a majority but by a plurality), the Deep South lived up to its promise to leave the Union. The bottom tier of states began to fall away.

In a final effort to reroute the nation toward a tranquil resolution of its problems before the inauguration of Lincoln and the Republican Congress made reconciliation impossible, a peace conference convened at the Willard Hotel in Washington, D.C., on February 4, 1861. Delegations from 21 states, a total of 131 men, attended the conference. Kentucky's contingent consisted of six men, including James Guthrie.

When a subcommittee was appointed to draft a proposal to send to the U.S. Congress, Guthrie was selected to be its chair. The result, presented to the convention three weeks later, was little more than a reiteration of Senator John J. Crittenden's earlier proposal for a national compromise. Senator Crittenden was no Henry Clay. His compromise failed. So, too, did the compromise offered by the peace conference. Though the proposal was passed by a vote of the peace conferees, it was rejected soundly by the U.S. Senate and was never even given the courtesy of a vote in the House of Representatives.

The delegates returned to their homes, but Guthrie may have lingered in Washington to visit with the president-elect and possibly to attend the March 4 inauguration. He was one of a group that met with Lincoln shortly before he took office to discuss how to mollify the border states. For Guthrie, this was also a chance to take measure of a man who might become either an ally or an enemy to the interests of the L&N. The meeting was not without some rancor. As the guests began to leave, Lincoln said,

"Well, gentlemen, I have been wondering very much whether if Mr. Douglas or Mr. Bell had been elected President you would have dared to talk to him as freely as you have to me."

"Mr. President," Guthrie replied, "if General Washington occupied the seat that you will soon fill, and it had been necessary to talk to him as we have to you to save such a Union as this, I, for one, should talk to him as we have to you." And the guests left, having accomplished nothing.[4]

For the L&N, the best hope was that the Upper South would remain in the Union. If Tennessee and Kentucky remained loyal, the L&N could continue its business without interruption.

Then in April 1861, Fort Sumter was fired upon. Lincoln responded by calling for volunteers to put down the rebellion. Now the states of the Upper South, Tennessee among them, began to secede. Suddenly, the L&N found itself in an unprecedented predicament. As Maury Klein pointed out, excepting only the Mobile & Ohio Railroad, "no other major line in the country traversed both a Union state and a Confederate state.... Like the Union itself, the L&N was split down the middle." Klein might have mentioned the unfinished Memphis & Ohio Railroad as well, but his point was well taken. As the only centrally located railroad serving both loyal and seceding states west of the Appalachians, the L&N was in a situation of unique peril. The north-south axis that had been considered to be a geographic advantage in the 1850s might become an invitation to destruction in the 1860s.[5]

The situation was profoundly confusing, but in that confusion James Guthrie perceived an opportunity. The L&N could double its profits by trading with both Kentucky, a loyal state, and with the seceded state of Tennessee, which was starved for manufactured goods of all descriptions. On May 2, 1861, the U.S. Treasury Department declared that transporting goods to the rebellious South was prohibited and that all contraband was to be seized, but Guthrie openly ignored the order. The *New York Tribune* clucked in disapproval, "There are not many nations on earth that would thus feed their enemies."[6]

Louisville's streets were clogged with freighters' wagons loaded with goods for the L&N Railroad depot and ultimately for Nashville. Trains rumbled out of the station every few minutes, but even with fully loaded boxcars they could not keep up with the volume of goods piling up on the L&N platforms. False rumors spread through the city that so many foodstuffs were heading for Dixie that Louisville's own citizens might be on the verge of desperate shortages. Other Louisville citizens worried about the doubtful wisdom of providing the South with tons of goods that would supply and strengthen them to make war against the North. When Unionists tried to prevent the L&N's treasonous trade by ripping up tracks south of the city, the company responded by sending armed guards ahead of the trains to drive off saboteurs. Plainly, the company would defend with deadly force its right to carry on what was essentially a black-market trade with the enemies of the nation. The profits were simply too tempting. By summer, freight receipts actually tripled what they had been in the spring and thus exceeded Guthrie's fondest hopes. The L&N directors avowed their determination to continue the illicit trade in their meeting of July 3, 1861, but they knew that the end was coming. A test case was pending. On July 11, 1861, Circuit Court Judge P.B. Muir declared in the case of *Brady and Davis vs. the Louisville and Nashville Railroad* that the Treasury Department did indeed have the authority to enforce a railroad blockade of the South.

By then, the point was moot. Concerned that such Southern commodities as sugar and cotton were being shipped north, the Confederate government prohibited trade north of the Tennessee line. The governor of Tennessee, Isham Harris, was a more scrupulous patriot than his neighbors to the north and enforced the law by a simple but effective stratagem: he placed a government man aboard each train as an inland customs agent. Then on July 4, Governor Harris took a more drastic step when he seized the L&N from Nashville to the Tennessee line, plus five locomotives, 70 freight cars, a handful of passenger cars, and miscellaneous equipage. The total value of the property commandeered was over $110,000. The *New York Times* saw the actions of Governor Harris as portending something more ominous. The newspaper said, "Tennessee's seizure of the Nashville end of our railroad, and of some of its rolling stock, is intended as a preliminary to Confederate seizure and control of the entire road and all its rolling stock.... If they are not watched and prevented, they will destroy all its important bridges and trestle-work in Kentucky." Note that the *Times* referred to the L&N as "our railroad," another sign of its singular importance to the Union.[7]

Though Guthrie and his board of directors howled about the loss of the southern portion of their route, Governor Harris refused to back down. He and Guthrie did negotiate, but in the end, the Louisville & Nashville Railroad Company had to accept that, for the foreseeable future, trade was restricted to Kentucky, and with a reduced supply of rolling stock.

2 — The End of Peace, 1860–1861

The Confederates had bitten the hand that fed them so well and had made an enemy of James Guthrie.

• • •

A recitation of the business narrative of the Louisville & Nashville Railroad in 1861 does not begin to convey the turbulence of the early months of the war in the Bluegrass State. While the L&N was happily trading with both North and South, Kentucky was trying to maintain an awkward political and military neutrality. Governor Beriah Magoffin was pro–Southern and the General Assembly was increasingly strong for the Union. Some in the legislature saw that Kentucky would never be able to remain neutral; trouble was coming and probably sooner than later. Lovell Harrison Rousseau, a state senator representing Louisville, had spoken for many when he warned Southern apologists from the floor of the Senate on May 12, "When Kentucky goes down, it will be in blood. Let that be understood. She will not go down as other States have done.... We have more right to defend our government than you have to overturn it."[8]

Now Rousseau was out of office, having resigned to raise first a Home Guard unit for Jefferson County and then a Union regiment. He was soon forced to move his camp across the Ohio River to the Indiana bank because of the objections of James Guthrie, Jeremiah Boyle, Garrett Davis, Joshua Fry Speed, and other Kentucky Unionists to the War Department in Washington, but he continued to quietly raise troops on his native soil. General William "Bull" Nelson was playing somewhat the same role in the Bluegrass Region near Richmond, Kentucky.

At the same time, the Lincoln administration was sneaking rifles down the Ohio into Louisville by paddle wheeler. The guns were stored in the basement of the Jefferson County Courthouse until they could be distributed under the direction of Joshua F. Speed. In the end, 5,000 "Lincoln Guns" ended up in the hands of Home Guard units across the state.

Some were alarmed at what they considered reckless behavior on the part of the Unionists, but the Confederates were active as well. It was not unusual to see two columns of eager-faced, young men marching in column down the sidewalks in Louisville, one column marching south to the Rebels, while on the opposite side of the street, the other column marched north to join Rousseau at Camp Joe Holt.

On balance, it appears that the Confederates had somewhat more respect for Kentucky neutrality than did the North until September 3, 1861, when forces under the command of General Leonidas Polk moved north from Tennessee to occupy Columbus, Kentucky, a powerful position overlooking the Mississippi River.

A few guns and a little recruiting were one thing, but this was an invasion. And it was all the excuse the Union needed. General U.S. Grant immediately moved across the Ohio River from Cairo, Illinois, to occupy Paducah, and General Robert Anderson moved the headquarters of the Department of the Cumberland to Louisville. Events were tumbling out of control, and even conservative men began to think that the time had come for drastic measures. Garrett Davis, one of Kentucky's political leaders, was concerned about the safety of the shining spine of Kentucky's rail system. He wrote on September 16 to General George H. Thomas, "The Louisville and Nashville Railroad ought to be taken possession of at once by the military authorities as far south as Bowling Green."[9]

Davis' moment of psychic clarity came too late. The very next day, on September 17, Brigadier General Simon Bolivar Buckner moved up from Camp Boone, Tennessee, on the Memphis Branch of the L&N to occupy Bowling Green the next day. Josie Underwood, a young diarist living in Bowling Green, recorded, "On detraining, one of the soldiers climbed to the depot's roof and lowered the American flag. Not satisfied with tearing it down, the lad also trampled Old Glory. While doing so he fell from the roof and broke both of his legs." Miss Underwood learned several days later that the boy had died of his injuries.[10]

This unnamed young soldier may have been the first Confederate to die in Kentucky.

3

The Federals Advance

Bowling Green was a handsome little town of 2,500 residents who lived and worked in 30 central blocks served by a web of ten roads, not counting the L&N Railroad which bordered the western edge of the community. The people lived a quiet, cultured life until Buckner's Rebels showed up. They transformed the town, first by scattering out through the neighborhoods begging for food, and then by using the town's trees and cabins to erect forts on the surrounding hills. Fort Underwood, at the homeplace of Josie Underwood, was a short distance northeast of town. Miss Underwood's wonderfully evocative diary, edited with skill by Nancy Disher Baird, was published by the University Press of Kentucky in 2009, and it gives a glimpse of the kind of trouble an occupation army meant to the civilian population. After several aggravating days of putting up with Rebels begging for handouts, the Underwoods looked out one afternoon to see hundreds of men trudging into one of their best pasture fields, 100 acres of clover, to practice their drills under the eye of General Buckner. From the saddle of a fine white horse, Buckner watched as his soldiers trampled the Underwoods' clover to ruin. Worse occurred a few days later when one of Buckner's infantry brigades came to make camp at Mt. Air, the Underwood property. They filled up the barn lot and the orchard and began right away to tear down the Underwoods' rail fences for kindling and campfires.

If they had minded their manners, the Confederates might have been a tolerable (if expensive) presence, but they were rude to the Underwood servants who were going about their chores, and one morning some of them even broke into the kitchen and stole the family's breakfast. Mr. Warner Underwood went to confront Colonel Lucius L. Rich about the conduct of his men. The colonel showed a nonchalant attitude about the theft of the morning meal. Mr. Underwood, said "He had hoped southern men might retain their honesty even though they had lost their loyalty and was grieved to find himself mistaken." His admonishment had no effect on Colonel Rich, and the family did not get their breakfast back.[1]

Neither did the soldiers' behavior get any better. They milked the Underwoods' cow and did not share the milk, and they stole eggs from under the laying hens. When a Mississippi brigade came to join their comrades at Mt. Air, the Underwoods must have despaired of having anything left of their farm once the war was done. The men from the Deep South were more polite than those first Rebel trespassers, but they were just as hungry, and soon pigs began to disappear from their sties and potatoes vanished from the garden.

The Underwoods soon saw why the additional soldiers had come. General Buckner's engineers had decided to place a fort on the crest of Underwood Hill. A hundred men with axes went to work chopping down a grove of walnut and oak trees near the barn lot for logs to build the fort. They tore down the cabin of one of the Underwood slaves and soon erected Fort Underwood. That the Underwood name was given to the fort was a dubious honor at best.

Their property had been seized to create one of five forts built during the Confederate occupation of Bowling Green. The financial loss was staggering. But the Underwoods had not suffered their last sorrow.

• • •

The day he occupied Bowling Green, General Buckner threw 600 infantrymen and an artillery battery forward to Munfordville "to cover the bridge and the line of defense of the river." He instructed Major J. M. Hawes to contact prominent Rebel sympathizers in Elizabethtown and to "seize any United States arms which may be at [the] Munfordville depot. Send all trains to Bowling Green, after establishing communication with Elizabethtown, except one locomotive and a few cars to keep up communication with your pickets." He especially advised Major Hawes to "establish a strong picket at Bacon Creek Bridge, eight miles in advance of Munfordville, on Green River."[2]

Munfordville was Buckner's hometown, and he instructed Major Hawes to make contact with Union captain William Brown, saying, "Endeavor to make his acquaintance as a friend of mine and give him my most friendly assurances." In some ways, it was an oddly polite war.[3]

3 — The Federals Advance

Buckner placed another small force under Joseph H. Lewis at Cave City, on the railroad between Bowling Green and Munfordville. On his arrival, Lewis issued a recruiting broadside, urging the young men to "come to the camp.... Come at once. Delay is sure destruction." His response was well met. The recruits who responded were combined with those who came down from Elizabethtown with Colonel Martin Cofer to become the 6th Kentucky Infantry, one of the regiments of the storied Orphan Brigade.[4]

General Buckner had many matters demanding his immediate attention. Needing arms for his occupying army and for those young Southerners who continued to arrive (before the occupation was done, there would be upwards of 25,000 graycoat soldiers in Bowling Green), he issued a decree that every Warren County man had to supply one gun to the Glorious Cause or pay a fine of $20. Buckner issued business licenses in the name of the Confederate government and levied taxes. It is said that he raised a quarter of a million dollars in this way. He ordered the Bowling Green banks to turn over to Kentucky's new Confederate government all of the public funds in their keeping; private accounts were apparently safe from seizure.

Buckner wrote to Governor Beriah Magoffin to say that his advance to Bowling Green was purely defensive in intent, and he also opened what amounted to diplomatic relations with James Guthrie. From his Bowling Green headquarters, Buckner sent the L&N president a long message.

> Sir: It is my purpose to reopen the traffic recently suspended by direction of the President of the United States on such portions of the Louisville and Nashville Railway as may be under the control of the forces under my command, and also to re-establish the running of the regular passenger trains. The counties through which this railway passes are largely interested in its stock, and are charged with heavy burdens to pay the interest on the debts which they have contracted in the construction of the road. The cessation of this traffic, under the orders of the President, was an act of injustice to the people, who were already sufficiently taxed, for it deprived the citizens of these counties of the very means relied upon to pay the largely-increased taxation demanded by the policy of the Government. As far as rests in my power, I propose to secure to the people of these counties their just rights in this respect, by permitting the traffic on the road to continue as it existed before the illegal interference of the President. With this view I have possessed myself of a considerable portion of the rolling stock of the road, and now propose to you that, as president of the company, you continue the management of the portion of road within the limits of the influence of the forces under my command, and conduct

it, as before the existence of the war, in the interest of the people who are interested in its stock. I propose that you will continue your agents and employees, with the single restriction that they shall be men who are not inimical to the people of these counties, and that the stockholders shall enjoy all the benefit to which their railroad charter entitles them. In order to secure the rights of the stockholders, I have directed an account to be kept of the earnings and expenses of the road, including the amount to which the company will be entitled for transporting the troops under my orders. This account will be rendered to you, and the balance paid over on the single condition that it shall be applied to the purposes contemplated by the charter. If this proposition should be declined, I propose transferring the rolling stock to such agents as may be appointed by the counties through which the road passes. This will insure an equitable distribution of the property of the road in the interest of the stockholders.[5]

Guthrie refused to negotiate with Buckner. But Buckner must have anticipated that outcome, for he had already dispatched men to burn the bridges north of Bacon Creek. Captain Phillip Lightfoot Lee of the 2nd Kentucky Infantry burned the bridge at Nolin, and Thomas Hayes burned the bridge over the Rolling Fork River just south of Lebanon Junction.

The timing of Buckner's actions is curious. He wrote Guthrie on the 18th, the morning *after* the bridges were burned on his orders. He must have known that burning the bridges would antagonize Guthrie, but if the letter to Guthrie was just a courtesy in the first place, then antagonizing the L&N president wouldn't matter so much. Maybe he was giving Guthrie a small sample of the kind of damage the L&N could expect to receive unless it co-operated with the Confederates who controlled its southern half. Then again, maybe Buckner knew that Guthrie would realize that he was merely taking the military precaution of protecting his northern perimeter.

Since the end of neutrality, Louisville had existed in a kind of stunned paralysis. Reporter Henry Villard of the *New York Tribune* wrote of the dazed city, "The streets were very quiet and had a deserted look. The hotel [the Galt House] too was almost empty." A modern writer, Robert E. McDowell added, "Business was dead, steamboats lying idle at the wharf." However, the burning of the Rolling Fork bridge shook Louisville awake. Lebanon Junction was only 30 miles south. The city was in a small panic.[6]

Immediate action was needed. General Robert Anderson summoned his second-in-command, General William Tecumseh Sherman to his office. There, Sherman found James Guthrie closeted with Anderson. Guthrie showed Sherman the dispatch that he'd only just received that the Rolling

Fork bridge had been burned. As Sherman remembered it, Guthrie went on to explain "that in the ravine just beyond Salt Creek were several high and important trestles which, if destroyed, would take months to replace, and General Anderson thought it well worth the effort to save them. Also, on Muldraugh's Hill beyond, was a strong position ... and we all supposed that General Buckner, who was familiar with the ground, was aiming for a position there, from which to operate on Louisville."[7]

Anderson ordered Sherman to gather all available troops and to move south to contend with the Rebels who seemed to be advancing en masse toward the northern terminus of the L&N. Sherman assembled 1,000 men of the local Home Guards and also the regiments under Colonel Lovell Harrison Rousseau at Camp Joe Holt. Sherman's patchwork command left Louisville by train at 2:00 A.M. on the 18th and arrived at Lebanon Junction at daylight. The home guards remained near the train while Rousseau's men moved forward on foot. The bridge was down, and the ruins were still smoldering. Rousseau led a scouting party wading across the waist-deep river, but a search of the far bank failed to find any of the enemy. The Rebels had burned the bridge, and now they were gone.

The Federals bivouacked at Lebanon Junction for nearly a week before Sherman ordered Rousseau's men up the Clear Creek Valley to the crest of Muldraugh Hill. They advanced quietly toward the outskirts of Elizabethtown when, according to a soldier who was with Rousseau, "the band struck up a fine national air, and after marching and countermarching through the town, we encamped in a beautiful grove near it.... The day after, we changed our encampment and marched to a forest within about gunshot of Elizabethtown." The men set up their tents and waited for further orders.[8]

Rousseau did not know it, perhaps, but his approach to Elizabethtown had the same effect on the locals as the news of the Rebels at Lebanon Junction had had on Louisville a week earlier, namely, panic. Basil Duke, soon to become famous as the second-in-command of General John Hunt Morgan, was in Elizabethtown on a recruiting mission the morning Rousseau reached the top of Muldraugh Hill. Duke remembered that a bug-eyed man in a jeans coat and baggy britches came tearing through town crying, "Save yourselves, gentlemen, Rouser's in town."[9]

In the interest of military preciseness, Duke reminded his readers that the advancing force was actually under Sherman's command, but "the people of Kentucky had never heard of Sherman and they believed it to be commanded by Rousseau, of whom they had heard a great deal."[10]

Duke continued, "I have rarely witnessed such a stampede as then ensued.... There was a general disposition to leave town and 'take to the woods,' in which ... I heartily shared."[11]

Sherman joined his command at Muldraugh Hill a few days later and made an immediate impression on the men as a genuine eccentric. He was a scruffy, fidgeting, loose-jointed man, none too clean, his head crowned in a perpetual wreath of cigar smoke. Officers learned not to lend him their cigars for a light; he would light his own cigar from theirs and then throw theirs in the mud before absent-mindedly wandering away.

His uniform had not yet arrived, and he was dressed in civilian clothes, complete with a stovepipe hat. Yet, he was a stickler for military niceties. It led to an exchange that was remembered by R. M. Kelly for an article in *Battles and Leaders of the Civil War*. Kelly wrote:

> Sherman's attention was attracted to a young man without any uniform, who was moving around with what he considered suspicious activity, and he called him up for question. The young fellow gave a prompt account of himself. His name was Griffiths, he was a medical student from Louisville acting as hospital steward, and he had been called out in such a hurry that he had no time to get a uniform. As he moved away he muttered something in a low tone to an officer standing by, and Sherman at once demanded to know what it was. "Well, General," was the [officer's] reply, "he said that a general with such a hat as you have had no right to talk to him about a uniform." Sherman was wearing a battered hat of the style known as "stove-pipe." Pulling it off, he looked at it, and, bursting into a laugh, called out, "Young man, you are right about the hat, but you ought to have your uniform."[12]

Sherman was involved in every detail of life at Camp Muldraugh. Once, when he disapproved of the slow way a bread ration was being handed out, he took over and began throwing bread at the surprised men.

Though he paid attention to the details of camp life, Sherman's worries were more serious than the appearance of his men or the distribution of bread. The people of Hardin and the surrounding counties were not supporting his troops materially, and the young men were not coming to enlist in the numbers he needed and had hoped for. He had only about 4,000 troops on hand, almost all of them untrained. Further, he was worried about his lifeline back to Louisville. It was said that because of Confederate seizures and normal wear and tear on the rolling stock, "the Louisville and Nashville Railroad has but eighty cars, all told, and not reliable for military transportation."[13]

So, Sherman fretted. No one denied that his troubles were serious, but they were about to get much worse.

4

The First Drops of Blood Are Drawn

On October 8, 1861, General Sherman succeeded the ailing General Robert Anderson. Now he was in command of the Department of the Cumberland, and he took to the task with his typical vigor. Sherman wanted to make a move against the Rebels without delay, not enough of one to bring on a premature engagement, but enough to put pressure on the Rebels and show that the Federals were not cowed. On October 9 he ordered Rousseau, now a brigadier general, to "move his camp as soon as practicable forward to the vicinity of Nolin, selecting with the advice of Captain [Frederick E.] Prime, a position for a large force. He will cause scouts to be sent forward towards Green River."[1]

Sherman chose well in selecting Rousseau for the assignment. A 43-year-old native of Lincoln County, Kentucky, Rousseau was the epitome of the self-made man. One of eleven children, he had had to quit school before age ten; by age 14 he was earning a man's wages by breaking rocks for a construction crew working on the Lexington-to-Lancaster turnpike. Almost entirely self-taught, a taste of learning gave him an appetite for more, and he eventually moved to Louisville where he read law. He was admitted to the bar in Bloomfield, Indiana, and in 1844 was elected as a Whig to the Indiana House of Representatives. At the start of the Mexican War, Rousseau resigned his seat, was quickly commissioned a captain, and saw action at the Battle of Buena Vista. While he was in the service of his country, Indiana voters elected him to the state senate. He took up the seat after his return, but he served for only one year before deciding to return to Louisville. As a resident of Kentucky, he was ineligible to continue as a Hoosier legislator, but his constituents refused to accept his resignation, and he continued to serve his district across the Ohio River until the end of his term.

In Louisville, he gained a reputation as a defender of the poor and even, on at least one occasion, served as counsel to four blacks (at a time when blacks in the South were routinely denied a trial) who were accused of murder. It speaks to his skill as an attorney that he won their acquittal. He was also a loud critic of the Know-Nothing Party, a hateful presence on the American political landscape in the 1850s. Rousseau was elected to the Kentucky Senate in 1860, but as had happened before, when war beckoned, he resigned. After Fort Sumter was fired upon, Rousseau was commissioned a colonel and was authorized to raise 20 companies, though he was ultimately forbidden to actively recruit them in Kentucky. He established Camp Joe Holt near Jeffersonville, Indiana. He and his men were welcome to enter Kentucky only when it appeared that Louisville was threatened by General Buckner's forces. Now, he was ordered forward from Muldraugh Hill to Nolin, within 15 miles or so of the most advanced Confederate videttes at Bacon Creek.

General Rousseau and Captain Prime soon found the site they were looking for; the farm of Mr. David Nevin was ideal for the Federal campsite. Nevin was lately a resident of Louisville, the owner of a marble shop that had stayed busy with private business and city contracts. In 1860, Nevin and his family moved south of the city. Mr. Nevin had bought a 600-acre farm on the Nolin River about nine miles below Elizabethtown. These 600 acres would do nicely, Rousseau and Prime decided. There was abundant water, good transportation via the L&N Railroad and the Louisville and Nashville Turnpike, and those wide, flat fields sloping gently down to the river.

It also helped that Nevin was a "violent secessionist," so the confiscation of this land would not cost the loyalty of a Union man. Rousseau's keen sense of irony often found expression in his humor, and when he quickly named the selected site "Camp Nevin" as a tribute to his Southern-leaning host, he was just needling the unhappy Mr. Nevin.[2]

Rousseau did not, however, take the brick home of the Nevin family as his headquarters. He selected a nearby cabin instead. From there, he could direct the building of the new L&N Railroad bridge to replace the one Captain Lee had burned and also a stockade with two-story blockhouses on the corners.

The first units of the Army of the Cumberland began setting up camp at Nevin's Nolin farm on October 9: the 5th Kentucky Infantry, Co. C of

4 — The First Drops of Blood Are Drawn

the 6th Kentucky Infantry, the 2nd Kentucky Cavalry, Battery A of the 1st Kentucky Artillery (Stone's Battery), the 6th Indiana Infantry, the 38th Indiana Infantry, and a battalion each of the 15th and 16th U.S. Infantry. The 30th Indiana Infantry was close behind and arrived before the end of the day. The next day, October 10, three more infantry regiments rattled into Camp Nevin: the 39th Indiana, the 15th Ohio, and the 49th Ohio.

More continued to arrive, by foot and by rail, including three regiments from Pennsylvania, until there were upwards of 14,000 men at Camp Nevin, which now overspread the boundaries of Mr. Nevin's farm and stretched six miles from end to end. The regiments were divided into four brigades and were commanded, not by Rousseau (who led the 1st Brigade), but by General Alexander McDowell McCook. His was the 1st Division of the Army of the Cumberland. McCook did take the Nevin house for his headquarters.

The Nolin River was the front line and these brigades on its northern bank were the spearhead of the Union effort in the West. The size of the force at Camp Nevin was an encouragement to George D. Prentice, editor of the *Louisville Daily Journal*. From his office in Louisville, Prentice flung down a challenge to the Confederates at Bowling Green: "If Buckner's troops are half-starved, let them come across to Camp [Nevin], and McCook and Rousseau will give them a bellyful."[3]

• • •

The Confederates had no intention of coming across to Camp Nevin. The Federals straddling the L&N Railroad were more than they could handle. Wild rumors had been circulating among the Yankees that there were as many as 45,000 Confederates in South Central Kentucky, but it was not so. Recruits continued to arrive, but as late as October 4, General Buckner said that the number was not over 6,000 "at all points." Rather than advance, the Rebels withdrew to the Green River line at Munfordville, burning the railroad bridge at Bacon Creek behind them as they went.[4]

One of the Confederate newcomers to Bowling Green was Brigadier General William J. Hardee, a career army man whose book *Rifle and Light Infantry Tactics* was the basic training manual of both armies. He outranked General Buckner and superseded him in command at Bowling Green. Hardee had been on the scene only shortly when on October 12 he wrote to Albert Sidney Johnston, the Confederate commander of the Western Department, "The enemy is reported to be advancing from Elizabethtown. Your presence here is much needed. Hurry forward the troops in the rear."

Soldiers were ordered to Bowling Green from Nashville and Columbus, and Johnston himself arrived on or about October 13.[5]

Albert Sidney Johnston was a native Kentuckian and a graduate of West Point Military Academy. He had fought in the Black Hawk War in 1832 but did not remain in the service of the U.S. much after that. He resigned his commission to join the Texas Revolution. Promoted to brigadier general, he went on to serve the new republic in the Mexican War and fought at the Battle of Monterrey.

Johnston returned to the U.S. Army in 1849 and once again became a brigadier. He maintained his home in Texas, however and his subsequent service was almost entirely in the West. At the start of the Civil War he was in California and was the leader of the Southern men who partied with Winfield Scott Hancock on the evening of June 16, 1861, before heading east at midnight to offer their services to the Confederacy. Johnston's loyalty to the Lone Star State was the deciding factor in his choosing the South, and he found a certain wry amusement in that. He said, "It seems like fate that Texas has made me a Rebel twice."[6]

The journey overland from the West Coast to Richmond took two and a half months. Arriving at the executive mansion in the old city, he had barely been ushered into the entry hall when he heard a loud voice from upstairs say, "That is Sidney Johnston's step! Bring him up!" It was President Jefferson Davis calling down.[7]

Davis idolized Johnston, had done so ever since their days at West Point when Johnston was the upperclassman. Now the plebe was in a position to show his admiration. Johnston learned that while he was still en route Davis had forwarded, and the Senate had approved, his commission as a full general. He was outranked by only one other in the Confederate military, Samuel Cooper. Robert E. Lee was immediately behind him on the list. Johnston was a proud man and was vexed that he was second to anyone in the military hierarchy, but what should have upset him, instead, was his assignment as commander of all the CSA forces west of the Appalachians. It was a sprawling, undermanned military department with every manner of land-mass, each one with a unique set of problems to test Albert Sidney Johnston's talents. Jefferson Davis was satisfied that he had the right man for the job, however, and still had not changed his mind years later when he described Johnston as "the greatest solder, the ablest man, civil or military, Confederate or Federal, then living." In the fall of 1861, others were waiting to see just how able Johnston really was.[8]

Johnston quickly comprehended the Federal strategy. He wrote to

Richmond on October 27, "The enemy seem to design to operate on at least three lines in Kentucky: one against Zollicoffer on the route to Cumberland Gap ... another on the Louisville and Nashville Railroad ... and the other against Polk, and will, perhaps, endeavor to use the Tennessee River in aid of the movement."[9]

Johnston issued an appeal to the governments of the Confederate states farther south for reinforcements and did what he could to accumulate supplies of all kinds, even if it meant interfering with their intended destinations. On or about October 18, he stopped a load of blankets at Nashville and rerouted them as he saw fit. The secretary of war, Judah P. Benjamin, forgave him that small larceny, for another load of smuggled blankets had arrived soon after from Bermuda.

However, Johnston's subordinates were following their commander's lead in taking whatever they wanted, and the situation was becoming untenable. Secretary Benjamin warned Johnston not to "permit in your department a system of action which cannot fail to produce the most unfavorable results in every possible aspect of the case." Benjamin explained, "Our means are inadequate to furnish everywhere all that is required. We divide out to the best of our ability, as fairly as possible, according to the exigencies of the service, such supplies as we can command. This equitable system can only be conducted from one common head. Let me pray you to give such instructions to your subordinates as shall put an end to this reprehensible practice."[10]

Benjamin did reassure Johnston that a sloop loaded with arms was expected from Liverpool and that he would be able to send the Western Department 10,000 of them. Benjamin soothed Johnston's anxieties and bruised ego as often as he could. On November 14, he wrote to Johnston, "I have ordered 4500 Enfield rifles sent to you, being half of all that were received by the recent arrival from England. You see you are not forgotten."[11]

Still, the trickle of supplies was so slow that Johnston, though desperate for reinforcements, could not hope to arm and equip the new men as they arrived. He had to ask Governor Isham Harris of Tennessee not to accept any volunteers who could not supply their own arms and confessed that he would have to disband some of the troops already accepted. That decision was later reversed, but it goes to prove how impoverished the Rebels were. Until greater quantities of supplies and arms were on hand, any thoughts of an offensive were out of the question and even defense was mostly a matter of bluff.

There was one officer, though, who was ready to carry the war to the enemy. He was John Hunt Morgan, the future "Thunderbolt of the Confederacy," and more than any other man, the nemesis of the Louisville & Nashville Railroad.

Morgan was 37 years old. He had a dark moustache and goatee and was rarely seen in uniform. He much preferred tall cavalry boots, brown britches and shirt, and a blue coat. His hat was black and, cavalier-like, he had the brim pinned up on one side. One would not think so from his jaunty appearance, but Morgan was a man carrying an emotional burden. His wife had died in 1861 after years of invalidism following the birth of a stillborn son. Morgan's Lexington businesses could not distract him from his grief, and nothing else could either until the war came to Kentucky. Morgan and his Lexington Rifles militia unit moved south and west to Hart County to enlist, but even before they were mustered in, Morgan was leading small patrols north to harass the Federal pickets at Camp Nevin on the Nolin.

Morgan's second-in-command, Basil Duke, wrote later that camp duty "did not accord with his nature, which demanded the stimulus of adventure." So four or five times a week, Morgan would ride north at dusk with ten or 12 picked men, slip through the Federal lines, and spend the night wandering behind enemy lines "gathering intelligence and trying to catch inattentive pickets whom they would stalk like game, locating them in the dark and then waiting until just before sunrise to gun them down with shotguns."[12]

For the young pickets of Camp Nevin, who were sometimes stationed ten miles out, the prospect of an encounter in the dark with Morgan or one of his men was terrifying. But to Morgan, it was all a great lark. He is said to have repeatedly passed into the very heart of Camp Nevin in Federal disguise or posing as a woodcutter or a miller. Once, he even went to headquarters, wrangled an audience with General McCook, and then earnestly presented a plan describing how the guerrilla Morgan could be caught.

Morgan seemed to come and go at will, and bloody death always followed after.

• • •

Aside from the potentially fatal requirements of picket duty, the men at Camp Nevin seemed to enjoy it well enough. Sergeant William C. Robinson of the 34th Illinois wrote, "Our camp is located in a splendid place, a very swift and beautiful stream running near."[13]

4 — The First Drops of Blood Are Drawn

There were four full brigades at Camp Nevin, commanded by Brigadier General Alexander McDowell McCook, a career army man from Ohio, a veteran of campaigns against the Apache in New Mexico and of the Battle of Bull Run. It was his opinion that he had "command of the most important army in the field" and that he was "ready to meet and whip him [the enemy] at our ... convenience."[14]

General Sherman in Louisville did not quite share McCook's view that the men of the 1st Division were ready to meet and whip the Rebels at Bowling Green. He warned McCook on October 15, "You must be prepared for anything.... Push the drill." And push the drill they did. William Sumner Dodge wrote in 1864 that "Camp Nevin became a grand school of instruction."[15]

A typical day for an infantryman was loud with no fewer than 26 bugle calls or drum rolls, beginning at 6:00 A.M., in a winter camp, when reveille sounded and the First Sergeant called roll. Thirty minutes later came a bugle call signaling breakfast, then another bugle blast for sick call, followed by another for fatigue duty. At 8:00 A.M., the guards for the day were assigned to their posts. The other men drilled until time for the noon meal. The men at Camp Nevin were well fed in the early stages of their encampment with donated food, both staples and delicacies, but they were soon reduced to living on the soldier's usual diet of hardtack, salt meat, and coffee, plus what they could buy or forage from local farmers.

After the noon meal was a short period of free time, followed by more drill. Colonel August Willich of the 32nd Indiana was said to be especially fond of having his men drill with the bayonet. Michael Peake, historian of the regiment, wrote, "Intricate fencing maneuvers of the drill, actuated by bugle command, seemed all the more deadly by the ferocious bellowing of the men than by the highly polished saber bayonets fixed on their weapons. Willich's men performed with tremendous precision, exhuberances [sic], and pride."[16]

The hours devoted to drill would be fewer as the men gained experience, but now they needed the training, and their sergeants put them through the paces. Some recruits were so ignorant that they did not know their right foot from their left, and the loading and firing of a rifle, requiring 12 distinct commands, was well beyond the ability of many young men in the fall of 1861. Firing practice was frequent if the 79th Pennsylvania was typical. The men of that regiment were given twenty rounds of ammunition on October 25 and 20 more on October 29. With these cartridges, the men were expected to hit a target at a distance of 125 yards.

It was natural that giving firearms and bayonets to 14,000 inexperienced young men would lead to some accidents, and there were some. One man in Co. K of the 79th Pennsylvania shot off his own forefinger, and a trooper in the 78th Pennsylvania was struck in the thigh by the careless shot of another's gun. His leg was amputated, but he died anyway.

Lyman Widney, 34th Illinois, wrote in his diary for October 25, "For want of an enemy to shoot, we shoot ourselves occasionally. We use pistol and musket balls or iron ramrods, which whistle recklessly through camp, fortunately without injury, until today, when the fusillade was equal to a slight skirmish, resulting in two casualties."[17]

In the 49th Ohio, Captain George E. Lovejoy accidentally fired a round from his own pistol into his upper jaw, but he seems to have survived the wound. Lewis H. Jones and George Staggerwall, Co. M of the 79th Pennsylvania, also survived what might have been a more serious accident. They were on picket duty while the artillery batteries were practicing. A solid shot from one of the cannon roared past them and smashed into a foot-thick tree before it struck another tree and was stopped. The men were lucky not to have suffered serious injury. But then Staggerwall picked up the cannonball, and he and Jones began throwing it around. Jones tossed it up to catch it but missed, and it came down and hit him above one eye, giving him a bloody wound. The rumor went around camp that Jones had survived being struck in the head by a fired round.

When afternoon drill was over, the men were dismissed by company in time to get ready for "retreat" (another roll call), an inspection, and "dress parade." Any new orders or decrees from above were read at dress parade. Once the bugle announced the end of dress parade, there was "tattoo," when the men answered roll call for the third time that day. An evening meal followed, then a return to quarters, and a little free time to write letters or wash clothes in the river before the bugle call that announced another day was done.

Of course, there were other duties, such as working on the stockade and the rebuilding of the burned L&N Railroad bridge. And there were occasional small forays against the enemy. Near Upton on October 14, the 39th Indiana surprised and scattered a band of Rebels at the log cabin home of a man named John Murrell. The same day, Co. I of the 2nd Kentucky Cavalry fought some Rebel horsemen and again on the night of the 15th. Sometimes the patrols were led by a contraband named John who had come into camp. "Redstick," a soldier in the 49th Ohio, wrote to his hometown paper in a letter dated November 13, "Capt. James Patterson

4 — The First Drops of Blood Are Drawn

and John, the scout, are now out scouting.... John is a negro and makes a valuable man in the scouting service."[18]

The men were anxious to join a general advance against the enemy, and when weeks passed with no forward movement, some saw an ominous reason. A soldier in the 6th Kentucky wrote to the *Louisville Anzeiger*, "We have continually put off going to Bowling Green and Nashville.... The contractors appear to run the supreme command, that is, the longer the war, the fuller the purse."[19]

While waiting to move against the enemy, the men found other diversions. Improving the living quarters was always a profitable use of one's time. There were concerts of the regimental bands, religious services, shopping trips to the sutlers' tents, and the visits of such dignitaries as Senator John J. Crittenden and Governor Oliver P. Morton of Indiana. There was a memorable visit at Thanksgiving 1861. The 6th Indiana marched to the nearby railroad village of Sonora to share the holiday with 200 citizens from Louisville's Sixth Ward, who ran the steel gauntlet of checkpoints on the L&N Railroad and came down, bringing with them a banquet, a singing troupe, railroad president James Guthrie, and a banner which they wished to present to the regiment. Generals McCook, Rousseau, and others were invited to attend, as well as a correspondent for the *New York Times*, who wrote an account of the festivities. The flag was presented to Colonel Thomas T. Crittenden, whose remarks were gracious in the 19th-century style. Mr. Guthrie delivered a "fervid" address in which he "reiterated over and over, with all his sledge-hammer power and Jackson-like firmness, and positiveness, that this Union must and should be preserved, that the Union Flag must never be disgraced, and must conquer." The feast was eaten and the appreciative men of the regiment immediately rechristened their part of Camp Nevin with the name "Camp Sixth Ward."[20]

More serious were the official visits of General Sherman, who visited Camp Nevin at least twice. The last time, November 17, he brought with him another general, the stern-looking Don Carlos Buell. All of the men may not have yet heard the news, but they certainly knew by the end of the generals' visit that for the past two days General Buell had been their commander. General Sherman was relieved of his Kentucky command and was on his way to Missouri.

5

The Stalemate Is Broken

From the first, General William T. Sherman's worries were overwhelming, and he was not good about keeping them to himself. He complained to Garrett Davis that he had been made to take command against his will, to Washington that he was not well supplied with "arms, clothing, or anything," and he complained to his wife Ellen that the sentries on the L&N were "volunteers who cannot appreciate the true State of the Case, and who are off their Guard and might be surprised and taken any night. This thought alone disturbs my sleep, and I cannot rest. Every night I fear this railroad may be broken."[1]

L&N president James Guthrie seems to have been Sherman's confidant during the fall, and he was in attendance at Sherman's insistence when Secretary of War Simon Cameron came with his entourage to visit at headquarters on October 16. Asked what he needed in his department, Sherman began a long analysis of his situation and then blurted out that he needed 60,000 men immediately to save Kentucky and would ultimately need 200,000 in order to push the enemy back to the Gulf of Mexico.

His visitors were stunned. No one else had envisioned the need for such numbers. Assistant Secretary of War Thomas A. Scott bluntly expressed the opinion of them all when he later said, "Sherman's gone in the head, he's luny."[2]

The direction of Sherman's career suddenly but quietly turned at the moment he gave his estimate of the numbers needed to fight the war to a successful conclusion in the West. However, it would be a little time before the result of his candor was seen. In the meantime, he continued to have an important ally in James Guthrie. President Lincoln ranked Guthrie, along with James and Joshua Speed, as being among his top advisors on the delicate situation in Kentucky. Political prisoners in Louisville were released if and when Guthrie thought they should be. One sees in the letters or telegrams from President Lincoln and Secretary of State Seward the frequently repeated phrase, "Consult with James Guthrie." In December 1861, when suggestions began flying that Lincoln needed a new cabinet, James Guthrie's name was put forward as a potential appointee. The cabinet shake-up did not occur, but the fact remained that Guthrie's word carried weight in Washington. It was important to have his support, and Sherman had it. Guthrie lobbied the government continually for support for Sherman, warning Washington that the enemy was stacking up against Sherman and that defeat was certain unless he got more in the way of men and arms. More than that, Guthrie suggested in an October 19 letter to President Lincoln that the proper strategy was to attack the enemy in the center of his line, i.e., Bowling Green. Guthrie wrote, "The Rebel force is rapidly enlarging upon this line.... If they force our centre Kentucky is lost for the present. If we force their centre Tennessee is saved. If possible, give us more men and abundance of arms."[3]

It was not by coincidence that the line of attack that Guthrie advocated happened to be along the route of his railroad. It seems to have been a common theme of the L&N president's correspondence. Railroad historian John E. Tilford wrote, "Undoubtedly, Guthrie played an important part in the decision of Federal military authorities to invade the South from Louisville along the line of the L&N." Union victory in the center would mean that the L&N was redeemed from enemy control.[4]

Guthrie's support was not enough to save Sherman. Apparently, the treatment for a general who had become "luny" was exile in Missouri, and that is where Sherman went after a final tour of his forces in the field with his successor, Don Carlos Buell, a man as deep as Sherman but much calmer. Buell reorganized his forces in what was now called the Department of the Ohio while he nursed a cold he had caught while touring the camps with Sherman. General McCook's former 1st Division at Camp Nevin on the L&N was now called the 2nd Division.

As an ally of Sherman's, James Guthrie might have been considered unwelcome in Buell's headquarters, but the evidence is that the L&N president easily worked his way into the new general's confidence and was soon at his elbow, successfully exerting upon him pressure to plan his southern advance along the route of the railroad.

Buell was a meticulous, slow-moving man, but events were about to start breaking across a broad front very quickly, and Buell was going to have to respond with what, for him, was unnatural speed.

• • •

When General Rousseau led the first regiments to David Nevin's farm in October 1861, the Confederate videttes at Bacon Creek were recalled. They burned the railroad bridge as they left.

The Federals had been rebuilding the bridge under the spying eyes of Confederate General Thomas C. Hindman (whose headquarters were at Cave City), and had nearly finished when, after dark on December 5, John Hunt Morgan and some 40 of his men rode out from the shadowy woods and burned it again.

General Buell was livid. This was an intolerable insult. He ordered General McCook to lead his division down to Bacon Creek and to send a brigade with artillery support forward to Munfordville, "leaving a small guard over the bridge at Nolin."[5]

General McCook moved three of his brigades to Bacon Creek and sent General Richard W. Johnson's 6th Brigade along with the 1st Kentucky Artillery on to Munfordville. The great bridge there had been destroyed, too. Simon Bolivar Buckner had been against destroying the Green River Bridge. He was a Munfordville native, felt the pride of a hometown boy in the engineering wonder, and knew that the locals shared that pride. Buckner said, "The destruction of so fine a work would injure us very much politically." His superiors saw more benefit than injury in dropping the bridge, however, and the bridge came down.[6]

That is, part of it came down. Stonemason Alex Key and his brothers and father were ordered to blow up the stone piers that supported the spans above. Ironically, these were the same men who had built the massive pillars only three years earlier. To destroy the bridge, they drilled holes in the two pillars on the south end, packed them with explosives, and lit the fuses. Luckily for the Federals, only one of the charges detonated and two spans (out of five) crashed into the river below — serious damage, to be sure, but not insurmountable. The railroad construction engineer Albert Fink had designed the bridge, and he could rebuild it.

General Richard W. Johnson's 6th Brigade arrived at Munfordville on December 10, along with the 1st Kentucky Artillery. Two companies of the 32nd Indiana were sent to the south bank of the Green River while the other companies of the regiment under Lieutenant Joseph Pietzuch went to work on a pontoon bridge. It was the 32nd Indiana, commanded by Colonel August Willich, who had drilled so impressively with the bayonet while at Camp Nevin. Within five days, the pontoon bridge was done, and two days after that, engineer Albert Fink arrived to supervise the rebuilding of the great iron bridge.

The Confederates, however, had other ideas. At noon on December 17, Company B, the right flank of Willich's southbank picket line, came under the fire of Confederate sharpshooters, part of General Thomas C. Hindman's forces from Cave City. A Federal patrol advanced to drive them off. When they ran into a larger force of Arkansas infantry and Texas cavalry, the patrol quickly fell back the way they had come. Colonel Willich had been called to headquarters shortly before, and Colonel Henry Von Treba was in command on the field, but like Willich, Von Treba was a veteran of the Prussian Army, and he knew what to do. He hurried forward Company C, the other company of the southbank picket and at the same time had his bugler blow a summons for help. Soon, the other companies of the 32nd were hurrying over the pontoon bridge. Von Treba formed his battle line, holding Companies E and H and part of Company D in reserve, and as Willich reported, "now ensued the most earnest and bloody part of the struggle."[7]

Colonel Benjamin F. Terry's 8th Texas Cavalry ("Terry's Texas Rangers") charged upon the Yankee line, holding their fire until they were within 15 yards. At this deadly close distance they fired with their shotguns and revolvers. The Germans were staggered and fell back, but they did not break.

Colonel Von Treba moved forward with the left and center of his line. The Rangers responded with another charge. They broke through the blue line but were themselves charged by Von Treba's reserve. Now, the Confederate guns began to throw "balls and shrapnels ... with great precision" among the Yankees.[8]

The fighting on the right was not at an end. A body of Rangers approached to within 15 yards (Willich called this an advance, not quite a full charge) before the Federals fired at them and drove them back. At another time, the Northerners might have enjoyed watching the Texans ride, for they were wonderful horsemen. As they attacked, they "sheltered themselves behind their horses, and shot over their necks, being all the while mounted." Under the circumstances, however, it was hard to find entertainment in the westerners' equestrian skills. Neither was there time, for here they came again.[9]

A body of perhaps 200 Texans charged and, typically, got very close before they fired on the Yankees. The Yankees fired a return volley into them and forced them back. The Rangers charged again, testing the front and both flanks this time. The Germans stood their ground and the Rangers fell back, but not before coming "close to our bayonets." It may have been during this charge that a Ranger who got especially close became involved in a battle of the blades. He struck at one of the Germans with his saber. The German parried the blow and ran the Ranger through with his bayonet.[10]

A final charge was noticeably weaker and once more ended with a repulse of the Rangers. But now, a Rebel infantry regiment approached with their band playing and pushed the Federals back. It was at this moment that Willich arrived on the scene. He took charge and, fearing that his line of retreat was about to be cut off, "ordered the signal 'fall back slowly' to be given." The 39th Indiana and the 49th Ohio came pouring across the river about this time, and General Hindman saw that he was soon to be outnumbered two to one. He called off the attack, fell back 2½ miles, and prepared for a counterattack. When none came, he returned to Cave City."[11]

It had been a hot 90 minutes. The Federals reported a loss of nine killed and 16 wounded. General Buell's forces had met the enemy in their largest engagement yet, and if they did not win exactly, neither did they break. The Rebels had left them in possession of the field. Their officers felt that they had acquitted themselves nicely their first time under fire. General Buell wrote to his friend General George B. McClellan, "The little affair in front of Munfordville was really one of the handsomest things of the season." From Camp Nevin, the Federals had now reclaimed another 23 miles of the L&N.[12]

General Hindman reported a loss of four killed, including Colonel B. F. Terry, and nine wounded. General Hardee, from his Bowling Green headquarters, wrote a congratulatory order in which he remarked upon the "impetuous valor" shown by the Confederates at what came to be called the Battle of Rowlett's Station. He hailed "the brilliant courage shown in the affair as a bright augury of their valor when the actual hour comes for striking a decisive blow."[13]

• • •

But when would that hour come? Albert Sidney Johnston seemed content to bring in more soldiers and stockpile supplies at Bowling Green and at Nashville, where he had also ordered works to be constructed against an overland attack. Major J. F. Gilmer, the chief engineer of the Western Department, complained to Johnston that "the agents employed under the sanction of Governor Harris to engage the services of negroes from their masters to work on the entrenchments for defending the city ... have failed to procure a force at all adequate to the magnitude of the work contemplated.... It is not probable, therefore, that any material progress can be made in the construction of the proposed defenses during the present month [December] unless other labor can be applied." There were other problems. Forage was running out at Bowling Green and had to be carted in from as far as 12 miles out. The soldier's clothes were wearing out and so was their patience. It was reported that the soldiers were chafing at the inactivity.[14]

All of the progress appeared to be on the political front. As a result of a secessionist convention held at Russellville on November 18–20, Kentucky was now a provisional Confederate state, and Bowling Green was its provisional capital. George W. Johnson was the provisional governor and three provisional delegates were sent to the Congress in Richmond.

However, there was nothing provisional about the Yankees at Munfordville or of those under U. S. Grant at Paducah or under George H. Thomas at Lebanon. They were very real and a worry to Johnston.

There were now more than 22,000 Confederates in Bowling Green. As the town filled up, space became precious, and more and more private homes were taken for military use. A few days after Christmas, the rude colonel of the 1st Missouri Infantry, Lucius L. Rich, took as his quarters Mt. Air, the home of Mr. Warner Underwood and his family. As the family packed to move out, soldiers came in to pilfer and to call dibs on the rooms they hoped to occupy once the Underwoods were gone. Colonel Rich persuaded the Underwoods to leave some of their furniture so that he could use it when his wife arrived. He promised to pay for it, but when Henry Underwood and his Uncle Lewis returned the next day for a few small things and for the promised money, Rich laughed and said, "Did your mother think I was going to pay Union people for anything? That's a good joke."[15]

In contrast to her negative opinion of the bullying Colonel Rich, diarist Josie Underwood called General Hardee a "gentleman." He refused on December 23 to permit the women to come back on Christmas Day to deliver "something nice" to the Union prisoners, but he said that he would allow them to come on New Year's Day. "He was so polite and courteous and escorted us himself to the carriage, helped us in, and said he wished the rebel ladies were half as anxious to do something for the sick soldiers and rebels in the guard house."[16]

As the officer responsible for Bowling Green, Hardee had reason to be concerned about sick soldiers, for measles were epidemic in the town as 1861 drew to a close. Three large buildings near the L&N Railroad were requisitioned as hospitals and, according to the report of a spy in the employ of General McClellan, were "so crowded that the stench coming from the outside doors was almost unbearable." William C. Davis, historian of the Orphan Brigade, wrote that there were as many as 840 Kentuckians alone in the infirmaries "in a single day."[17]

One of the most commented upon deaths at Bowling Green in December was that of Henry, the toddler son of Simon Bolivar Buckner. Buckner had brought his family down from Louisville to be with him at the beginning of the Confederate occupation of Bowling Green, but their happy sojourn was a short one. The child died, and Buckner requested of General Buell that his wife, accompanying the body of the dead child, be allowed to pass through the lines back to Louisville, along with two friends and an army surgeon. General Buell, through McCook at Munfordville, declined the request. It is said that Buell later apologized and that the funeral party was allowed to go through to Louisville where the child was buried.

Meanwhile, at the top level of command, Albert Sidney Johnston, while he continued to preside over the building of the five forts surrounding Bowling Green, the accumulation of supplies, and the placement of reinforcements, pondered the Federal strategy. On December 21 he wrote to Secretary of War Benjamin, "The movement of the enemy indicate[s] the design to turn my right by the turnpike road from Glasgow, through Scottsville to Gallatin and Nashville. They are concentrating in great force at Munfordville ... and at Columbia." To counter the enemy's moves, he shuffled troops around and waited and reinforced Bowling Green some more. He told Benjamin, "The day after tomorrow ... two Tennessee regiments from Camp Trousdale will reinforce the garrison of this place, and on the 24th another is promised."[18]

Then, after the first of the year, things began to break loose. On January 19, 1862, General George H. Thomas, commander of the 1st Division, Army of the Ohio, moved south to Mill Springs and defeated the Confederates there and killed their general, Felix Zollicoffer. The disorganized Rebels fell back into Tennessee. Johnston had lost the anchor of his eastern flank. At the same time, the Federals on the western flank were making

5 — The Stalemate Is Broken

menacing moves. To defend against a Yankee surprise, General Buckner and General John B. Floyd (who had brought a brigade from western Virginia) were dispatched to Russellville. Three weeks later, General U. S. Grant, along with a flotilla led by Flag Officer Andrew Foote, moved along the Tennessee River and forced the CSA evacuation of Fort Henry. Johnston's western flank was collapsing. It would be gone altogether if Fort Donelson fell. Johnston ordered Generals Buckner and Floyd to make a hard winter march to reinforce General Gideon Pillow there. It was of no use. On February 16, Fort Donelson unconditionally surrendered to Grant.

By that time, with Buell moving in his front, his right flank gone and his left flank hard pressed, Johnston had decided to abandon his Kentucky line. The orders went out on February 11 to the troops at Bowling Green to begin the move to Nashville the next morning. The hospitals were evacuated first. Some 850 of the worst cases made the trip to Nashville on the L&N. Those who were ambulatory had to endure a 60-mile march. They left behind a thousand graves of their comrades-in-arms.

The move required two full days, and on the last day, as they pulled out, the work of destruction began. The retreating Rebels demolished the L&N depot, engine house, and machine shops. They dropped the railroad bridge into the Barren River. They set fire to the town itself and burned the western side of the town square, including the store that belonged to Mr. Warner Underwood. Worse for the Underwood family, Colonel Rich's men burned Mt. Air before they left. The Underwoods found the ruins still smoldering when they returned to Bowling Green from their Simpson County exile. Bowling Green had lost its savor for the Underwood family, and they would move away before the end of the year.

The Rebels were on their way to Nashville. Some of them took out their anger at leaving the Bluegrass State without a fight by plundering homes and farms at Franklin, but it was important to keep moving. A short distance farther south, in a symbolic gesture, the officers dismounted and walked across the state line into Tennessee.

• • •

At Munfordville, General McCook took as his headquarters the home of Hart County deputy sheriff Alec Edwards and his wife Durenda. Dispossessed by the general and his staff, Mr. and Mrs. Edwards loaded their children and belongings in a wagon and went to Barren County, leaving their place to the Federals, who did not treat the house as a home. When the Edwards family returned, nothing was the same as it had been before they left. Even their cookstove had been carried out and left standing derelict in a field.

The enlisted men and junior officers camped on the farm owned by the father of General Thomas J. Wood, the commander of the 5th Brigade. Their jobs were: to clear and repair the Louisville and Nashville Turnpike, to rebuild the collapsed railroad tunnel near Horse Cave, to build defensive works overlooking the Green River (these works were on the farm of Mr. Anthony L. Woodson), to rebuild the L&N Railroad bridge, and all the while to scour the countryside for approaching Confederates.

Lyman S. Widney, a soldier in the 34th Illinois, left a vivid entry in his diary describing the work on the Green River Bridge. Widney wrote:

> It soon became an interesting sight to stand at the water's edge and look up at the massive timbers stretching like a spider's web from pier to pier. A work locomotive, darting back and forth on the frail temporary track reaching halfway across the span reminded me of a spider, so small it looked as it tugged away at a rope to which were attached heavy timber, being elevated from the water to their aerial supports. These sturdy timbers, so bulky at the start of their journey, seemed to shrink as they ascended until they dwindled to the size of matchsticks.[19]

Repairs were completed by Fink and his construction gangs on the ninth day of January, but the infantry did not receive orders to cross over for another month. When it did, it was not General McCook's division that advanced but rather the 3rd Division of General Ormsby M. Mitchel, fresh from Bacon Creek. In an irksome turn of events, McCook's men, who had led the way ever since leaving Camp Nevin, were ordered to turn about and march north, through Hardin County to West Point on the Ohio River, where steamers would be waiting to take them to U. S. Grant. The 2nd Division was going to help reduce Fort Donelson.

Freezing and thawing and a midwinter snowstorm had turned the Louisville and Nashville Turnpike into apple butter. The boys from the North always found Kentucky's mud unbelievable. A soldier in the 1st Wisconsin described it "as heavy as stone and as tough as putty.... Besides it is as slippery as ice and dirtier than any mud this side of Egypt. I suppose, by Darwin's theory of adaptation, one could easily account for the extra length of limb which distinguishes Kentucky horses. They need it to keep their heads above the mud."[20]

The foot soldiers had no extra length of limb, and they were having an awful time of it, so General Rousseau, at least, ordered his men to march up the ankle-twisting, ballasted bed of the L&N Railroad. At

5 — The Stalemate Is Broken

Upton, the column received an order to halt. General Buell had decided that there was time for McCook to reverse direction, march overland, and still reach Grant in time for the battle at Donelson. So, the men turned south again.

Miles ahead, Ormsby Mitchel's division struggled over a country filled with sinkholes and caves. There were no streams, and the only drinking water was found in ponds, which the retreating Rebels had filled with dead dogs, horses, and mules. Colonel John Beatty freely admitted that "when the Major sipped his coffee in a doubtful way and remarked that it tasted soupy, my stomach quivered on the turning point."[21]

When the 3rd Division came within sight of Bowling Green, they saw Confederate cavalry still setting fires in the town. Quoting Beatty again, "I rode ahead as rapidly as I could, and reached the river bank opposite Bowling Green in time to see a detachment of rebel cavalry fire the buildings which contained their army stores. The town was ablaze in twenty different places." To drive the arsonists off, Mitchel ordered Captain Cyrus Loomis' guns to unlimber on Baker Hill and to fire a few shells into the town. Colonel Basil Turchin's brigade moved down to the river bank and began crossing by means of a flatboat. At five o'clock the next morning, they entered the town, accompanied by a detachment of cavalry. The people rushed out to greet their liberators, thinking that they were Kentuckians, but recoiled when they discovered that Turchin's men were a group of "hungry, coarse Dutchmen."[22]

If the townspeople hoped that the behavior of the Federals would be any better that that of those who had just left, they were soon disappointed. Turchin's men spread out and went to looting. Colonel John Beatty said that they "gutted many homes." It seemed that Bowling Green was fair spoils for the men of either side, being considered too Northern by the Confederates and too Southern by the Federals.[23]

Mitchel threw pickets five miles south on the Louisville and Nashville Turnpike, on the L&N Railroad, and out toward Russellville on the Memphis Branch, while the bulk of the division made their camp north of the Barren River.

Much of Mitchel's subsequent report of the occupation of Bowling Green had to do with the condition of the L&N, which was so important not only to supplying his men but also to the upcoming advance on Nashville. He wrote, "Our victory is a bloodless one, but not the less important.... Our effort to drive the enemy from the town by artillery fire did not prevent them from firing the depot and several other public buildings.... One locomotive on the track was injured badly by firing the wood in the tender. Five or six locomotives in the engine house have been partially destroyed by the fire. Three of them it is thought may be repaired. We found on the track at the depot several platform cars, some house cars, several hand cars, with a piece of artillery mounted upon a platform car ready for removal, but which the enemy was compelled to abandon." Mitchel also mentioned that the railroad between Bowling Green and the Horse Cave tunnel was in "perfect condition," but that, north of there, a section of track 4½ miles long had been damaged by heating and bending the rails. He estimated a week's work by a regiment could reopen the railroad all the way to Bowling Green. In the meantime, he asked that supplies be sent via the L&N "as far as the railway is in order." Mitchel ended his report by asking General Buell to "please announce to the country the fall of Bowling Green and its present occupation by U.S. troops."[24]

Two days later, the infantrymen of the 3rd Division were able to cross into Bowling Green by a footbridge built on the ruins of the Barren River railroad bridge, and cavalry scouts reported that the road all the way to Franklin was open and the last Rebels were leaving the state.

The Louisville & Nashville Railroad was clear of Rebels all the way to the Tennessee line. When the repairs were completed, the railroad would be ready to resume business in Kentucky.

6

On to Nashville

With all of the Kentucky lines redeemed and with the reasonable hope that the L&N all the way to Nashville would soon be inside Union lines, 1862 promised to be a better year than 1861. True, the L&N had a daunting amount of damage to repair: depots and water tanks, machine shops and engine houses, culverts and permanent replacements for the Green River Bridge at Munfordville and the Barren River Bridge at Bowling Green. And this did not even take into account all the locomotives and rolling stock that had to be replaced. It was going to take money, but the L&N had a reserve and more would soon be coming in.

Then, in February 1862, government officials and railroad magnates held a summit meeting in which they negotiated a schedule that basically set passenger rates of two cents per mile per soldier and freight charges of between three and five cents per mile, depending on the distance. The government would receive a 10 percent discount and top priority would be given to government shipments.

James Guthrie was not included in the summit meeting, and he refused to accept these rates without a fight. They were unfair to the L&N, he argued. The L&N occupied a uniquely hazardous geographical setting and had consequently suffered more damage than other railroads. The lowball government rates would cripple the L&N in its efforts to repair the destruction and resume anything like a normal business climate.

To fill the financial gap, Guthrie hurriedly negotiated a contract with the Adams Express Company to simultaneously haul private freight, along with the military cargoes. It was a practice that would lead to controversies.

The fight over rates that began between Guthrie and the government in 1862 did not really end until the war did. Until then, the United States found itself fighting a war not only with the Southern Confederacy but with James Guthrie and the L&N Railroad.

• • •

The fall of Fort Donelson on February 16, 1862, left Nashville in an indefensible position, vulnerable to forces that might launch an overland attack and also to gunboats that might steam up the Cumberland River to shell the city to pieces. The rocking-chair strategists could see it, and it threw the city into a state of alarm only slightly greater than that of the high Confederate command. General Albert Sidney Johnston himself estimated that the Federal gunboats would arrive at Nashville within six hours.

It appears that General Johnston never had any intention of ending his retreat at Nashville. As early as December 4 of the previous year, his headquarters had received a discouraging report from Major J. F. Gilmer that although defensive positions had been prepared near Edgefield on the north bank of the Cumberland River, none of the fieldworks could accommodate "more than two or three regiments." In fact, "No one point sufficient in extent for encompassing a large number of troops has been found." The defensive posture of the city had not been improved, and Nashville would have to be sacrificed.[1]

The fact was that beginning on February 15, when the cold and ragged soldiers from Bowling Green began to arrive, followed two days later by the bloody survivors of Fort Donelson (including Generals Gideon Pillow and John B. Floyd, who had ignobly left Simon Bolivar Buckner behind to surrender), the people of Nashville were convinced that the Confederacy was collapsing in on them from all sides. They didn't need the men with stars on their collars to tell them that Nashville was in trouble. Citizens who could do so fled the city; so did the public officials. The Tennessee legislature took the train south; Governor Isham Harris paused long enough to make a valedictory speech in which he urged Nashvillians to burn their property, and he then joined the lawmakers. Those who remained were driven by a careening panic into outrageous behavior and normal life came to an end. The post office closed, as did many stores. There were no daily editions of the city's newspapers, leaving an information vacuum that was filled with rumors instead of facts. The streets were crowded with roaming looters.

When General Floyd arrived at the city on the morning of February 17, General Johnston put him in charge and immediately left the city for

Murfreesboro. Floyd had the remnants of his own command from Fort Donelson and was reinforced by Colonel Lucius Rich's 1st Missouri Infantry and, shortly afterward, the cavalry of Nathan Bedford Forrest and John Hunt Morgan. Floyd later claimed that he placed guards over the government property and put the rest of his men to work loading the railroad cars of both the Nashville & Chattanooga and the Tennessee & Alabama. It might be so, but when Nathan Bedford Forrest arrived on the morning of the 18th, he found the doors of the quartermaster and the commissary warehouses wide open and throngs of citizens carrying away whatever they could. It was Forrest who finally restored order. He was one of the most competent men in the Confederacy.

Forrest charged into the looters to drive them away from the warehouse doors and began the removal of all descriptions of property. He confiscated every wheeled vehicle he could find to trundle loads of goods through the streets to the waiting trains. On February 19, when it was deemed unsafe to wait any longer, cattle on the hoof and troops and conveyances were ordered to be brought over from the north bank of the Cumberland and the bridges to be destroyed. But the removal of government property continued. Over the next five days, hundreds of boxes of clothing and meat, machines for rifling gun barrels, and a laboratory for making percussion caps were saved. Even when Yankee scouts appeared across the river on February 20, the work continued. General Floyd left Nashville that day, but Forrest remained. In the last hours, 30 wagonloads of ammunition were carted away. Only then were the citizens invited to come back and take what they wanted. On February 23, Forrest burned whatever was left and led his cavalrymen south.

The defeats at Fort Henry and at Fort Donelson and the evacuation of Bowling Green and of Nashville were not what was expected of General Albert Sidney Johnston. All the man seemed to do was surrender territory to the enemy. He had an explanation, of course. He said that he had only 11,000 effectives to face Buell's 40,000, and outnumbered as he was, he had to decide which part of the Confederacy to let the Yankees occupy, Middle Tennessee or the Mississippi Valley. He decided to defend the Mississippi Valley and consequently abandoned Nashville with the intention of moving toward Decatur.

The explanation was not altogether satisfactory. A special committee of the Confederate Congress was appointed to investigate the reasons for the string of setbacks in Johnston's department. Johnston, though, still had the confidence of President Davis, and he kept his command until his death two months later at Shiloh, where he did, at last, stand and fight.

• • •

General Ormsby Mitchel had enjoyed the bloodless glory of occupying Bowling Green and was anxious to surge ahead to Nashville and add even more luster to the name of the 3rd Division. General George B. McClellan, too, was urging General Buell to order an advance. "Time is now everything," said McClellan. "If Nashville is open, the men could carry their small rations and bread, driving meat on the hoof.... If you can occupy Nashville at once it will end the war." A week later, McClellan was still waiting for word that Buell had stepped off.[2]

Buell refused to be prodded. He feared that Nashville was going to receive heavy reinforcements for its defense and was not willing to move against the Tennessee capital until everything was ready. That included having the railroad south from Bowling Green in perfect working order.

At last, on February 22, the 3rd Division moved out, some regiments marching by way of the turnpike, and some, including the artillery batteries, moving by way of the L&N. The train, because of washed-out bridges along the way, was no faster than the infantrymen on the turnpike, and both shoe-leather and steel-rail contingents arrived at Edgefield on the 24th. Across the river, they could see the American flag flying over the capitol building. General William "Bull" Nelson's 4th Division (which was part of the Army of the Ohio, but had been temporarily assigned to Grant) had beaten the 3rd by taking river transports up the Cumberland. It was of no matter except to those with an excess of unit pride. The important thing was that Nashville was safe in the hands of two Federal divisions. General Buell led the first elements of the 3rd Division into Nashville on February 25. The Federal presence was strengthened when the water-borne 5th Division arrived and began debarking, also on the 25th.

But just to remind the Yankees that there were Confederates still in the neighborhood who were not all that intimidated, John Hunt Morgan led a squad of 12 men back into Nashville on February 26 and burned the ferryboat *Minnetonka* while she rested, moored to a tree.

• • •

It would be several days before the rest of the Army of the Ohio came forward. General George H. Thomas' division arrived by steamer on or about March 1. General Alexander McDowell McCook's 2nd Division

6 — On to Nashville

came overland from Bowling Green and reached Nashville about the same time as Thomas.'

McCook's division had had a strange journey. On February 15, one day after having been ordered to march north to the mouth of the Salt River, the 2nd was suddenly stopped in its tracks near Upton and ordered to turn around and move south again. A day's worth of struggling through the snow and mud had been for nothing. Worse, it deprived the 2nd Division of the satisfaction of being the first to enter Bowling Green and also of any share of the pride in the Fort Donelson victory. Instead, the division was detailed to the heavy, unglamorous work of repairing the L&N. On February 23, it was reported that "railroad repairs between Cave City and Bowling Green progress slowly," but McCook's men were opposite Bowling Green by the end of the next day. It was further reported that they were having trouble crossing the Barren River, which was swollen by the recent heavy rains.[3]

The division finally managed to enter Bowling Green and remained there for several days before pushing on to Nashville. It is not recorded that McCook's men had any violent encounters with the people of northern Tennessee, but other units did. A few weeks later, when the 1st Kentucky Cavalry was marching south, it had some skirmishes with Champ Ferguson's irregulars, and when approaching Nashville, someone fired at the column from ambush. By good luck or bad aim, only a horse was wounded, but the bushwhacker obviously had hoped for a more tragic outcome.

Entering the city, the 1st Kentucky was somewhat safer from the danger of ambush, but it was made plain to the men that they were not welcome. The historian of the regiment, Sergeant E. Tarrant, wrote, "We found no observable welcome among the citizens. The businessmen remaining, unless they were newcomers from the North, treated us with freezing politeness; the pretty maids were shy and occasionally showed disdain in a quiet way. Even the children intimated by their actions that they were taught to despise us."[4]

Spillard F. Horrall of the 42nd Indiana found the atmosphere of the city to be oppressive. Horrall wrote, "It looked like a deserted city indeed.... The appearance on the streets was that of the most absolute loneliness. You might walk for blocks and blocks and not see a human being, except, perchance, you were to meet a Federal soldier. The citizens remaining kept indoors for days."[5]

When the citizens did eventually emerge, Horrall had much the same experience as Tarrant. He wrote, "The men were sullen and the women spiteful, full of 'spit-fire.' Some of them gratified their spirit by literally spitting on the soldiers as they passed under second-story windows, from which the 'little dears' looked with proud defiance and disdain."[6]

The soldiers who wandered the city were generally not impressed by the streets but thought the buildings showed some promise. The comments of Major J. A. Brents, 1st Kentucky Cavalry, were typical. He wrote, "There are not many Union citizens in Nashville. It cannot be called a handsome city, nor is it as large as Louisville. The capitol at Nashville is one of the finest buildings in America." Nashville was the first Southern capital to fall, and almost all the men made a point to see the new state capitol, an odd building, shaped like a marble boxcar with a lighthouse on top.[7]

Some of them also made a point of going to see one Southern lady who had not remained in the city only to insult them. She was Sara Childress Polk, the widow of President James K. Polk, and though she was Tennessee-born, she was gracious to all the Federals who came to visit, beginning with General Buell, who paid a courtesy call soon after he set up his headquarters. Neither Buell nor any other Yankee suspected that Mrs. Polk's house was a depository of treasures that her fleeing neighbors had pleaded with her to keep hidden until their return, but they knew that the grand old lady was herself a treasure of Southern womanhood, and they honored her and repaid her civility in kind.

• • •

When Buell moved south on March 15 to join in the general advance on the Confederate stronghold of Corinth, Mississippi, he left in charge of the post of Nashville General Ebenezer Dumont, but the real power in Nashville was the dour East Tennessean Andrew Johnson. The disheveled-looking Dumont was the military authority in Nashville only until June, when he was succeeded by Colonel Stanley Matthews who, after a month, was replaced by the longer lasting Colonel J. F. Miller.

Military authorities came and went, but Andrew Johnson was a more fixed and permanent force in Nashville. Lincoln appointed him on March 3, and Johnson left Washington right away for a trip that took him to Cincinnati on the B&O and down the Ohio to Louisville by paddle wheeler. From there he proceeded on a rattletrap of an L&N train pulled by a jury-rigged locomotive that had neither cowcatcher nor cab. He arrived in Nashville on March 12 and remained until the spring of 1865, when he traveled back to Washington, D.C., to be sworn in as vice-president. The vice-presidency is widely regarded as a job with little authority,

6 — On to Nashville

but as wartime governor of Tennessee, Johnson was a power to be reckoned with. He took control of the Bank of Tennessee and ordered the arrest of civilians, including some teachers, and either imprisoned them or banished them to Louisville or beyond. He had an ongoing feud with Nashville's ministers, and when many of them refused to take the oath of allegiance to the federal government, he imprisoned them. He replaced city officials who would not take the oath, and he controlled the press. The *New York Times* praised Johnson's "firmness and prudence." Insofar as his relations with the military authorities in Nashville were concerned, there was no question about what the administration expected. The order came directly from Secretary of War Stanton on March 22, 1862, that the officer in command of Nashville would "report to him [Johnson] and execute his orders."[8]

Johnson was fiercely loyal to the Union. He was the only senator from a seceding state who never gave up his seat, and his appointment as military governor of Tennessee was a fitting reward. But his tenure was not a happy one, either for himself or for those who had to deal with him. He constantly quarreled with General Buell and with the military authorities in the city. He was touchy about any perceived trespass upon the boundaries of his power — at times, even President Lincoln had to step in to sooth Johnson's ruffled feelings — but he was not so careful about the boundaries of other men's power, eternally offering advice about what needed to be done in other areas, especially East Tennessee.

Moreover, Johnson constantly carped that Nashville was undermanned, virtually abandoned, and about to be attacked. General Buell wrote to Johnson, "I have not apprehended an advance upon Nashville…," but Johnson was not reassured. He complained all through the spring and summer.[9]

He need not have worried so. The L&N Railroad was entirely within Union lines now. Troops were stationed all along its length, and thousands more were arriving in Louisville every day. Before Nashville would be in any real danger, the L&N would have to be so badly broken up that troops could not be funneled south. Nashville might be annoyed on its outskirts by Confederate raiders, there might even be acts of vandalism inside the city, but if the L&N could remain operational and in Federal hands, Nashville would be relatively safe.

The question was: could the L&N remain operational? John Hunt Morgan had something to say about that.

7

The Year of the Thunderbolt

The Federal campaign to reach Corinth met an obstacle. The Rebels did not sit at that important Mississippi railroad town and wait to be attacked. Instead, they moved up to the Tennessee River and surprised General Grant at Shiloh. The Confederate fought Grant to a frazzle for an entire bloody day before General Buell's army arrived on the scene. On the second day, April 7, the fresh troops of the Army of the Ohio helped to turn the tide. The Confederates fell back to Corinth, and the Federals took some time to catch their breath before moving out again, headed for their original destination. When they appeared in three columns on the outskirts of Corinth, General P. G. T. Beauregard slipped out of town without a fight, and the Federals moved in. It was an easy victory and an important turning point.

John Hunt Morgan played little role in the Battle of Shiloh or in the defense of Corinth. Morgan was a destroyer of railroads, the "Thunderbolt of the Confederacy." There was an obvious military benefit to be gained from disrupting the enemy's transportation and communications, but there was another reason that Morgan specialized in behind-the-lines raiding. He had little appetite for battle. General Jacob D. Cox explained Morgan with considerable insight in his *Military Reminiscences of the Civil War*. While acknowledging the "boldness" of Morgan's raids, Cox wrote, "It cannot be said that he showed any liking for hard fighting. Like boys skating near thin ice, he seemed to be trying to see how close he could come to danger without getting in."[1]

He had shown the same characteristic at Camp Nevin when, with a dozen or so men, he would sneak through the lines and attack unsuspecting pickets in the dark. Morgan chose as his special target the L&N Railroad,

7—The Year of the Thunderbolt

not only because it was the primary artery of supply for the United States forces in the West, but also because striking the railroad meant that he would have a numerical advantage in every encounter and could perform his acts of destruction without having first to win the right to do so by means of a stand-up fight. When he could strike by surprise, Morgan was fearsome, but when the element of surprise was lost or the odds against him grew too long, he sidled off to fight another day.

Eighteen sixty-two was Morgan's year. On March 16, the day Buell's army stepped off for southern Tennessee, Morgan struck Gallatin. It was nearly perfect for his inaugural raid; the town was on the L&N and it had no garrison. Forty men rode with Morgan as he approached the small town that was to play such a large part in the legend of the "Thunderbolt."

His first stop was the telegraph office where, ironically, the operator had just been receiving reports of Morgan's whereabouts. Morgan made a prisoner of the man and collected all the books and papers in the place. He captured and destroyed a train, and after spending the night in a comfortable home in the town, he destroyed the L&N water tank and burned some boxcars. Then he returned to Murfreesboro with five prisoners in tow. The destruction of railroad property in Gallatin might have been worse except for the intervention of Judge Joseph C. Guild, who stepped forward and persuaded Morgan to spare the depot.

The Southern reading public did not care about what was spared in Gallatin. They were more interested in the newspaper reports of what was destroyed and in details of the dashing style with which it was done. Morgan was popular, a fact he touched upon in his report of the Gallatin affair. He wrote, "The whole country through which we passed turned out en masses to welcome us. I have never before witnessed such enthusiasm and feeling.... All expressed themselves gratified at the presence of Southern soldiers in their midst. A handsome flag was presented by the ladies of Gallatin and some accompanied us even to the ferry." The Southern people might have felt glad to have Confederate soldiers in their town under any circumstances, but it was John Hunt Morgan who made it an event and he was the one that they followed out of town to the ferry.[2]

The many admirers of Morgan would have been thrilled to know that this first Gallatin raid was only a rehearsal for what was to come.

• • •

After Shiloh, both the North and the South struggled, not only to absorb the enormity of the loss of life, but also to care for the wounded survivors. In Nashville, no fewer than 14 hospitals were begun to accommodate the bloodied survivors of Shiloh, and even in far away Louisville, the mayor was warned that he needed to prepare to receive 2,000 wounded. It was during this period, when a stunned public began to realize the unthinkable cost of the war, that Morgan struck again.

This next raid was longer and involved more men. During the second week in May, Morgan rode out of Tennessee at the head of 150 Raiders. He planned to hit Bowling Green, but a reported garrison of 500 troops there discouraged him. Instead, he held to the east, bypassed Bowling Green, and headed for a smaller railroad town, Cave City. There he captured the telegraph office, as well as the L&N station, and a train, which he set on fire and sent roaring on south. There was not much more to do in such a small town, but the Raiders lingered, hoping to capture a trainload of Confederate prisoners on the way to Louisville. The next train that approached, though, was not the prisoner train but a southbound express. Morgan and his men blocked the track to stop the train and, when it did stop, loaded the track behind it with debris to prevent its escape. The passengers on this second train included both Union soldiers and women, some of them military wives. Morgan arrested and paroled the military men, emptied the express box of $6,000, and, caught up in a chivalric impulse, indulged the ladies' comfort by allowing them to return to Louisville on their train. If James Guthrie had loaded a delegation of women on every train, he might have saved a lot of rolling stock and a good many locomotives.

There was no great consequence of the Cave City raid. The damage was so slight that Morgan does not seem to have even filed a report. It was, however, the second successful hit-and-run operation Morgan had conducted — both of them against the L&N Railroad — and he was encouraged. He began right away to plan an even more ambitious foray into his native state.

• • •

As a reward for his initiative in carrying war to the enemy, Morgan was allowed to raise a regiment, the 2nd Kentucky Cavalry. An increase in rank was not authorized, but Morgan now began calling himself a brigadier general. Ostensibly he was attached to General Edmund Kirby Smith, but that was only a technicality, for Morgan was too independent minded to take orders from Smith or anyone else. "Brigadier General" Morgan kept his own schedule and went where he wanted. Where he wanted to go in July 1862 was home to Kentucky. His 900 men would

7 — The Year of the Thunderbolt

ride deep into the northern Bluegrass Region and return to Tennessee in 24 days. This time he would strike the L&N twice, the main stem at Horse Cave and the Lebanon Branch at its terminus, Lebanon.

As Morgan finalized his preparations, relations were becoming strained between the government and the L&N. Officers in charge of the U.S. warehouses in Nashville were chafing about the poor service they were getting. On June 16, the assistant quartermaster at Nashville protested to General Buell's chief of staff, Colonel James B. Fry, that army requisitions were not being filled at Louisville and also complained about the railroad's slowness. He did acknowledge, though, that there was a possible explanation. He wrote, "The Louisville & Nashville Railroad has not enough rolling stock to bring forward all the supplies." The commissary of subsistence at Nashville, however, insisted that there was another cause for the shortages: the L&N was giving priority to car loads of private commodities. He wrote to Fry, "Four hundred thousand rations received last night by rail; more than one million rations en route by river, which ought to have been sent by rail, and over two million for which bids have been accepted in Louisville. The Louisville & Nashville Railroad commenced to bring sutlers' and citizens' freight, while subsistence stores are sent by river. I saw several car loads of private freight in depot to-day."[3]

Whatever damage that Morgan inflicted on the railroad would only reduce further the tonnage of supplies the L&N could deliver and harden Northern officials' attitudes toward a railroad that, in their view, was not doing its job and that seemed more interested in hauling private cargo for profit than government cargo for victory.

On Independence Day 1862, Morgan led his cavalry out of Knoxville toward Sparta and from there almost due north to Tompkinsville, Kentucky, where he had a small fight and captured 300 men. From Tompkinsville, the Raiders veered west and hit Glasgow, where they burned commissary stores and medical supplies, and captured a small arsenal of guns, which the "Brigadier" distributed to 200 of his unarmed men.

Beyond Glasgow, the Raiders rode north to Horse Cave. Now Morgan was deep behind enemy lines, and he needed to know what the Federals were up to. To that end, he ordered his telegrapher, a Canadian-born Rebel named George A. Ellsworth, to tap into the wires and listen in. Ellsworth was the kind of man who helped enhance the Morgan legend for élan. Daring the meteorological gods, Ellsworth sat for several hours with his telegraphic key on his knee, in a thunderstorm, with a pool of water creeping up his shins. From this time on, he was "Lightning" Ellsworth.

At Horse Cave, Ellsworth discovered that, with Morgan on the prowl, all shipments of money via the L&N had been suspended. No gold in the cars, and no nuggets of intelligence coming over the wires, it was disheartening. Ellsworth reported that he spent some time reading the latest telegraphic news from Washington and New York. After a few hours, Ellsworth was ordered to send a bogus dispatch reporting that Nathan Bedford Forrest was attacking Murfreesboro and that Morgan, moving to support him, was somewhere between Scottsville and Gallatin. It was a small but effective deception.

However, it was at Lebanon that Ellsworth really shined. There, Morgan and his butternut Cossacks had a festival of destruction. They burned the Rolling Fork Bridge and two warehouses, which included in their inventory 500 sacks of coffee. While the aromatic black clouds swirled above, Ellsworth sat in the telegraph office, where he pretended to be the usual operator. He learned that a train carrying 500 troops had passed through Lebanon Junction at 8:30 the previous night. Luckily, Morgan had anticipated such a Federal move. From Horse Cave, he had sent a detachment of three companies in the direction of Lebanon Junction, and now Ellsworth learned that these men had intercepted the train and fought a 20 minute skirmish with the troops on board. The train had reversed course and returned to Lebanon Junction, never having gotten any closer to Morgan than New Hope. This was useful news. It meant that Morgan had the time to finish his business in Lebanon. He robbed the Commercial Bank of public money. He torched the hospitals, 35 wagons, 53 ambulances, and quantities of clothes, boots, and surplus weapons and ammunition, before proceeding toward Springfield and Harrodsburg. En route, at Midway, Ellsworth again pranked the Yankees when he sent telegraphic intelligence that Morgan was attacking Frankfort, thus directing the enemy away from Morgan's actual route.

Morgan later reported that he enjoyed a grand reception at Harrodsburg — the people even threw a picnic for him and for his dusty men — and another gratifying welcome at Georgetown, where he rested for two days. The raid was becoming a joy ride, and while Morgan scattered Home Guards and burned property and stole saddle mounts at his pleasure, the Yankees fumed. Kentucky adjutant John W. Finnell yelped, "They are playing Hell all through the Central Counties. Are beating our forces in detail. We have no one in the field worth a damn."[4]

Even the president in Washington became aware that things were not right in his birth state. Lincoln wired Major General Henry W. Halleck

7 — The Year of the Thunderbolt

A stockade on the L&N. *Harper's Weekly.*

in Corinth, Mississippi: "They are having a stampede in Kentucky. Please look into it."[5]

Morgan just laughed. His primary opponent in this statewide game of tag was General Jeremiah T. Boyle in Louisville, and for Boyle, Morgan only felt a growing contempt. Boyle had been in command of the 11th Brigade in the 5th Division under General Thomas L. Crittenden, when he was assigned to take command of the troops in Kentucky beginning May 27. Perhaps the timing of his appointment had something to do with Morgan's jab at Cave City in May.

Boyle was a soft-eyed, pudgy-faced man with a tendency to exaggerate every little threat into certain doom, a weakness he tried to cover up with a brave line of talk. His shortcomings would become obvious in time, but immediately after his appointment, the war critics were willing to give Boyle his chance. George D. Prentice, editor of the *Louisville Daily Journal*, felt an optimism at Boyle's appointment, which he expressed by a terrible pun. Prentice wrote, "Our Kentucky rebels had better look well to their conduct, or they will get in hot water and find themselves badly Boyled."[6]

General Boyle understood the importance of protecting Union interests in Kentucky. What he did not understand was how to accomplish this by any method other than oppressive force, and once he assumed command in the District of Kentucky, he wasted little time in implementing a campaign of suspicion, suppression, and enforced obedience. He decreed, "When damage shall be done to the person or property of Loyal citizens by marauding bands of guerrillas, the disloyal of the neighborhood will be held responsible and a military commission appointed to assess damages and enforce compensation." He composed a loyalty oath for suspected Rebel sympathizers and imposed a death penalty for those who violated it. He interfered in elections, tamped down freedom of the press, and locked up at least one editor. He appointed provost marshals for each of Kentucky's counties and, three days before Morgan began his raid, authorized them to start imprisoning disloyal women. War against women! How could one not have contempt for such a man?[7]

If he had at least been a worthy opponent, Morgan might have had a grudging respect for him as a military man, but Boyle soon made it plain that he was no match for a bold raider like Morgan. The convalescents at Louisville were mobilized to protect the city and its bridges. The 9th Pennsylvania Cavalry was dispersed across the region south of Louisville to watch for Morgan, and the 1st and 2nd Kentucky Cavalry (USA) combed the Bluegrass, but all to no avail; Morgan would not be caught. And all the while, Boyle cried that he needed reinforcements (at least two cavalry regiments and more infantry from Buell, and "all forces in Ohio and Indiana") and complained about the quality of the Gallagher rifles with which some of his forces were armed. In Boyle's imagination, Morgan had 3,000 men loose in Kentucky. Boyle asked the mayor of Cincinnati to send him artillery and warned that all the Rebels in the state were about to rise in insurrection.[8]

Boyle's superiors tried to steady him. From his headquarters at Huntsville, Buell reassured him that two companies behind fieldworks could protect the railroad bridges on the L&N "against any attack likely to be made by any force of cavalry," and instructed him to build stockades with loopholes for rifles and send a guard of 40 soldiers on every train. He added that, "The force of the enemy is doubtless greatly exaggerated." President Lincoln also tried to stiffen Boyle's spine and sent him a wire from the War Department telling him, in essence, to handle the situation and forget about getting help from Buell. "We cannot venture to order troops from General Buell," Lincoln said. "We know not what condition he is in. He may be attacked himself." But Boyle knew that Buell and Lincoln were far away; he was the only one who knew the true situation, and it was dire.[9]

Beyond Georgetown, Morgan continued a bit farther south to Cyn-

7—The Year of the Thunderbolt

thiana, where he had the sharpest fight of the raid. Detachments of the 18th Kentucky Infantry, the 7th Kentucky Cavalry, and several companies of Home Guards made a stand on the road leading into town. After one and a half hours of fighting, the Federals fell back into the streets of Cynthiana, where they continued fighting until sundown, when they surrendered. An undetermined number of prisoners were captured along with their artillery. The railroad bridge leading into town was burned before Morgan turned south again. He led his men through Paris, Winchester, and Richmond, where he learned that four separate cavalry columns were converging on him. He hurried through Crab Orchard to Somerset, where he inflicted the last destruction of the raid, burning the government stores there and 120 wagons. He also had Ellsworth tap into the telegraph lines to cancel, in the name of General Boyle, all orders to pursue Morgan. He also took a moment to fling a Morse code insult back at General Boyle. As Morgan dictated, Ellsworth tapped out, "Good morning, Jerry! The telegraph is a great invention. You should destroy it as it keeps me posted too well. My friend Ellsworth has all your dispatches since July 10 on file. Do you want copies?"[10]

While he was at it, he also sent a message to George D. Prentice of the *Louisville Daily Journal*: "Good morning, George D.! I am quietly watching the complete destruction of all of Uncle Sam's property in this little burg. I regret exceedingly that this is the last that comes under my supervision on this route. I expect in a short time to pay you a visit and wish to know if you will be at home. All well in Dixie." From Somerset, Morgan continued through Monticello south and soon really was back in Dixie.[11]

In his summary of what was afterward known as the "First Kentucky Raid," Morgan wrote, "I left Knoxville on the 4th day of this month with about 900 men and returned to Livingston on the 28th instant with nearly 1200, having been absent just twenty-four days during which time I traveled over one thousand miles, captured seventeen towns, destroyed all the Government supplies and arms in them, dispersed about 1500 Home Guards, and paroled nearly 1200 regular troops." In doing so, he had lost only 90 men killed, wounded, and missing. However, something did not quite jibe. Considering all of his talk of frenetic welcomes in one town after another, why didn't he recruit more than a measly 300 men during his month in Kentucky?[12]

• • •

While Morgan was raiding, General Don Carlos Buell and his army were struggling across North Alabama on their way to Chattanooga. General Halleck had ordered it. Chattanooga was a worthy goal, no one denied that; it was the route that was poorly considered. The enemy was not strong in North Alabama, but the country itself was hostile. It was cotton country, not well-suited to supplying the ration and forage needs of an army on the march. In other years, paddle wheelers on the Tennessee River would have been a way to supply the army, but in the summer of 1862 a drought descended on the South that dried the Tennessee to a relative trickle, and steamers could not keep pace with the Army of the Ohio, especially as it moved farther and farther upstream. That left only the railroads.

Buell's line of march paralleled the Memphis & Charleston Railroad. It was fed from the north by the Nashville & Decatur Railroad and the Nashville & Chattanooga Railroad. They, in turn, were fed by the Louisville & Nashville Railroad. A break, or combination of breaks, in any of these and Buell's army was going to be in real trouble.

The L&N was a worry for another reason: it still was not meeting expectations, and complaints about its unsatisfactory service continued. On July 15, Captain Robert MacFeely in Nashville complained to General Buell's Huntsville headquarters, who passed it on to Louisville, that he had "no provisions in Nashville and has received none for six days, and ... the railroad from Louisville has been occupied in carrying forage and private freight. The general is discouraged at having to urge this matter. The army will starve unless there is more activity and success in throwing forward supplies."[13]

In Louisville, Colonel Thomas Swords replied, "The road has been wholly occupied by General Boyle for the movement of troops. The collision last week crippled four locomotives. The road is exclusively used for military purposes and trains commenced going through every morning. I am [also] sending supplies by water as fast as possible."[14]

It was undoubtedly true that the L&N had equipment failures and accidents and that, at the time of Captain MacFeely's complaint, it had been busy responding to the emergency in Kentucky. However, it is also easy to believe that James Guthrie, dissatisfied with the going government rates for passengers and freight — even with the 25 percent bonus that the government had authorized for his railroad, alone, to receive — was favorably inclined to give priority to private, more lucrative fares. This is especially true in light of the previous complaints in June against the L&N.

It is also true that the Rebels did not need the help of a recalcitrant railroad president like Guthrie to hinder Buell. This was the kind of warfare for which the Rebels were perfectly suited. Small bands of men had a vast area in which to roam, hitting isolated targets, such as bridges and tunnels, with a minimum of risk. By their sabotage miles away, they could halt the forward progress of Buell's army and wreck the North Alabama campaign.

At the beginning of the campaign, Buell's columns traveled with twelve wagons per regiment, plus an additional 75 wagons carrying food for the men and forage for the animals. They were full at the start, but they were soon rattling empty down the dusty roads.

By necessity, the men could not be farther than fives days' travel from the railroad. Yet, the railroad proved — as Buell had feared — almost completely useless, for guerrilla raiders and cavalrymen, such as Nathan Bedford Forrest, kept it torn up. There were not enough wagons to deliver supplies from the breaks. The campaign quickly became more of an exercise in engineering than in fighting. Rebuilding the railroad both slowed down the advance and used up the energy of men who were now on half rations. On June 29, elements of the Army of the Ohio entered Athens. There were supposed to be supply wagons waiting there, but there were not. The advance creaked to a complete stop. Buell kept some of his divisions in Alabama and sent others to strategic points in Tennessee where they could guard and repair the railroad. Besides the obvious defensive benefits of this deployment, far-flung units would have an easier time finding food and forage.

On July 12 came some good news at last. All the railroad repairs to the north were finished, and Buell would soon be receiving a gush of supplies. Unfortunately, the expectation of full rations and new uniforms was short-lived. The next news that arrived said that Nathan Bedford Forrest had hit Murfreesboro, destroyed the railroad bridge there, along with 200,000 rations, and had captured 1,400 men. A week later, he wrecked two bridges between McMinnville and Nashville. The Memphis & Charleston Railroad was broken again, too.

Buell was with the advance at Stevenson, Alabama, when the news came that trains could get through again. Stevenson was the terminus of the Nashville & Chattanooga Railroad, so relief would be coming directly to the men. Over 200,000 rations arrived by rail on July 29 and a like amount the next day. Shoes, uniforms, and a full allowance of food must have transformed Buell's army and also sparked an optimism that the march could continue and Chattanooga still be won.

Then came the news from Gallatin.

• • •

If John Hunt Morgan had really wanted to do some harm on his First Kentucky Raid, he would have concentrated on the L&N Railroad. By destroying the main line to Nashville, he would have turned off the tap, depriving General Buell of the supplies his army needed in Alabama. The railroads from Nashville to Decatur and to Chattanooga would not have had to have been broken, for they would have had nothing to haul without the loads from Louisville via Nashville. The trouble was that the L&N was too well protected in Kentucky. Munfordville, for example, had a garrison of 1,800 men, plus a company of artillery—too strong to tempt a raider like Morgan—and it was a similar picture at nearly every stop along the railroad. So, Morgan flickered around the state, annoying Home Guards and burning supplies, while the hard work of stopping Buell fell to Nathan Bedford Forrest.

It is ironic, then, that the coup de grâce to the Federal campaign was delivered by Morgan.

The Federals were busy building stockades to protect the railroads both north and south of Nashville in compliance with General Buell's orders of July 30. Regarding the L&N, he sent word to Colonel J. F. Miller at Nashville:

> Order stockades built at every bridge or other important point occupied by troops on the road north of Nashville. It must be done without an hour's delay. Properly fortified in that way a guard of from twenty to forty men, according to the importance of the bridge, is amply sufficient at any point and two companies at Gallatin.
>
> I will send plans and specifications for stockades by mail. In the meantime order the posts to be cut and hauled immediately. They should be eleven feet long and from eight to ten inches thick. At least three hundred posts will be required at every point.[15]

Colonel Miller replied that the work on the stockades had already begun. Miller was a capable man, but on August 6, Buell sent his engineer, Captain James St. Clair Morton, to oversee the work. "Don't lose an hour in completing the stockades," Buell told St. Clair. "The work must go on night and day, and if it cannot be done well it must at any rate be done quickly." Captain Morton pushed the work but complained that his gang of slave laborers was much smaller than he had requisitioned. He had asked for 1,000 hands and had received only about 150.[16]

Nashville itself was in no danger. Colonel Miller had an aggregate of almost 4,100 men present and ready for duty, but Buell worried about the approaches. He wanted a stockade built at the north end of the railroad

7—The Year of the Thunderbolt

bridge over the Cumberland River. It had only been reopened since the second week in June, and Buell feared that Morgan might creep in to burn it. Even more worrisome was Gallatin. Buell had specified in his July 30 order that two companies be posted there, almost five times more men than at any other of the stockades. Buell was right; Gallatin was a weak spot on the L&N because of two tunnels about seven miles north of there. The northern most of the tunnels was called "Little South," 600 feet long, and the southern one was called "Big South," nearly 1,000 feet long and so close to the other that they were referred to as the Twin Tunnels. A contingent of the 28th Kentucky Infantry protected the town of Gallatin and the tunnels, 375 men under Colonel William P. Boone.

About dawn on August 12, Morgan's cavalry showed up in Gallatin. They came in quietly, slipped through a rather porous picket line and captured the drowsy pickets from behind, and buttoned up the town before anyone knew they were there, including Colonel Boone. He was caught in the comfortable hotel room where he slept with his wife. Gallatin was suddenly in Southern hands, and not a shot had been fired.

Morgan's men were too busy to celebrate. "Lightning" Ellsworth was in the telegraph office sending false reports to confuse the enemy and trying (but failing, this time) to intercept some useful Yankee messages. Others burned government stores, as well as a freight train of 40 cars, and when a second train pulled into the station, they burned it too, after offloading some horses and Springfield rifles.

Now, as was his custom, Morgan scattered his men in small bands to spread the destruction over a wider area. One bunch went south a few miles to destroy the Pilot Knob Bridge. Another was sent north to the Twin Tunnels. They easily overpowered the guards and prepared to destroy Big South. Some men piled crossties inside the tunnel as an obstruction while others stacked flammables on flatcars behind a locomotive. They set the flatcars on fire, opened the throttle on the locomotive, and sent it screaming into the tunnel where it hit the crossties and overturned. The heat of the fire inside the tunnel was incredible. The supporting timbers were consumed and 800 feet of the tunnel collapsed. The L&N Railroad was blocked by an underground plug of locomotive and flatcar parts, and thousands of tons of shattered, superheated rock.

Before they left, the tunnel destroyers threw another hindrance in the path of any work crews that Colonel Miller might send up from Nashville. They tore up 600 feet of track below Big South and burned a small bridge.

After about 18 hours in Gallatin, Morgan looked around and saw that there was nothing more to do. Everything of military value was burned or stolen, every captured Federal was paroled and walking north toward Bowling Green, and the railroad was critically broken. He led his triumphant men back to Hartsville. Only a small rear guard was left behind in Gallatin.

Morgan could not have known it, but he would never do anything greater than what he had just done for the Confederacy. The railroad was closed for 98 days, but its importance is seen in the context of the larger picture. For the first time Morgan had conducted a raid, not only to satisfy his personal craving for adventure and attention, but in co-operation with a major military objective, stopping Buell.

And Buell was stopped. His only source of supplies had been shut off once and for all, and the North Alabama campaign could not continue. Stevenson, Alabama, was as close to Chattanooga as General Buell ever got.

The story of Gallatin, however, was not yet completely told. On August 13, Colonel Miller came as far north as the Pilot Knob Bridge with a brigade of infantry and a battery of artillery. It was the right move, as far as his military reputation was concerned, but Miller must have known that it was unlikely that foot soldiers could catch any of Morgan's horsemen. And they would not have, except that they suddenly came upon Morgan's unsuspecting rear guard just south of Gallatin. A short skirmish followed and three of the Confederates were killed. Miller went into town, searched the houses, and warned the citizens against helping the Rebels, before marching back to Pilot Knob and taking the train home to Nashville.

After the destruction of Big South, the L&N responded quickly. Work crews sent by Albert Fink showed up on August 13, the day after the raid, to begin repairing the damage. They found that they could not do much in the tunnel, for the rock was still too hot to remove and a seam of coal had caught fire and was still burning. As they inspected the work site, a band of Morgan's cavalrymen appeared and drove them away with gunfire. The L&N men came back the next day with a military escort and began working on the downed bridges. The Rebels attacked again. In the fire fight that followed, they killed a railroad carpenter and chased the others down toward Nashville. Morgan had made his point. He had won back 50 miles of the L&N and was now in control. He added a punctuation mark on August 17 when he cut the telegraph lines.

In response to the assault on civilian employees of the railroad, Lieutenant Colonel Horace H. Heffren led a second punitive force of 300 bluecoats to Gallatin. Since the people there had evidently not followed Colonel Miller's advice about not co-operating with Morgan, Heffren ordered the arrest of every man over age 12 and began herding them back down the L&N toward Pilot Knob and the railroad to Nashville.

Three hours later, at about midnight on August 20, the news reached Morgan's camp of this outrage in Gallatin. He sent Captain J. B. Hutcheson ahead to burn the Sandersville trestle, and thus cut off the Federals, while he led the rest to Gallatin. By morning, he was at the now familiar town, but there were no Federals to be found, only women and small children who begged Morgan to bring back their husbands and fathers and who told horror stories of atrocious Yankee behavior on both this and the previous occasion.

Morgan took up the trail of the Yankees and their prisoners. The sequence of events is difficult to follow from accounts of the action, but it appears that Heffren intended to return to Nashville by rail. Soon realizing that he was cut off, he was forced to move his prisoners toward Nashville on foot. They seem to have become strung out on the march, for Morgan soon caught up with them and began picking the Yankees off, one by one, and rescuing the prisoners. If the bluecoats had been in a compact column, Morgan would not have had such an easy time of it, but they were scattered and isolated, and they panicked when they saw the Raiders thundering down on them. Even if they tried to surrender, they were killed. Morgan had declared to his men at the beginning of the ride that there would be no quarter given, and there was none. James Ramage, the pre-eminent Morgan biographer, quoted the general as saying, "There were so many of them that when they threw down their arms we couldn't shoot them all." Atypically for Morgan, he also ordered attacks on all of the new stockades along the way, successfully reducing them and capturing the small garrisons.[17]

Morgan was able to recapture 40 of the prisoners en route, but 20 were still in Union custody when they reached Edgefield. These final 20 were hurried into the stockade by their guards. The Edgefield stockade was defended by twenty men of the 50th Indiana under Captain H. N. Atkinson. Morgan ordered an attack, but Atkinson's men beat Morgan back three times over a span of three hours, and the Thunderbolt finally withdrew to Gallatin, returning the 40 prisoners who had been rescued to their homes and grateful families. He and his men were exhausted, so Morgan chose to spend the night at Gallatin. It turned out to be a small mistake.

All this time, a combined force of 800 cavalry, infantry, and artillery men under General Richard W. Johnson had been moving toward Morgan. Johnson was one of the Camp Nevin generals, and as such, he was one of those who had felt Morgan's sting from the earliest days of the war. He must have remembered how Morgan had moved through the autumn nights, killing the pickets along the Nolin River and always evading capture. He wanted very badly to catch his fellow Kentuckian, boasted that he would, and had every reason to be confident that he could. Before the war, Johnson had chased Comanches on the Texas Plains as an officer of the 2nd U.S. Cavalry, the same unit that carried on its rolls the names of Albert Sidney Johnston and Robert E. Lee. Certainly, he could meet and whip a miscreant like John Hunt Morgan. On the morning of August 21, he had his chance; the Confederate chieftain was at Gallatin and Johnson moved quickly to make a prisoner of him.

Alerted of the Federals' approach while he was still in bed, Morgan hurriedly got his men in the saddle and moved north toward Kentucky on the Scottsville Road. They had not gotten far when the first of Johnson's cavalrymen came into view. Morgan's first instinct was to run, but he suddenly turned to Basil Duke and said, "We will have to whip these fellows sure enough. Form your men."[18]

Morgan's men dismounted and prepared to meet the charge. There was some preliminary skirmishing before it came, but when it did, it was against the left. The Rebels on that flank showed good discipline, letting the bluecoats ride to within 30 yards before they opened up with their Enfields. The charge fell apart. The Yankees retired, reformed, and came at them again. The Rebels repulsed them. General Johnson reported, "Some horses were wounded, riders killed, and confusion began to appear." The unengaged Confederate right flank advanced. Their brethren on the left came out to join them. Their combined weight was too much for the Federals, who fell back a half mile before digging in on a hillside.[19]

They lacked the fortitude of their grayback opponents. When the Rebels charged them, they gave up their position, threw down their weapons, and ran for it. A few staff officers tried to rally them but failed. Morgan's men caught and captured some of them; the others were too fast.

After three or four miles, Johnson got his men somewhat under control and sent a flag of truce to Morgan, asking for time to bury his dead. Morgan answered that the internments were already being attended to; he demanded Johnson's surrender. Johnson declined. Instead, he retreated

7 — The Year of the Thunderbolt

toward Cairo on the Cumberland River. Now, Morgan was the pursuer. When Johnson turned to fight, his men stood fast for only 15 minutes, when the majority broke and ran, leaving only about 75 to continue the fight. Those who ran littered their escape route with their rifles, cartridge boxes, canteens — and pride.

The regimental officers advised Johnson that surrendering the resolute 75 was the best option left. Johnson stayed and continued to fight for a short time longer before capitulating. The fight was over. Johnson calculated his losses as 30 killed, 50 wounded, and 75 taken prisoner, including Johnson himself. In addition, 200 horses were lost. Morgan's estimate of the enemy's losses was somewhat higher. He claimed to have taken 200 prisoners and killed or wounded 180.

Johnson later reported, "The conduct of the officers and men as a general thing was shameful in the lowest degree, and the greater portion of these who escaped will remember that they did so shamefully abandoning their general on the battle-field, while if they had remained like true and brave men the result of the conflict would have been quite different."[20]

Back in May, even before the First Kentucky Raid, the *New York Times* had run a long article about Morgan. The article spoke of the Thunderbolt's braggadocio and verbally shook its head in wonder at the ability of Morgan and his Raiders to strike at will and escape with ease. "He and his men turn up everywhere," whined the *Times*. Morgan was a stick in the Northern eye, but he was the Southerners' gleeful avenger, and he was on his way to becoming a legend. His name was in every Southern newspaper. Robert E. Lee's daughter named a pet squirrel for him. Little Southern boys playing cavalryman recited: "I wish I was a cavalryman/And did with John Hunt Morgan ride/A Colt's revolver in my hand/And a saber by my side."[21]

And it was only August. The year of Morgan had four months more to go.

8

Confederate Kentucky?

On July 31, 1862, there was a meeting in Chattanooga between General Braxton Bragg and General Edmund Kirby Smith, who had come down from his headquarters at Knoxville. The men were encouraged by "General" John Hunt Morgan's reports of ardent Confederate feeling in Kentucky, dammed up and just waiting for an opportunity to burst forth in a decisive wave of support. Bragg and Smith planned to open the spillways of that dam and release a human tide of perhaps 30,000 recruits. It was agreed that Smith would move north toward Cumberland Gap; about ten days later (once his artillery arrived) Bragg would move north out of Chattanooga. Somewhere in Middle Tennessee the generals would combine their armies and, if things by then had gone as they hoped, they would continue north into Kentucky.

Smith, an aggressive Floridian, stepped off first. He left Knoxville on August 13 and headed toward Cumberland Gap. He left a small force to pin down the intimidated Federals there, then unexpectedly swung around a few miles west to Big Creek Gap, where he crossed the mountains and pushed for Kentucky. Any linkup with Bragg in Middle Tennessee was quickly forgotten; indeed, Smith may have planned from the very start to make a unilateral invasion of Kentucky. In quick sequence, he picked off Barbourville, London, Richmond, and Lexington, where he stopped. Detachments were sent to the state capital at Frankfort and other smaller towns, while Smith rested.

Bragg began leaving Chattanooga with his Army of the Mississippi on August 26. He was the this hard luck army's third commander. First was Albert Sidney Johnston, who was killed at Shiloh. His successor, the elegant P. G. T. Beauregard, served only long enough to abandon Corinth without a fight and reward himself with a vacation at the stylish health resort, Bladon Springs, just north of Mobile. While he relaxed, he was relieved. Braxton Bragg was Beauregard's replacement. Like Albert Sidney Johnston, Bragg was a favorite of President Jefferson Davis, who had met him during the Mexican War and had admired his performance as a young artillery commander at the Battle of Buena Vista. Bragg was a stern North Carolinian, cursed with stomach troubles and a sour disposition, but he was a soldier, in Davis' view, and it was Davis' view that counted. Now the Southern Confederacy would see if Bragg could live up to expectations. His Army of the Mississippi was divided into two wings, commanded by a pair of major generals who were mismatched in talent. Leonidas Polk, who commanded the right wing, was the lesser and William Hardee, commanding the left wing, was the superior, by far. Reaching Middle Tennessee, Bragg selected Hardee to shear off to the west, toward Nashville, while Polk pushed for the Kentucky line.

Bragg's opposite number on the Union side, Don Carlos Buell, had already dispatched General Lovell Harrison Rousseau to assume command at Nashville, while the garrison under Colonel J. F. Miller moved south to Murfreesboro to cover the southern approaches to the Tennessee capital and to guard against dashes by Forrest and Morgan. Meanwhile, from scattered sites in Alabama and Tennessee, the Army of the Ohio began to pull itself together. No one in Buell's officer corps was sure of either Bragg's destination or his route, though each man had his opinion. One consideration dominated the commanding general's thinking: the Federal supply base must be protected. Ultimately, Buell ordered all the far-flung elements of his army to converge on Nashville.

It was a controversial move and one that occupied much of the testimony of the Buell Commission, which later investigated the army commander's actions of August, September, and October 1862. Some of Buell's subordinates thought that the army should concentrate at McMinnville; others thought Sparta was the place, and still others favored Murfreesboro. Buell chose Nashville and opened himself up for criticism from military as well as civilian observers. A Cincinnati newspaper opined, "It seems incredible that Bragg has succeeded in scaring so powerful a body as the Army of the Ohio into seeking refuge behind works around Nashville."[1]

If there was one person who agreed absolutely that General Buell had made the right choice in moving to Nashville, it was Governor Andrew Johnson. It is no wonder, perhaps, that Johnson felt Nashville to be at risk. He had never been comfortable with the small number of troops defending his capital city, had complained often, and must certainly have taken great comfort in the thought that an entire army would soon be there to save the city from Bragg. Relations between Buell and Johnson had not been of the friendliest nature, but from Decherd, Tennessee, while the segments of the army were still moving toward the Nashville rendezvous, the general sent the governor a long, explanatory message detailing the background of the decision. He began by acknowledging that it was "proper and due" that Johnson should be informed of the military situation, and went into why it had proven impossible to attack Chattanooga, as had been ordered after Corinth. In part, Buell said:

> At first it was necessary to rebuild the bridges over a long line of railroad, and in some cases it has had to be repeated several times. So constant has been the interruption of our communications that it has been with the greatest difficulty the troops could be sustained at all, and even then some 15,000 men were required to occupy positions and guard our communications, which starting necessarily from Louisville, extended in all over some 400 miles of railroad.
>
> From this cause the force which I can bring to bear so far in advance of the source of supplies is reduced to 25,000 or 30,000 men. This force is not only very much less than that which is now crossing the mountains under Bragg, but labors under all the difficulty and peril of operating virtually in an enemy's country surrounded with an immense force of irregular cavalry. Braggs's force I apprehend does not amount to less than 50,000.... By falling back to Nashville my force will increase to 40,000 of the Army of the Ohio proper, and including troops that are coming from Corinth it will be about 50,000.
>
> These facts make it plain that I should fall back on Nashville, and I am preparing to do so.... That we shall triumph in the effort to preserve Tennessee I do not for a moment doubt.[2]

Soon after Buell arrived in Nashville, he and Governor Johnson had the first of three contentious interviews. Buell's courtesy in writing to Johnson did not mollify the touchy Tennessean. He wanted further assurances that the Union retrograde movement would not include Nashville and that his city was to be protected. One senses a real irritation on the part of Buell, who had already told Johnson that he intended to "preserve Tennessee," and was too busy just now to repeat what he had already made plain. He decided to just let Johnson stew. He refused to directly answer the governor's entreaties, saying only that Nashville had little military importance. It was not until the third interview that Buell told the governor that he had decided, after all, to leave a force for Nashville's defense. Johnson later wrote that Buell went on to say that "in leaving a force for the defense of Nashville that he did not do it so much from military as from political considerations which had been pressed with so much earnestness upon him." In other words, Buell had only seen the light of day when Johnson opened his eyes.[3]

Other evidence, less self-congratulatory than Andrew Johnson's, makes it clear that Buell had always intended to include the defense of Nashville in his plans. General Thomas J. Wood later testified before the Buell Commission that he met with Buell on the afternoon of September 6, and "there was not the slightest intimation of his intention to abandon Nashville but on the contrary, a statement of his intention to retain Nashville if possible." The next day Wood was in the room when Buell asked General George H. Thomas to remain and defend Nashville. "There was no intimation at that time of an intention to abandon Nashville, but every evidence given to induce me to believe that it was General Buell's fixed determination to hold it.... So far as I know this opinion and intention of General Buell was not influenced by any other person."[4]

General Alexander McDowell McCook went even further. He testified that he and Buell had discussed the numbers necessary to defend Nashville. When he, McCook, had expressed the opinion that Nashville was not very defensible and should be burned to the ground, Buell strongly disagreed and said that "Nashville must be held at all hazards."[5]

Johnson should have been reassured that Buell took Nashville's defense seriously by the activity he could see going on, and which had been going on, all around him. In addition to maintaining Colonel Miller's usual garrison of about 4,000 men, Buell had ordered Captain James St. Clair Morton to initiate a massive construction effort, the building of a ring of defensive works around the city. By the time the Army of the Ohio arrived, Nashville was well protected by two completed forts built solidly of earth, wood and stone and, in the case of the fort on Capitol Hill, cotton bales. The star-shaped fort on St. Cloud's Hill, which "command[ed] the town and the surrounding countryside," would later be called Fort Negley. It was nearly 12 acres in size. Each fort had a complement of 60 men and presented four artillery pieces to any of the enemy who dared to challenge. In addition to these, Captain Morton was urging his work crews to finish two additional forts. General Buell believed strongly in the value of defensive works; he thought that a contingent of 40 men inside a railroad stockade could hold off any number of Confederate cavalry. That he had ordered the erection of such substantial works in and around Nashville was proof that Nashville was going to be defended until the bitter end.[6]

The Fortified L&N bridge across the Cumberland River at Nashville. Library of Congress.

However, Nashville was a city that in other ways had been weakened by war. A reporter for the *New York Times* whose byline was C. V. S. wrote, "Nashville, of course, is not what it was before the war. Much of its beauty has been marred by grim war's effacing fingers.... Military law and military necessities have stamped their rigid impress everywhere, paying slim regard to the exercise of elegant tastes or aesthetics." Two weeks later, another newspaperman added, "The condition of the town ... does not credit to loyal officials. The streets even surpass those of New York in accumulated filth, dirt, and garbage, and, under this tropical sun, steam with odious exhaltations."[7]

The L&N bridge over the Cumberland River had been long since rebuilt (at the expense of the U.S. government), but since the collapse of

8 — Confederate Kentucky?

Another view of the L&N Bridge at Nashville. Library of Congress.

the tunnel at Gallatin, it had served only foot traffic. No trains were reaching the city and foodstuffs were scarce. Stores closed their doors at 9:00 A.M., having exhausted their meager inventory even at that early hour. A temporary rail terminus had been established at Mitchellville, a town almost right on the Kentucky state line and 30 miles distant from the capital. At Mitchellville, the contents of the boxcars were unloaded onto wagons, sometimes as many as 500 at a time, which began a creaking and treacherous journey to Nashville. The road was rough and the wagons were prone to breakdowns and, worse, were virtually sitting targets for guerrillas. An armed escort traveled with each wagon convoy, so most of them did eventually roll into Nashville, but the flow of supplies was not enough.

Naturally, Nashville's civilians were unhappy with the shabby condition of their once proud city, unhappy with the shortages, and unhappy with the galling reality of military occupation and martial law. In a city whose population was inclined to favor the Confederacy anyway, attitudes seemed to be growing more bitter with each passing month. General William Nelson thought that hostility had grown 1,000 percent under Andrew Johnson's heavy hand. General Alexander McCook McDowell essentially agreed; he believed that Nashville was "the most treasonous place in the southern country, except the little place of Murfreesboro."[8]

• • •

General Buell was wrong on two related questions. The first was the size of General Braxton Bragg's army. The dyspeptic old North Carolinian never had more than approximately 36,000 men behind him, although he intended to add many thousands more in the Bluegrass. In fact, he was taking along wagonloads of crated Enfield rifles to distribute when he arrived in Kentucky.

Bragg's destination was the second point about which Buell was wrong. The Confederates were never headed for a showdown at Nashville. They passed far to the east of the city and crossed the Cumberland River at Carthage and at Gainsboro, and struck due north for Glasgow, Kentucky. Seeing by Bragg's route that Kentucky was the Confederates' destination, Buell started five divisions of his army north; the first two, led by Lovell Harrison Rousseau and Thomas J. Wood, left on September 4. Those of Jacob Ammen, Alexander McDowell McCook, and Thomas L. Crittenden followed at intervals, skirmishing along the way with General Joseph Wheeler's 700 Rebel cavalrymen. General George H. Thomas was left behind with three divisions to protect Nashville.

Buell was too far west of where he needed to be. The detour to Nashville had put him out of his proper relation to the Army of the Mississippi. Buell might have angled eastward to encounter Bragg en route. Instead, he moved along a parallel route and marched due north to Bowling Green. His concern about the safety of the L&N Railroad took precedence over catching Bragg, according to the recollection of General Thomas.

When he learned that General Buell had decided to move north from Nashville, all of Governor Johnson's worst fears were confirmed. A visit to Johnson by the Methodist preacher Granville Moody during this time revealed the governor's emotional turbulence. Johnson blurted out to the minister, "Moody, we are sold out. Buell is a traitor! He is going to evacuate the city and in forty-eight hours we shall be in the hands of the Rebels!"

8 — Confederate Kentucky?   83

A bizarre scene followed. The two men fell to their knees and prayed and at one point Johnson actually crawled across the floor to embrace the preacher. As their passions cooled, Johnson said, "Moody, I feel better.... Damn me if Nashville shall be surrendered."[9]

• • •

On September 11, the Federal vanguard began to reach Bowling Green. Until Buell arrived three days later, General Rousseau took charge of the defenses of the city and the surrounding area. He began immediately to repair the now-decrepit fortifications that the Rebels had built the previous winter and also to supplement the stockpile of 1,200,000 rations. He reported on September 13, "I am foraging for grain, etc., for the stock, and have ordered beef instead of bacon while in camp here, and will send train at daylight in the morning to Franklin for $17,000 worth of flour with guard of 300 men. Have ordered the seizure of 100 barrels of salt now here."[10]

The Federals were not the only ones scrambling for supplies. The march had been brutal for both armies. The boys in both blue and gray were parched and famished. They were sick from the heat. Their bare feet were blistered, and their insides rumbled and cramped from the putrid water and green corn that had sustained them on the march. The Confederates began reaching Glasgow on September 11, the same day that the Federals arrived in Bowling Green, but significantly closer to the supposed goal of Louisville. Hardee's wing arrived first, followed closely by Polk's, which began arriving the next day. For some of the men, the march was not quite ended. Brigadier General James Chalmers' brigade of Polk's wing staggered on to Cave City on the L&N. They tore up the track, took over the telegraph office, and went looking for supplies. Chalmers reported, "At Cave City [on September 12], we captured three boarding cars, one box car, two hand cars, one telegraph machine and battery, two boxes new clothing (uniforms), six boxes worn clothing (uniforms), one box boots, and one barrel salt." Chalmers' Rebels also seized a gristmill at Horse Cave. It was full of wheat, and in no time the men were grinding it for flour.[11]

Sam Watkins, a private in the 1st Tennessee Infantry, wrote of the Confederates' arrival in southern Kentucky, "I remember how gladly the citizens of Kentucky received us. I thought they had the prettiest girls that God ever made. They could not do too much for us. They had heaps and stacks of cooked rations along our route, and wine and cider everywhere, and the glad shouts of 'Hurrah for our Southern boys,' greeted and welcomed us at every house."[12]

The signs pointed to the veracity of John Hunt Morgan's report. Kentuckians really were enthusiastic about supporting the Confederate cause. On the 14th, General Bragg issued a noble-sounding proclamation from Glasgow that began, "Kentuckians, I have entered your State with the Confederate Army of the West, and offer you an opportunity to free yourselves from the tyranny of a despotic ruler. We come not as conquerors or as despoilers, but to restore to you the liberties of which you have been deprived by a cruel and relentless foe." He must have believed that those 20,000 Enfield rifles would soon be issued to sharpshooting Bluegrass boys, 20 regiments worth of fresh recruits who just might be the decisive factor in the campaign for Kentucky.[13]

• • •

While Bragg was hoping for reinforcements, Buell was getting them, in the form of Major General George H. Thomas' division, which was ordered to move to Bowling Green on September 12. Predictably, Governor Johnson was beside himself, certain that Buell had doomed Nashville. He wrote Buell on September 14, "It is all-important that Major General Thomas and his forces, as now assigned, should remain at Nashville. There is the utmost confidence in his bravery and capacity to defend Nashville against any odds.... I express the strong and earnest hope that the present assignment of forces under General Thomas for the defense of Nashville may not be disturbed." Buell had the gift of ignoring noisy politicians (sometimes to the great irritation of the War Department) and he ignored Johnson now; the order was not rescinded. General James Negley took charge of Nashville, and Thomas remained with the army during the course of the Kentucky Campaign.

Thomas' eminent arrival in Kentucky was a comfort, but a dispatch that arrived at Buell's Bowling Green headquarters was not. Colonel John T. Wilder at Munfordville was under attack and was requesting reinforcements.

• • •

Munfordville was a pretty little village of about 60 homes and 270 citizens. The town had grown up in the first decade of the 1800s around the Munford Inn, a log hostelry where, residents proudly pointed out, Andrew Jackson had once spent the night. Munfordville grew at a slow pace during the first two decades of the century, but in the 1830s there was a small economic boom and the cabins of the pioneer settlers began to vanish, replaced by some exceptionally fine brick homes and houses of worship. The Presbyterian church would have been an ornament in many a larger town. It was a two-story brick building with a square tower through which the worshipful entered. Large stained-glass windows looked out on a community whose future seemed bright. The Louisville and Nashville Turnpike ran right through the center of town and was busy with traffic of every kind and, in the 1850s, the L&N Railroad came, assuring an attractive level of sustained prosperity. The L&N bridge over Green River became the nationally-known trademark of a progressive town.

Soon after the war began, Munfordville's pride was hurt by the destruction of the Green River Bridge and its peace of mind disturbed by the fight between Colonel August Willich and General T. C. Hindman. The garrison of over 1,000 Union men, who had arrived soon after to take up residence around town, was a reminder that a war was still raging, but when months passed with no further trouble, it began to seem as if Munfordville had seen the worst of it. Even John Hunt Morgan had bypassed the town in his recent raids. The permanent replacement for the great bridge would be rebuilt, and soon the town could resume its forward momentum, the war only a temporary distraction.

Then, Braxton Bragg led the Army of the Mississippi into Kentucky, with Louisville his apparent objective, and Munfordville was directly in his path.

On September 8, Colonel John T. Wilder arrived by the L&N with 204 men of the 17th Indiana to take command of Munfordville's defenses. Wilder had the features of a pugilist. His face was crosshatched by a short, straight nose and a wide, no-nonsense mouth. Until just a year ago, he had been an Indiana manufacturer, but despite the brevity of his military career, he was a remarkably clear-thinking young officer, and arriving at Munfordville, he saw that the simple stockade that General McCook had erected the previous December was in no way sufficient for the present emergency. Wilder had the men of his own regiment, plus those that were already in Munfordville: the 67th Indiana, the 89th Indiana, two companies of the 74th Indiana, a battery of the 13th Indiana artillery, 60 men of the newly organized and completely unarmed 33rd Kentucky, one company of the 18th U.S. Regulars, one company of cavalry, and the Louisville Provost Guard (who may have arrived in Munfordville with Wilder). While the unarmed recruits of the 33rd Kentucky Infantry scouted and foraged in the surrounding countryside, Wilder put the other regiments to the task of improving and adding to the shambling fortifications.

These fieldworks were on the farm of Mr. Anthony L. Woodson, just south of Green River. It was a 400 acre farm, well fenced, with 265 acres under cultivation and 93 in timber. The rest was in pasture and orchards. The buildings included the Woodson dwelling house, a stable, barns, cribs, and slave quarters. It lay astraddle of both the railroad and the turnpike, which made it doubly attractive to the Union forces. General McCook took some timber for his stockade and rail fences for firewood, but that was only a patch to what Wilder ordered. He clear-cut acres of Woodson's timber for his defenses and to clear a field of fire. The treetops were laid out front for abatis and chaveaux-de-frise. Many of Woodson's outbuildings and his barn were burned to prevent their use as nests for Confederate sharpshooters.

When Wilder was done, his works stretched across Woodson's farm for a half mile from the river to the turnpike. On the right, overlooking Green River (and the all-important railroad bridge), was a semicircle of rifle pits, complete with a head-log, and anchored on its extreme flank by McCook's original stockade. The 89th Indiana was posted here. Proceeding left, there were more rifle pits rising gently in elevation and terminating in an earthen bastion (Fort Craig), manned by the 67th Indiana. In all, there were 2,122 men to defend the works and ten artillery pieces, including a Parrott gun, two Napoleons, and seven six-pounder "rifles." The rising and dipping ground in front of the works added a natural element to its defense.

Almost anyone would have judged the Union position at Munfordville to be formidable, but one observer was not impressed. He was Colonel John Scott of the Confederate cavalry. General Edmund Kirby Smith sent Colonel Scott and his horse soldiers westward to try and make contact with General Bragg. There was a linkup to arrange, and though Bragg was the ranking officer, Smith hoped that Bragg would come east to join *him*. On September 13, when Scott spied the Federal outpost at Munfordville, he saw, not an obstacle, but an opportunity. In his estimation, the garrison was small and isolated and ripe for the plucking. Scott did not keep his presence a secret. To the contrary, he sent Wilder a demand for immediate surrender. Wilder declined, and Scott sent a dispatch to Brigadier General Chalmers at Cave City, urging him to hurry forward and take advantage of the chance to easily take an isolated Federal outpost. Chalmers moved out that night.

At 3:00 A.M. on Thursday, September 14, Scott launched an attack, but the effort was not very vigorous. One senses that Scott was just feeling the enemy, testing his resolve. While the fighting was going on, Colonel Wilder took the precaution of burning the Baptist church outside his works to further clear the field of fire. General Chalmers saw the smoke from a distance and feared that Wilder was retreating and burning the L&N Railroad bridge behind him. He hurried his Southern infantry forward. They arrived about dawn, found a small battle under way, and went into line.

By this time, Wilder had been fighting Scott for three hours, but now, with Chalmers on the scene, Wilder could see that the fighting was going to go on awhile longer. At about 6:30, three Mississippi regiments moved against the Federals' stockade. They advanced to within 30 yards before the Yankees opened fire and delivered to them "a very avalanche of death." Three more Mississippi regiments launched a simultaneous attack, this one converging on the redoubt. They advanced to the burned church, formed their line, and plunged forward. An eight-foot-deep ditch surrounding the earthworks slowed them down at exactly the wrong spot. Wilder wrote that "they were literally murdered by a terrible fire from the gallant defenders of the work." Showers of rifle slugs and salvos of grapeshot and canister ripped through their ranks. Not all of the fire was from the redoubt. Chalmers' attacking men found themselves caught between the artillery fire from Fort Craig and incoming rounds from their own big guns. Some of the men took cover in sinkholes, but no place was safe. In the confusion resulting from artillery fire from two directions, the attack was called off, and the survivors of the charge hurried back toward their lines.[14]

At 9:30, General Chalmers called a truce and sent a message to Wilder complimenting his defense but demanding a surrender "to avoid further bloodshed." Wilder still had plenty of fight in him. His men had inflicted four times their own losses. Besides that, the Confederates had carelessly failed to cut the telegraph lines to the north, and Wilder had wired for reinforcements, who were just then beginning to arrive. Moreover, General Buell was no farther away than Bowling Green. Wilder had sent riders south with news of his situation; indeed, Buell might already be on his way. Wilder saw every good reason for hanging on. In his reply, he thanked Chalmers for his compliments but refused to surrender, saying, "If you want to avoid further bloodshed keep out of the range of my guns." Wilder's sassy reply to Chalmers notwithstanding, this was an oddly affable battle. It was during this lull in the fighting that Wilder allowed Chalmers the use of some shovels for CSA burial parties. In addition, some Yankees lent a hand in loading wounded Rebels on flatcars and then helped push the cars down the L&N tracks to nearby Rowlett's Station and the Confederate field hospital there.[15]

Chalmers later reported that his losses were 35 men killed, three of them officers, and 253 men wounded. Wilder initially said that he had 37 killed and wounded, but the number was later adjusted upward to 72.

The 420 reinforcements who began arriving during the last minutes of the battle came in response to Wilder's telegram to headquarters in Louisville. They were led by Colonel Cyrus Dunham, and they rode the L&N down to within six miles of Munfordville. The train derailed when it hit a break where Colonel Scott's cavalrymen had torn up the track. The men had to walk the rest of the way, leaving boxes of ammunition behind. After the fight on September 14 ended, loyal citizens of Munfordville and Hart County took their wagons to the derailed train to get the ammunition and bring it to the fort. There, they found the weary soldiers busy repairing the stockade and the earthen bastion.

Colonel Dunham outranked Colonel Wilder, and he assumed command. One of his first acts was to send out a request for reinforcements and more ammunition. Though General Chalmers had withdrawn, Dunham suspected that the Confederates were not finished at Munfordville.

And they were not. Chalmers, upon his return to Cave City on the night of the 14th, wired Bragg the news of his setback at Munfordville. Bragg was livid. He called the attack "unauthorized and injudicious." He had not wanted to bring on an engagement yet, but his ambitious subordinate had not only brought one on, but had been repulsed, and now Bragg had a problem. It would be unwise to discourage his army at the very beginning of the campaign by allowing Chalmers' defeat to be the final outcome of the Munfordville affair. It had to be made right. Yet, to make it right would cause a delay in the drive north, and delay could be fatal. There were several reasons he had to keep moving. His army was low on supplies, and this country was foraged to a nub. Enemy forces were very likely coming up behind him, and he must link up with Edmund Kirby Smith. Ultimately, Bragg decided that his timetable would have to be sacrificed: Munfordville had to be taken.[16]

The soldiers were ordered up and forward. Sam Watkins must have spoken for many of his less articulate comrades when he described the march, "We marched the whole night long. We, the private soldiers, did not know what was going on among the Generals. All that we had to do was to march, march, march. It mattered not how tired, hungry, or thirsty we were.... Every staff officer who would pass, some fellow would say, 'Hey, mister, how far is it to Munfordsville [*sic*]?' He would answer, 'Five miles.' It seemed to me we traveled a hundred miles and were always within five miles of Munfordsville."[17]

On Tuesday, September 16, Bragg showed up at the Federal defenses and fired a few rounds into Fort Craig to let the Yankees know that the entire Army of the Mississippi had arrived. There was some minor fighting through the day; then Bragg sent in the third demand for surrender.

Colonel Wilder was back in command. Colonel Dunham had made the mistake of informing Louisville that he doubted that his men could hold out against all these butternuts massing in front of them on the south side (Hardee's wing) and behind them on the north side (Polk's) of Green River. Dunham was immediately ordered by return wire to turn over command to Wilder. When Dunham made matters worse by protesting that he outranked Wilder and could not properly serve under his junior, he was placed under long-range arrest.

Thus, it was Wilder who responded to Bragg's demand for surrender. Wilder wanted proof that Bragg's whole army was, indeed, in front of him and asked to meet with General Simon Bolivar Buckner, who was a division commander in Hardee's wing. Buckner was a Munfordville native and, Wilder knew, a gentleman whose word could be trusted. The young colonel asked Buckner bluntly if he should surrender. This was a first. For a defending officer to ask an enemy officer who was about to attack whether or not he should surrender showed admirable candor, but also a certain lack of military tradition. Buckner did not answer Wilder directly; what he did agree to do was conduct Wilder on a tour of the Confederate position so that he could see for himself. There was something in this for Buckner, too. By showing Wilder the Rebel firepower, he might prevent a battle and spare his hometown the inevitable death and damage that would ensue.

What Wilder saw was eye-opening. He counted 46 artillery pieces and multitudes of graybacks stacked against him. There were more on the north bank. Wilder was a businessman and could read the bottom line. He said, "Well, it seems to me, General Buckner, that I ought to surrender." Buckner warned him, one uniform to another, that it was his duty to hold out if he thought it would serve the greater interests of the Union cause. Wilder could think of no benefit to be gained by the sacrifice of his men. He said, "I believe I will surrender," and this he did on September 17. The vanquished Federals were paroled, given four days' rations, and sent to Bowling Green while the Southern army moved into Munfordville.[18]

9

Destination Louisville

At dawn on September 14, 1862, A. G. Craddock, a citizen of Munfordville, came to General Lovell H. Rousseau's headquarters in Bowling Green. He came with a request for reinforcements from Colonel Wilder. Craddock later remembered, "In about half an hour after I got to the hotel General Buell came to General Rousseau's headquarters and sent for me. He asked me then the situation in and about Munfordville, and said that Colonel Wilder had better evacuate the post. That, as well as I recollect was about the purport of his remarks to me."[1]

The observation that Wilder had better evacuate was a rather cold response to the situation of a fellow officer who was in trouble and only 40 miles away. There could have been no misunderstanding. Wilder had made it clear that he needed and expected help. In his testimony before the Buell Commission, Wilder stated several times in several different ways that he had sent word to Bowling Green of the straits he was in and that he had looked for relief from the south. "I had railroad communication to Bowling Green till Friday noon," he said. "I then sent out scouts. I sent one on Saturday 13th—Mr. Wash. Miller, and two or three others. I did not send written communications, only verbal ones ... stating that I must receive assistance." Two days passed. By the 15th, he still had had no word from Bowling Green. At dark that day Mr. Miller returned to Wilder's lines, "and told me I could expect no assistance from Bowling Green; that no troops had started to relieve me at the time he left." It was disappointing news, for as Wilder stated near the end of his testimony, "I supposed ... that General Buell's army would come to relieve me before Bragg could get there."[2]

It had become common knowledge throughout the Army of the Ohio

9—Destination Louisville

that Wilder was under attack. Those of General Buell's officers who expected him to hurry to the aid of Colonel Wilder at Munfordville were disappointed. Buell did not begin to move from Bowling Green until the afternoon of September 16. What explains the hesitancy to move rapidly?

The answer has several facets. First was Buell's organic timidity. He was a shy man in his personal life, and professionally he did not like to rush into action. He insisted on the luxury of time in which to think and to plan. It may be revealing that one of his best friends in the military was General George B. McClellan, another commanding officer who was notorious for having the "slows."

A second consideration was the poor condition of the Army of the Ohio after its march across North Alabama, followed by a hard march to Nashville, and then the equally taxing march to Bowling Green. If Louisville was the prize, these men had to be fit to win it, and the outcome of a hurried march to Munfordville followed immediately by a climactic fight with the Army of the Mississippi might be to lose both Kentucky's largest city—and Kentucky.

There was a third factor. Buell continually obsessed about his supply lines at Bowling Green and, Governor Johnson's accusations notwithstanding, at Nashville. Buell said, "I deemed it all important to force him [Bragg] further into the State, instead of allowing him to fall back upon Bowling Green and Nashville." Applying just the right amount of pressure by a slow pursuit, Buell could ease Bragg deeper into Kentucky and at the same time prevent a Confederate retrograde movement around the Union flanks that might result in a bitter loss somewhere farther down the L&N, in southern Kentucky or Tennessee.[3]

So, Buell lingered until the 16th when he moved, as he claimed, to catch the enemy at Glasgow. Here again is a mystery, for General Crittenden later said, "When we moved from Bowling Green, it was known that a considerable portion of Bragg's army had already left Glasgow." General Thomas J. Wood verified this, saying it was known that "by Wednesday morning the 17th, there was no rebel force at Glasgow."[4]

The railroad north of Bowling Green was broken again, so it was back to shoe leather, for those lucky enough to have shoes. The Army of the Ohio paused at Dripping Springs its first night out, less than 20 miles from Bowling Green, and proceeded from there to Prewitt's Knob. It was here that Wilder and his paroled men began to reach friendly lines. It is said that some of Buell's men cried at the sight of their defeated comrades who might have been saved, who had asked for help from Bowling Green and had received none. Colonel Wilder reported to General Buell the news of Bragg's occupation of Munfordville and that he had made the recently improved defensive works his own; he was dug in and waiting for Buell. From Wilder, Buell also learned for the first time of the true size of Bragg's army — about 38,000. Wilder had counted them. Wilder also told Buell that the Rebels had only three days' rations and that if their supplies were cut off from the east, they would have no choice but to fight or fall back.

Buell did not move forward to either trap Bragg or cut off his supplies. He lingered at Prewitt's Knob until the 20th, when his army took to the road again. The advance arrived at Munfordville in time to see the backs of the Rebel rear guard as they disappeared into the distance on the other side of Green River.

• • •

Soldiers question their commanders. It seems to be universally true, through all times in all armies, and it was as true of the Confederates in 1862 as it was of the Federals. If General Buell caught criticism for not hurrying to Munfordville, General Bragg came under fire for hurrying away from Munfordville.

One subordinate, the diminutive cavalry officer Joseph Wheeler, later wrote in an essay for *Battles and Leaders of the Civil War* that Bragg arrayed his troops

> in a strong position south of the river, using the [Federal] fort as a part of his line of defense. My command was thrown forward to meet and skirmish with the enemy....
> If Kirby Smith's command had been ordered from Lexington to Munfordville, even as late as the 12th, a battle with Buell could not have been other than a decided Confederate victory.... It is true our back was to a river, but it was fordable at several places, and we felt that ... having it on our rear was fully compensated by the topographical features which, with the aid of the fort, made our position a strong one for defense.[5]

Bragg pleaded in his own defense that it was a mere question of rations: "Reduced at the end of four days to three days' rations and in a hostile country utterly destitute of supplies, a serious engagement brought on anywhere in that direction could not fail (whatever its results) to materially cripple me.... I was well aware also that he had a practicable route by way of Morgantown or Brownsville to the Ohio River and thence to Louisville. We were therefore compelled to give up the object and seek for subsistence."[6]

9—Destination Louisville

Some have accused Bragg of shading the truth in referring to Hart County as "destitute of supplies." Hart County was rich farming country, but Bragg was undoubtedly speaking the truth. It was a season of drought, and the crops in the field were stunted and withered. Colonel Wilder told General Buell that Bragg had only three days rations. He noticed among the CSA dead in front of Fort Craig that their haversacks contained nothing but green corn. The civilians in Munfordville also noticed how impoverished the Rebels were for food and observed that Bragg came into town with empty wagons.

It is true, however, that the victory at Munfordville seemed to have affected Bragg's thinking. He made comments that led his listeners to believe that he had lost the will to fight. He began to complain about all those thousands of still-crated Enfields—the Kentucky recruits of which John Hunt Morgan had spoken were not materializing. And, General Bragg made two flatly untrue statements. The first, to his fellow officer Earl Van Dorn, then campaigning in Mississippi, "We have driven and drawn the enemy clear back to the Ohio," and the second to Adjutant General Samuel Cooper at the capital in Richmond, "My junction with Kirby Smith is complete."[7]

Perhaps Bragg believed that his projections into the near future were so certain to become true that there was no harm in announcing them a little bit ahead of time. In any case, what was true *now* was that he was out of supplies and that Buell was on the move, at last. On September 20, Bragg crossed the river, burned the bridge, and headed up the Louisville and Nashville Turnpike, immediately parallel to the L&N Railroad. Joe Wheeler, the Confederate "War Child," was ordered to take his cavalry and watch the rear. As the army left Munfordville, the horse soldiers had a little skirmish with the Federal vanguard, the latest of several small encounters they had fought over the last few days.

While Bragg was resting his infantry in Munfordville, his cavalry had stayed busy on the back trail, skirmishing with Buell's horsemen. They fought at Cave City, Horse Cave, Bear Wallow, and near Mammoth Cave, with more to come. The fights were brief but costly to the Rebels. A *New York Times* reporter who was traveling with Buell claimed that in the small actions on the turnpike between September 18 and September 26, the Yankees nabbed 700 prisoners.

As they moved north from Munfordville, the Confederates passed the wrecked locomotive and train of cars that Colonel Scott had derailed. They added to the destruction when they tore lengths of telegraph wires down from the poles. They marched past farms and woodlots familiar from one year ago, when Southern Kentucky was theirs. Albert Sidney Johnston was still alive then and their hopes were bright. Some of them had been in the Bacon Creek outpost; now they took it back from the small Yankee garrison and torched a train of cars and the oft-burned L&N bridge again.

From the dispatches they were receiving, the Rebels must have expected to find Hardin County a land of plenty. They knew that at Sonora on September 17, a scouting party led by Captain J. M. Wampler had reported finding "two hundred bushels of wheat bound for Louisville ... plenty of forage on and near the road, road good." And near Nolin, a captain named Pittman took charge of two gristmills, Eagle Mill and Red Mill, and ground corn day and night for a solid week to feed the men. They didn't even have to fight for it. The troops guarding the Camp Nevin stockade and the L&N Railroad bridge had fled as the Confederates approached.[8]

It is hard to determine precisely when Bragg's Rebels left the vicinity of Nolin/Camp Nevin, but they proceeded only a few miles up the Louisville and Nashville Turnpike when they made a move that baffled observers, both friend and foe. The long, gray columns left the turnpike, abandoning the road and, ultimately, the city of Louisville to Buell. They headed east, toward Hodgenville and Bardstown. Bragg left Wheeler's cavalry and one artillery piece a short distance behind at Vinegar Hill to cover the rear of his army as it tramped off eastward. Wheeler concealed his men and horses. About noon on September 22 when Buell's advance drew near, Wheeler attacked. In his report, Wheeler calculated that 1,500 Yankee cavalry had approached to within 350 yards when he sprang from ambush, "killing and wounding many men and horses" in an engagement that lasted until dark. For their part, the Federals reported that the fight lasted about 30 minutes and that their cavalry had gallantly driven Wheeler away. They made no mention of any Federals being killed but claimed to have killed seven Confederates.[9]

Whatever the truth, the Confederates faded back and the bluecoats continued up the turnpike. Bragg had relinquished the contest for Louisville, and Buell had a clear road to the City at the Falls.

Buell was surprised by Bragg's move. He had expected Bragg and Kirby Smith to effect their long-delayed linkup at Elizabethtown and that he would meet them in battle there to determine the fate of Kentucky. Now Bragg was sliding off to the east. There would be no battle at Eliz-

9—Destination Louisville

abethtown; there would be no contest for Louisville. The Army of the Ohio pushed on up the turnpike. A correspondent saw Buell about this time and wrote, "His dress was that of a brigadier instead of a major general. He wore a shabby straw hat, dusty coat, and had neither belt, sash or sword about him.... Buell is certainly the most reserved, distant, and unsociable of all the generals in the army. He never has a word of cheer for his men or his officers, and in turn his subordinates care little for him save to obey his orders, as machinery works in response to the bidding of the mechanic."[10]

Buell paused in Elizabethtown long enough to send a dispatch to General Thomas, far back in the line of march: "Leave your trains and push forward with your command as quickly as possible ... to Louisville by way of Salt River [West Point].... You will have to make marches of twenty-five miles a day. A brigade of cavalry will be left at this point to cover the advance of the trains."[11]

The brigade which Buell mentioned was the 1st Cavalry Brigade, commanded by Colonel Edward McCook (part of the Cavalry Division commanded by Colonel John Kennett, who was also in Elizabethtown). Edward McCook was the cousin of General Alexander McDowell McCook and one of the fifteen "Fighting McCooks" from Ohio.

The 1st Brigade's sojourn in Elizabethtown was not uneventful. At about 9:00 P.M. on September 28, a detachment of the brigade cantered out of town toward New Haven (on the Lebanon Branch of the L&N). Bragg's army had reached Bardstown by this time, but the 3rd Georgia Cavalry, under Colonel Martin J. Crawford, held New Haven as an outpost.

After riding most of the night, the 1st Kentucky Cavalry and the 2nd Indiana Cavalry arrived at New Haven about dawn on the 29th. The deep dust of the road muffled the sound of the horses' hooves so that the Yankees were able to approach and capture the enemy pickets without a struggle. As they handed over their weapons, the Rebels laughed and said, "You are so covered with dust and look so gray, we thought you were our own men charging on us to frighten us." The pickets farther in and closer to the main camp were likewise taken without gunfire.[12]

The guards in the main camp heard the horses of the Federals as they thundered over the wooden bridge across the Rolling Fork — but too late. The horse soldiers quickly surrounded the camp and began rounding up sleepy prisoners.

Captain Silas Adams looked into Colonel M. J. Crawford's tent and demanded his surrender. As Sergeant E. Tarrant recorded the conversation, Crawford said, "Who in the hell are you, giving me such peremptory orders?"

"I am commanding the 1st Kentucky Cavalry," said Adams.

"But what is your rank?"

"I am a captain in command of a regiment, but I have no time to quibble about rank."

"But let me have a few minutes to consider."

"Surrender in two seconds, or I will blow your damned head off."[13]

Adams' mastery of the situation proved once again that the talent for command is not strictly a matter of gilded eagles or stars on the shoulders.

At New Haven, every Rebel except for one distant vidette post was caught and not a single cartridge was burned in the doing. Three hundred Georgians were captured, their supplies and equipment either carried off or destroyed, within three miles of a substantial detachment of Bragg's infantry, cavalry, and artillery. Rather than risk being caught by them, the Yankee expedition quickly returned with their prisoners to Elizabethtown.

For the 1st Kentucky Cavalry, the neat little victory was spoiled, somewhat, by the fact that both Colonel McCook and division commander Kennett gave credit for the capture of the New Haven Rebels to Lieutenant Colonel Stewart and the 2nd Indiana Cavalry. In fact, said Tarrant, "Every man along knows that the capture was achieved before either Stewart or his regiment reached the enemy camp."[14]

The following December, after his exchange, Colonel Crawford was court-martialed and convicted for being caught so completely off guard. His punishment was a three-month suspension without pay and an official reprimand.

In his report of September 29, Colonel Kennett pointed out the measures he was taking to ensure that he did not become the Union equivalent of Colonel Crawford. He wrote, "Our horses are saddled nightly; we sleep on our arms, and will be drawn up in the order of battle tomorrow morning [as they were every morning, Tarrant said]. Such are our precautions to prevent surprise."[15]

Exciting as the occasional dash into enemy territory might be, Colonel Kennett was anxious to get on to Louisville to rejoin the army and be refitted there. On October 2, he sent a courier to headquarters in the City at the Falls with a message pointing out that "we require clothing, coats, and some arms," and subtly suggesting that perhaps he and his men had been forgotten. "Please ascertain ... whether [General Buell] intends us to move immediately to Louisville."[16]

The cavalry brigade never did get to Louisville. The men were left to watch the back door at Elizabethtown until October 4. By that time, the Army of the Ohio had left Louisville. Colonel McCook's brigade joined Buell's columns at Bardstown, en route to the showdown with General Bragg and the Army of the Mississippi at Perryville.

• • •

The men of the 1st Cavalry Brigade were deprived of the joyous welcome enjoyed by the others in Louisville. When General Crittenden's division marched into the city on September 24, crowds lined the streets to cheer them. The soldiers, dirty and footsore as they were, must have been refreshed by the enthusiasm of the greeting. Curtius, a reporter for the *New York Times*, called Louisville "among the most loyal of cities and her trueness and devotion to the cause of the Union has aided in keeping the war ... back from the Ohio River." There was none of the sullen acceptance here that the soldiers had noticed at the opposite end of the L&N at Nashville. The citizens of Louisville cried, "God bless you!" and handed the soldiers dippers and cups of water. The hurrahs rained down from every balcony and window. The Stars and Stripes waved everywhere.[17]

It was not just shouting. Curtius added, "Our men were taken to the houses of the citizens and feasted with much needed and more tangible rewards." However, there were not enough homes to feed every soldier, and what Curtius failed to mention was that some of those men who were not invited to share a meal broke into the abandoned homes of refugee families and helped themselves to what they found.[18]

By September 27, almost the entire combat force of the Army of the Ohio was in Louisville. The wagon train was still struggling over the rough country of western Hardin County but would soon arrive.

Aside from the many homes standing empty, the men who had known Louisville before the war could see the many changes in the city they left in 1861. They must have noticed some of these changes before they even reached the city proper. South of town was a line of rifle pits between the turnpike where they marched and the Louisville & Nashville Railroad. A short distance in, there was an eight-mile-long line of entrenchments, curving in a half circle around south Louisville and anchored at each end on the Ohio River.

The city itself looked a little worn and ill kept. Buildings were beginning to need a fresh coat of paint, and the windows were dirty. The streets required sweeping, and here and there a pothole needed to be filled. The wharf was busier than ever, not with brightly painted river packets, but with gunboats and Union supply ships. A spur line of the L&N had been laid right down to the river's edge so that offloaded cargoes could be stacked in railroad cars on site. A good many citizens had fled across the river to Indiana when they thought Bragg was approaching, but their absence was not felt. The city throbbed with thousands of Home Guards and soldiers hastily gathered up before the Army of the Ohio arrived and with uncounted refugees from the hinterland. Before the war, the city had a population of 68,000; there was no way to tabulate the number now.

The men with the gold braid on their sleeves tended to stay in the elegant Galt House, but the ordinary soldiers of the Army of the Ohio, when they arrived, pitched their tents a few miles southwest of downtown, near the Oakland Race Track, a predecessor of Churchill Downs. There they were to receive five-months' back pay and be outfitted with new uniforms and brogans.

Nearly every ingredient was in place to guarantee a soldier's happiness in Louisville, but one thing was bitterly missed. General Jeremiah T. Boyle issued a decree banning the sale of wine or spirits to soldiers. According to Robert E. McDowell, they were "horror-stricken" to learn that they were to be denied their liquor. But as resolute soldiers, they were used to outflanking the enemy. They soon scouted out those locals with whiskey-filled canteens who would sell a swig or two.[19]

Boyle was not so much an intentional enemy, just a blundering one. After Edmund Kirby Smith invaded the state and during the race between Bragg and Buell, Boyle, true to form, had spent his time predicting disaster and calling for reinforcements. "The enemy are likely to take the State," he wired General-in-Chief Henry Halleck on August 31. "The rebel force in Kentucky much larger than at first supposed," he wailed on September 17.[20]

Yet, as busy as he was populating Kentucky with phantom hordes of Rebels, all of them with through tickets to Louisville, Boyle had the time to pursue his vindictive policies toward the citizenry. James Speed wrote to Lincoln about him on September 15, saying, "Annoying arrests continue, very much to our detriment. Order Boyle to the field. He is a good man there. In his present position he is doing more harm than good. Our cause is weakening under his management."[21]

It is evidence, perhaps, of the influence the Speeds enjoyed with Lincoln that, the same day of the wire to Lincoln, Secretary of War Edwin Stanton ordered Boyle to quit making arrests without the consent of Governor James F. Robinson. Boyle answered Stanton later the same day and, without knowing who they were, called his critics "weak-backed Union men."[22]

Two days later, Joshua Speed was in communication with Lincoln. He fired with both barrels. He complained that Boyle had misused his military power, that he had ignored crooked provost marshals who were using their position for gain, and that he had gone back on his promise to take advice from civilian advisors, such as himself, his brother James Speed, and James Guthrie, on all "matters touching the public interest." Speed said, "Boyle I am satisfied is injuring the Government by his course. I have said so to him; he says he will persist in it so long as he has power."[23]

Luckily, at this point, General Boyle's authority was largely overshadowed by that of Major General William "Bull" Nelson. General Buell had sent Nelson north to take charge of the defense of the state on August 16. He was a big man for a big job. The native Kentuckian stood six feet, four inches tall and weighed 300 pounds. A deceptively youthful face belied his rugged years in the U.S. Navy and his fluency in the language for which sailors are famous. Lincoln himself had talked Nelson into leaving the navy in 1861 in exchange for a landlocked post in Kentucky's Bluegrass Region where he was expected to raise recruits and help keep Kentucky in the Union. He had done well at that task and at every subsequent duty, as well. However, he found himself in an awkward position when he arrived in Kentucky in late summer 1862.

In its mania for reassignment, the War Department had created the Department of the Ohio, which was separate from General Buell's army and which was commanded by Major General Horatio G. Wright. The meaning of all this was that Buell had no authority to put Nelson in charge in another general's department. Ignoring the departmental trespass, Wright seems to have been glad of the extra help, for he let Nelson take operational command of the task to which Buell had assigned him. Then, on August 24, Major General Wright reassigned Boyle and put him in charge of what was called the Department of Louisville, which gave him command of "the troops in and about Louisville, Kentucky and of such detached forces within the state of Kentucky as are not under the command of Major General Nelson." The long-suffering Boyle objected to what he considered a demotion, but General Buell intervened to reassure him, and Boyle accepted Wright's decision.[24]

In fact, it was a demotion. General Boyle's department encompassed only three cities: Bowling Green, Munfordville, and Louisville. The larger job of preparing the state to receive the Rebels belonged to Nelson. It was he who saw to the completion of the ring of works around Louisville, and it was he who began to gather Home Guards, convalescents, and whoever he could snag into an ersatz division to protect the city. Employees of the L&N shops were among those who had muskets thrust into their hands. Nelson told his troops, "We will give them a bloody welcome!" He imposed martial law on the city, and on September 22 he ordered women and children and citizens of questionable loyalty to leave the city by way of the coal-barge pontoon bridges to the Indiana shore. When the state legislature moved temporarily to Louisville in September, bringing with them the state archives and $1,000,000 in public monies, Nelson's responsibilities grew. It is little wonder that when Buell's army began marching into Louisville on September 24, Nelson exulted to General Wright in Cincinnati, "Louisville is now safe. We can destroy Bragg with whatever force he may bring against us. God and Liberty."[25]

• • •

Of course, the Rebels were not coming to Louisville. They had slid away to the east and satisfied themselves by merely annoying the Federals, as on September 26 when 500 butternut cavalrymen made a dash into the area of 18th and Oak Streets in a small action which yielded them 50 prisoners. But they were not massing for an attack on the city, and those lovely earthworks would never be stained with Rebel blood.

The Army of the Ohio was going to have to go out and either chase Bragg to ground or fight him wherever he turned to make a stand. Buell thought the fight would probably be at Danville. Before he went after the grizzled old Tarheel, though, Buell wanted to reorganize his army into corps. The First Corps would go to General Alexander McDowell McCook. The Second Corps would go to General Thomas L. Crittenden. The Third Corps would be commanded by General William Nelson. At least, that was the plan.

When General Jefferson C. Davis shot General Nelson dead in the lobby of the Galt House—the result of a short but intensely bitter feud— General Buell had to scramble to find a new Third Corps commander. He offered the job to several officers, but none was interested until he approached one of Nelson's staff officers, Charles C. Gilbert. Gilbert's actual rank was that of captain, but in these confusing times he had been

9—Destination Louisville

performing as an acting major general. Captain Gilbert was a veteran of the Battle of Shiloh. His most recent job had been to inspect the railroads and their defenses, an important but inglorious task. Gilbert eagerly accepted Buell's offer.

On October 1, 1862, the Army of the Ohio left Louisville, entrusting General Boyle to protect the city. McCook's corps traveled by way of the Taylorsville Road, through an area not directly served by the L&N. General Gilbert's corps kept snugly to the railroad. It traveled nearly parallel to the L&N on the Shepherdsville Road. General Buell, concerned perhaps about his newest and least experienced commander, traveled with Gilbert's column. The corps had no trouble at all between Louisville and Shepherdsville, but on October 3, when the men turned east to follow the Bardstown Branch to a rendezvous with Crittenden, they bumped into some CSA cavalry and skirmished all the way to the Nelson County seat. The sudden, always surprising crackling of Enfield rifles and the sound of bullets zipping through the leaves and underbrush kept the men's nerves drawn tight. That, combined with the continuing lack of water, made the march a memorably difficult one. When Gilbert's men reached Bardstown on October 5, they learned that General Crittenden's corps had had even more problems than their own on the march from Louisville.

Crittenden's corps had marched directly toward Bardstown and the enemy forces who were known to be there. Curtius, of the *New York Times*, was with the Second Corps. He admired the good-looking farms they passed on the first day out and called the section "the most prosperous and best-improved in Kentucky." He found something admirable, too, in the "glorious people" along the way. They were "as true and noble as their country is rich and exuberant." The people who came out to watch the soldiers pass were "frantic with delight." At one place, a pretty girl and several friends came out with some buckets of water for the thirsty soldiers. The men needed water more than the girls had imagined. What started as a gesture of kindness turned into a real job; the number of thirsty men seemed endless. Curtius noted that the girls had to scurry to keep refilling the bucket.[26]

There was some inconsequential skirmishing at Mt. Washington, a few miles out of Louisville, but at the end of the first day, the men discovered a problem they no doubt considered more serious. Buell had ordered all heavy baggage and staff wagons to be left behind at Louisville. Curiously, the directive did not come down until the men had already gone a mile. The wagons were stopped and not allowed to proceed. Curtius wrote, "The result is that we are here, and many of the regiments are without anything to eat.... A few raw onions, without bread or meat, has been the only ration of several of the Colonels and their messes this evening."[27]

The next day, there was a fight at the Salt River crossing, where the Rebels used artillery against Crittenden's hungry men. Twenty-five of them were killed. Another fight followed when the column drew closer to Bardstown, and a sharper one on October 4. Four miles out of Bardstown, at the Nelson County fairgrounds, Union cavalry encountered mounted Rebels and a battery of artillery under Colonel John Wharton. The Federals deployed and broke into a charge. At 50 yards, the Confederates countercharged with such force that they sent the Yankees reeling. In the confusion that followed, the Federals lost 50 killed and 40 captured, according to the Rebel officers' estimates. Wharton's cavalry had given the Rebels a good day, but a day was all it was. Not even an entire day, for Crittenden's column moved into Bardstown that night, and the Confederates moved out. The Yankees commandeered St. Joseph's College for a hospital. The several hundred sick and wounded Rebels they found were paroled by General George H. Thomas, who was second in command to Buell in this campaign.

On October 5, there was a conference at Bardstown between Crittenden, Thomas, and Buell. Buell had first thought that the Rebels would turn at Elizabethtown to fight him. When they turned off the Louisville and Nashville Turnpike toward Hodgenville, he believed that the great fight would be at Danville. Now, he had decided that it would come at Perryville, the country village that drowsed beside Doctor's Creek, in Boyle County.

On Sunday, October 6, the army moved out of Bardstown. A few miles ahead, they would resume contact with General McCook's corps, and then, on October 8, they would fight Braxton Bragg's Rebels, who they found arrayed for battle on the hills near Perryville, just as Buell had predicted.

10

Return of the Thunderbolt

The Battle of Perryville is beyond the geographical scope of this book. Suffice it to say that it was a very strange battle, in that Bragg's entire army spent the day pummeling one corps, McCook's First, on the Union left flank. Especially hard hit was the division of General Lovell H. Rousseau. General Gilbert's corps was in the center of the Federal line, within sight of the fighting, but he held his men out of the fight, except for the division of the irascible Philip H. Sheridan, who could not be completely restrained. McCook's defenders of the Union left flank had been forced back nearly a mile, and it was almost dark before Gilbert did, at last, send reinforcements. General Crittenden's Second Corps was on the Union right flank, six miles away from the fighting. General Joseph Wheeler demonstrated on Crittenden's front periodically through the day. Crittenden expected that he might come under general attack at any moment, and with no orders to come to McCook's aid, he remained on the right, ready but uninvolved. When the day was done, Bragg had won a tactical victory, but not a strategic one. His men were done in by the day's hard fighting and badly depleted in numbers, and they had been fighting only one corps. Tomorrow Buell might well send two fresh corps against him. His position unsustainable, Bragg slipped away in the night. He linked up with General Edmund Kirby Smith at Harrodsburg, and together they retreated toward Tennessee. General Joseph Wheeler's cavalry were the rear guard and skillfully kept the pursuing Yankees back.

Behind the contending forces, all of central Kentucky tried to cope with the consequences of the Perryville fight. At the battle site itself, there were hundreds of dead to bury and piles of horses to burn. Burned barns had to be rebuilt and houses damaged by artillery and small arms fire had to be repaired. Uncounted tons of debris — weapons, wagons, ammunition boxes, and the shattered treetops — had to be picked up before the land could ever again be put to the plow or cattle safely turned out to pasture. Towns 50 miles away began to receive the wounded. James Guthrie ordered that several L&N cars be converted into hospital cars to move the wounded, once they were carted to a railhead; Perryville was not on the railroad. Louisville (which also had to accommodate more than 1,600 prisoners) had to take in over 1,000 wounded. It was a real hardship on the city, considering that it was already swollen with wounded from the battle with Edmund Kirby Smith at Richmond. In the end, 19 hospitals staffed by 50 surgeons and nearly 300 nurses were established in the city. Even the so-called Asylum for the Blind (officially, the Kentucky Institution for the Education of the Blind) was commandeered, its 21 students dispossessed of their classrooms and dormitories, a thick layer of sawdust spread on the floors, and 300 wounded soldiers moved in. It created a small scandal. On November 7, the secretary of war ordered General Boyle to return the asylum to its proper residents and to move the wounded to the Marine Hospital and to the confiscated homes of secessionists. When it was not done quickly enough, General Halleck became involved. On November 15, Major General Wright, the departmental commander with his headquarters at Cincinnati, tried to reassure Halleck. He wrote, "By report from Louisville, I learn that the Blind Asylum has not yet been evacuated; that all the hospitals in the city are crowded to overflowing; 2800 sick at Bowling Green, 900 at Lebanon, and 1000 at Danville to be sent there. I have directed again that the asylum be vacated as soon as other accommodations can be provided at Louisville or the sick sent to other points; but, if I am correctly informed, the building is essential to the welfare of the sick and wounded at this time."[1]

Major General Halleck responded tersely that Wright's letter was "by no means satisfactory. You were directed to restore the building to the blind..."[2]

Wright protested in his reply that he had ordered Boyle to evacuate the asylum after the initial order, but "I did not imagine it possible that it could be done instantly," but that it "would be as promptly obeyed as the well-being of the patients would permit." A week later, when the asylum still had not been returned to the students and the staff, and undoubtedly anticipating another hateful message from Halleck, Wright wrote that "the medical director at Louisville asserts that the asylum could not up to this time be given up without jeopardizing the lives of the patients. I do

10—*Return of the Thunderbolt*

not, therefore, see what more I could have done without a palpable disregard of the lives or health of the sick and wounded soldiers..."[3]

Considering that there was no further mention of the matter of the Asylum for the Blind in the *Official Records*, the wounded soldiers were presumably moved out a short time later and the buildings and the campus returned to their rightful inhabitants. The short tale is a reminder of the cost of war to the civilian population, even those who lived in a community far removed from the scene of battle.

• • •

During the Perryville campaign, John Hunt Morgan was with Edmund Kirby Smith in the Lexington area. He had no role in the battle and only a very small one in the retreat. The southbound army had retreated no farther than Richmond before Morgan decided that he had had enough. He asked for permission to turn west. He argued successfully that he could hurt Buell by striking the L&N Railroad. Smith agreed, and by October 17 Morgan was on his way.

On or about October 19, he destroyed a column of supply wagons near Bardstown. On October 20, the Raiders attacked Elizabethtown where they looted the post office; sacked some homes, stores, and offices in the courthouse; stole fresh saddle mounts; and burned an L&N Railroad culvert. They camped that night in a grove of ancient hemlock trees on the Leitchfield Road, but it was a short night's rest. At three o'clock in the morning, a Yankee troop train approached the town. The burned culvert stopped the train but not the Yankees (1,800 men of the 91st Illinois Infantry), who continued on foot, their way lighted by the great lantern on the front of the locomotive. Near Morgan's camp they met resistance, and a brisk, indecisive two-hour fight resulted before the Raiders galloped away toward Leitchfield.

Morgan continued through the Pennyrile and Western Coalfield regions toward the Tennessee line, and did no further damage to the L&N until the Raiders were beyond Hopkinsville where some detachments tore up sections of both the Memphis Branch and the main stem.

For all of his talk about hurting Buell, Morgan had done very little damage to the Federal supply line. But he had another expedition in mind, and this next one would be more in keeping with the Morgan legend.

• • •

President Lincoln was adamant that General Buell should pursue Bragg into eastern Tennessee. Buell could not see the wisdom in it. He was more concerned about protecting his Nashville supply base, and at London, he broke off the chase and turned toward the southwest.

Since he left Corinth the previous June, Buell had pleased neither President Lincoln nor General-in-Chief Henry Halleck, and this refusal to keep close to Bragg's heels was one disappointment too many. Buell was relieved of command on October 24.

Word soon got out and Buell's supporters petitioned Washington to reconsider the order. From Louisville on October 27, James Guthrie sent General Halleck a wire that was full of alarms. It read, in part, "The renewed rumors of the removal of General Buell I hope are without foundation.... If he should be removed a winter campaign with his army—now the best in the service—will be lost, and perhaps Nashville and all Middle Tennessee and West Tennessee in danger without the possibility of relief to East Tennessee."[4]

Having sounded the warning, Guthrie next went into detail about why Buell deserved to retain his command:

> He has confidence of most, if not all, of his generals and of all thinking men here. When he could no longer get supplies by the Tennessee and Cumberland Rivers and the Louisville and Nashville Railroad was destroyed his army was put on half rations. In this condition he could not advance on the enemy. He fell back and saved Nashville; then fell back and saved Bowling Green and Southern Kentucky; then fell back and saved Louisville, and brought through all his baggage trains without loss, and now has driven Bragg and Smith out of Kentucky. The battle of Perryville proves the efficiency of his army and the character of his officers.... No general can now take his place without injury to the service and the cause.... I repeat again, I hope General Buell has not and will not be removed.[5]

Guthrie was still influential as a Border State leader. In September he had been suggested in some circles as a successor to Secretary of War Edwin Stanton (who did not leave office, however). But Guthrie's influence did not extend into the realm of military dismissals and appointments, and in the case of General Buell, his hopes were disappointed. Buell was replaced and there was no going back on the decision.

Buell accepted that his days as an army commander were at an end. He dutifully informed General Wright at the headquarters of the Department of the Ohio of the final deployment of his troops: "I have deemed it necessary to post a division at Bowling Green, with a detachment (a brigade) at Munfordville and a brigade at Lebanon, with certain bridge guards, well protected by stockades. I am putting a brigade of cavalry at

10—Return of the Thunderbolt

Lebanon and one at Bowling Green. I have assigned General Gilbert to command the brigades at Lebanon and Munfordville and the guards on the road between these points and Louisville..."[6]

On October 30, 1862, Major General William S. Rosecrans, a brilliant, profane Ohioan, assumed command from General Buell at the Galt House in Louisville. Though a West Point graduate, Rosecrans had left the army in 1853 to follow a career in the coal and kerosene business. At the beginning of the Rebellion, he re-entered the service and fought in western Virginia under General George B. McClellan, whom he called "that damned little cuss." Transferred to the Western Theatre, he had whipped Earl Van Dorn at the Battle of Corinth (October 1862). Afterward, he had shown a disturbing, Buell-like reluctance to pursue and destroy the enemy. Nevertheless, he was Lincoln's choice to lead the Army of the Ohio. It was a popular choice among the soldiers. Spillard Horrall of the 42nd Indiana wrote, "There was a dash about the man that took with the soldiers at the start."[7]

Rosecrans trained down to Bowling Green to establish his headquarters. He no doubt noticed signs along the route of the recent presence of armies, but his journey was not delayed by their vandalism. Bridges and culverts at Shepherdsville, Elizabethtown, Bacon Creek, and Munfordville had been destroyed, but Albert Fink and his work crews had repaired all the damage and the railroad was open, at least to the state line. There was still a lot of damage in Tennessee, at Big South Tunnel near Gallatin and all the bridges between there and Edgefield, but by the end of another month, even the Twin Tunnels at Gallatin would reopen and military traffic on the entire length of the L&N could continue as normal.

Rosecrans took as his headquarters the private home of a secessionist lady who refused to abandon her home. He might have been a general, but she was a housewife and ranked everyone when beneath her own roof. She remained in one part of her house while the general and his staff occupied two rooms and the parlor in another part. Buell was an energetic man, brimming with ideas, and he immediately began in Bowling Green to effect them. He did away with Buell's system of three corps in what was now being called the XIV Army Corps or the Army of the Cumberland. Instead, the army was divided into wings. The right wing was commanded by General McCook, the center wing by General Thomas, and the left wing by General Crittenden.

On November 4, Rosecrans threw McCook's wing forward to Nashville. The blue columns followed the L&N south and arrived on November

9, having sloughed off one brigade at Edgefield. However, it was not McCook's job to rest in Nashville and wait for the rest of the army to come up. His assignment was to usher wagon trains of supplies forward from the temporary supply depot at Mitchellville, to restring telegraph wire, to rebuild railroad bridges, and to help with the reconstruction of the Big South Tunnel. If he did not have skilled mechanics available, Rosecrans told him that he could at least put axes in the hands of his men to cut and shape timbers.

General Rosecrans retained some of General Buell's men in their assignments but replaced others. One of the replacements was Brigadier General Eleazer A. Paine, who was given the post at Gallatin, a particularly vulnerable point in the Tennessee stretch of the L&N. Paine was a 44-year-old native of Ohio, a West Point graduate, and a lawyer in private life. From his Gallatin headquarters, Paine was to protect the L&N from Mitchellville, near the Kentucky line, to Nashville. It was a big assignment, but he had the energy and the requisite cruelty to do whatever had to be done to suppress the local guerrillas, who were becoming more of a threat, and also to try and deal with John Hunt Morgan.

Morgan was active north of Nashville again. In the first week in November, he dashed into Edgefield with 200 men to destroy the railroad and pontoon bridges across the Cumberland River. He fought against several companies of Illinois troops, who killed five of his men and wounded 19. All that the Thunderbolt accomplished was to burn the L&N depot before he retreated. Nathan Bedford Forrest simultaneously attacked south Nashville to divert Federal attention from Morgan but with no more success. He tangled with General Negley on the Franklin Pike and handled the Union general pretty roughly until a shortage of ammunition for his fieldpieces forced him to retreat.

General Paine's job was to guard against such flagrant outrages and also against quieter forms of sabotage. Paine was warned that Confederate skulkers in civilian dress were loafing around the stations, looking for a chance to damage the railroad. In an early version of a conference call, an order went out from General Rosecrans to Paine in Edgefield; to General Thomas, who was in Gallatin with two divisions; to Brigadier General Robert S. Granger in Bowling Green; to Colonel Sanders D. Bruce in Russellville; and to Colonel Henry A. Hambright at Mitchellville to send patrols out to the "neighborhoods of their stations, to know the settlers, and arrest all interlopers. Whoever cannot give a good account of themselves shoot or hang on the nearest tree."[8]

10—Return of the Thunderbolt

Rosecrans entered Nashville on November 10 and immediately went into council with his wing commanders. The next day he reviewed General Negley's and General John M. Palmer's troops and paid homage to the men who had stayed behind to defend the city during the Perryville Campaign.

Normal life in the city was still depressed. A correspondent for the *Louisville Daily Journal* wrote, "Poor old Nashville — dull, dirty, and mourning. Two-thirds of her stores and business places are shut up.... People sour and uncomfortable ... one of the poisoned strongholds of secession." Commodities were available, but at prices higher than the people could ever remember: eggs cost $1 per dozen, a pound of butter was $1.50, a peck of potatoes cost $1.25, vegetables of all kinds sold at "fabulous rates," and wood was $20 a cord. Little wonder that the economy was sluggish.[9]

At least, the L&N Railroad yards were lively. Work on the obstructed tunnel at Gallatin continued from both ends, and the bridges between there and Edgefield were being rebuilt, not by the railroad company but by the U.S. Government, so trains were seen departing, headed north for the short distance to the work sites. A *New York Times* reporter wrote, "I notice at the depot long strings of freight cars and an engine or two going about, showing that the rebels have not entirely destroyed or stolen all the property which is owned by Northern and foreign capitalists, mostly."[10]

Big South reopened on November 25, and a great volume of supplies was expected to arrive from Louisville. Once again, the L&N disappointed. The railroad responded so sluggishly that a military takeover of the railroad was contemplated. William D. Bickham wrote in *Rosecrans' Campaign with the Fourteenth Army Corps*, "The railroad managers were urged to push their carrying capacity to the utmost. They had agreed to run through one hundred car-loads a day, but they hardly averaged one-fourth of that number. There was no alternative. The drought continued and the Cumberland River still remained at its lowest ebb."[11]

James Guthrie wrote directly to Rosecrans on December 8, confessing that he, too, was disappointed that his railroad had not been able to meet the commanding general's expectations. Guthrie assured him that the railroad would do all that it could, but its capacity was limited by a lack of water towers and wood and water for the boilers, especially between Bowling Green and Nashville. Additionally, Guthrie offered the rather feeble excuse that, while cars could pass through the Gallatin tunnels, the work there was not completed. Finishing the job was going to be difficult with the inadequate work force he had on site. Men had been pulled from the railroad north of Bowling Green and from the Memphis Branch, but when they arrived at Gallatin, the building materials they needed were not there, and 40 of them got scared and ran away. There were not enough mechanics to do the skilled work required to put the railroad back in shape. Guthrie had searched for mechanics from Cincinnati to Louisville and had not found enough, and engineers had to be brought in from Virginia to design the arches for Big South. Guthrie slyly pointed out at the end of his long letter that the military, too, bore some of the responsibility because it had given the L&N contradictory orders, which hindered efficiency.

It is unlikely that Guthrie's letter had much of an effect on Rosecrans' thinking. That the railroad was not nationalized may have been because of the influence of Assistant Secretary of War Thomas A. Scott, a friend of James Guthrie and a former railroad executive himself, or that of J. H. Simpson, a former L&N employee, who was now chief topographical engineer in the Western Theater.

Rosecrans knew that Buell's failure as a commanding general was partly attributable to his inability to adequately protect the railroad with blockhouses and stockades. Buell had ordered them, to be sure, but even he knew that the work was not being pushed to completion. Back on August 15, he wrote, "My orders are not obeyed. Instead of fortifying their posts and defending [them] manfully, the guards lounge about without vigilance and are gathered up by the enemy as easily as he would herd as many cattle."[12]

Rosecrans would not allow his orders to be so casually ignored, not when the welfare of the army in Nashville and the commencement of a new campaign depended on the L&N. At Rosecrans' insistence, crews were sent to the bridges where they erected octagonal blockhouses with peaked roofs and loopholes for rifles on each of the eight walls. The blockhouses presented an odd sight, perched awkwardly on the top of each corner of the bridge superstructure. At track level, square shacks were placed on the outside of the superstructure, where they could protect the central piers. They, too, looked like the nests of some large cliff-dwelling bird. At each end, the railroad bridges had heavy wooden gates that could be slammed shut against an assault on the middle spans of track. At such posts as these throughout Kentucky and Tennessee, there were 10,000 soldiers on duty guarding the L&N.

Rosecrans' attention to his supply line paid off. With the railroad safe for the time being and open all the way from Louisville, the required number of rations and other supplies were eventually delivered. The slow but steady delivery of supplies meant that, by the end of December, enough was laid by that Rosecrans' army was safe from starvation through February. He could now plan a campaign south. The Confederates sensed that a move was imminent and made plans of their own to prevent or at least to hinder it by strikes against the army's supply line. The agent of this smashup would be the man who specialized in attacks on the L&N, John Hunt Morgan.

There had been rumors of Morgan on the move all through the autumn. At one point, he and Edmund Kirby Smith were reported north of the Cumberland River with 11,000 men. It was not true, none of the rumors was true, but they did reflect the Federals' certainty that, while the L&N continued to pump supplies to Rosecrans, the Thunderbolt would not sit idle.

Nor did General Bragg want him to. On December 1, Bragg essentially cut Morgan loose with an open-ended order which read: "You will assail [the enemies'] guards and where your relative force will justify it, capture and destroy his trains; burn his bridges, depots, trestlework, etc. In fine, harass him in every conceivable way in your power.... You are not limited in the extent of your operations."[13]

December was a golden month for Morgan. The Confederate government had finally caught up with his personal (but not secret) evaluation of his talents and made his rank of brigadier general official. He had a new wife. And now Braxton Bragg gave him the whole length of the L&N to operate along and the authority to strike whatever target he chose. This was perfectly suited to Morgan's talents. He warmed up by leading a raid on Hartsville, Tennessee, where he surprised and captured an entire Federal brigade. Then, on December 22, he moved north out of Alexandria, Tennessee, with 3,900 men and seven artillery pieces behind him.

Morgan might have hit the Gallatin tunnels again. But Big South and its twin were guarded by two divisions, a force too strong for Morgan's taste. Instead, he set his sights on the lightly defended trestles on Muldraugh Hill, deep in Kentucky.

After Hartsville, the Federals knew that he was on his way, and probably sooner than later. Three days before Morgan moved north, General Wright in Cincinnati tried to prepare General Boyle and boost his confidence for what was coming. Boyle's district was now styled the District of Western Kentucky. Wright wrote the tremulous Kentuckian at his headquarters in Louisville, "If our force at Bowling Green and Munfordville fight, they can whip Morgan.... Our troops must understand that they are expected to fight, and if they do half their duty they can whip Morgan's rascals."[14]

Morgan wasn't any more interested in Bowling Green and Munfordville than he was in Gallatin. They were good targets but too well guarded. At Bowling Green, General Mahlon Manson had five infantry regiments, a regiment and one company of cavalry, and a section of artillery at his command. Munfordville was even better defended, with seven regiments of infantry, plus a battalion and a regiment of cavalry, and one section of artillery, all under Colonel E. H. Hobson.

Instead of these, Morgan first hit Glasgow. There he faced only three companies of the 2nd Michigan Cavalry, which he defeated on December 24. The Christmas Raid was underway.

Morgan, as was typical, scattered his men in various directions, both to maximize the damage and to confuse the enemy. On December 26, he sent Colonel Adam R. Johnson in a feint toward Munfordville, ordered Lieutenant Colonel John Hutchinson to attack the stockade at Bacon Creek, and sent Colonel Basil Duke ahead to Nolin to take the stockade and burn the bridge there, while he waited with a few men at Upton.

The stockade at Nolin was a remarkably easy victory. Duke merely displayed his artillery pieces, and the captain and 76 men of the 91st Illinois surrendered and were paroled. The bridge and the stockade were burned along with some nearby culverts.

Bacon Creek was a different story. Lieutenant Colonel Hutchinson and his Rebel detachment fought for five hours at Bacon Creek. Squads of men repeatedly crept forward with torches to burn the bridge, but December 26 was a rainy day, and the fire wouldn't catch. The rain kept putting it out, and it was dangerous to keep sending bridge burners forward with the Bacon Creek defenders shooting down at them the whole time. Basil Duke, who was not there and must have heard about it later, wrote, "This was a very obstinate defense. A number of shells burst inside the stockade.... Some shots penetrated the walls and an old barn, which had been foolishly included within the work, was knocked to pieces, the falling timbers stunning some of the men." Still, the Yankees would not capitulate.[15]

At Upton, Morgan had met no resistance at all. A young Raider, 17-year-old John Allen Wyeth, later recalled, "As we struck the railroad at Upton, we saw several Union soldiers walking along the track, each with his gun on his shoulder. Under orders, we spurred our horses rapidly forward. Captain Tom Quirk, pistol in hand, shouted to them to surrender, at the same time firing over their heads. Before anyone else could shoot, the men threw up their hands." Upton was captured.[16]

Lightning Ellsworth tapped into the telegraph and, as Morgan dictated, pretended to be General Robert Granger. He inquired of Boyle in Louisville about the location of Federal troops and told "some awful stories in regard to the large size of his own command and its movements." In the end, he assumed his own identity and addressed Boyle directly, sarcastically calling him "bright youth" and a "smart boy."[17]

After Colonel Johnson's men came up from scaring Munfordville, Morgan took them back down to Bacon Creek to see what was delaying Hutchinson. He found his exasperated colonel still fighting a low-grade battle with the stubborn Yankees.

Impatient to be on his way to rejoin Duke, Morgan identified himself and sent in a demand for surrender. Morgan's name was magic. Captain J. A. James and 93 men of the 91st Illinois instantly agreed to lay down their guns. The bridge and the stockade were torched.

The prisoners paroled, Morgan and his men inched toward Nolin, building along the way great bonfires upon which they laid the iron rails that they wrenched from the crossties. As the iron heated, it became soft, and the men bent and twisted the glowing lengths of rail into useless scrap.

The next day, Morgan's cavalry continued toward Elizabethtown, destroying railroad as they went. Some detachments, though, were sent out as flankers and did double duty as procurers of fresh saddle mounts. There is a locally told story, perhaps apocryphal, that shows at once the darker and the more chivalrous sides of Morgan's nature. Morgan and a junior officer named Ferguson were with a patrol looking for horses a short distance southeast of Elizabethtown when they spied a bunch of good horses tied outside a house. The men quietly unsaddled their own tired mounts, saddled the fresh horses, and rode away. A short distance down the road, they saw some young women walking toward them. Morgan swept off his hat, bowed low in the saddle, and jokingly asked the young ladies how they liked his horse. The girls knew their horseflesh. One remarked that the horse belonged to a Mr. Barr, who was at the funeral of Mr. Stephen A. Bridwell, who had died on Christmas Day. A funeral — this explained the gathering of people and the number of fine horses tied outside. Mortified that his men had stolen horses from a funeral party, Morgan ordered that the horses be returned at once to the Bridwell residence. This was quietly done, the saddles exchanged once more, and the raiding party rode off on their old, tired horses, leaving the mourners inside none the wiser until much later.

The scattered elements of Morgan's division seem to have rendezvoused on the Louisville and Nashville Turnpike south of Elizabethtown before moving into the town. Elizabethtown was defended by Lieutenant Colonel H. S. Smith and seven companies of the 91st Illinois; 652 men, in all, who until today had spent their time working on three (as yet) unfinished stockades. As Morgan drew near, Lieutenant Colonel Smith employed a bluff as old as the Bible. He moved his men out to an open field that slanted down from a small hill, then marched them in column around and around, so that, at any given moment, half of them were out of sight. As the never-ending column continued emerging from the backside of the hill, an inexperienced observer might have been convinced that the number of men was too large to challenge. Captain Tom Quirk was no inexperienced observer, however. He rode out to investigate and soon saw the truth; Lieutenant Colonel Smith had considerably fewer than 1,000 men. There was an exchange of gunfire and the Yankees withdrew into Elizabethtown.

Lieutenant Colonel Smith was not yet out of tricks. He sent out to Morgan a rider bearing a demand for surrender. It read, "Sir: I demand of you immediate and unconditional surrender of yourself and forces under your command. I have you completely surrounded, and will open my batteries upon you in twenty minutes and compel you to surrender."[18]

The sheer temerity of it tickled Morgan, who replied, in part, "The situation is reversed and it is you and your command and not mine that is surrounded.... Following your example I have, therefore, to demand and unconditional surrender of yourself and your command." He warned Smith that his guns would open fire in ten minutes.[19]

Smith refused to consider surrender. He said, "In reply, I would say that it is the duty of U.S. soldiers to fight and not surrender."[20]

The Federals took up position in the brick buildings near the center of town as Morgan's men finished their deployment. Colonel W. C. P. Breckinridge's brigade spread out on the left of the Louisville and Nashville Turnpike, Colonel Basil Duke's on the right, and an artillery battery unlimbered on Cemetery Hill, a few hundred yards south of the courthouse square. One regiment was ordered to skirt around the edge of town to the northern approach and prevent any attempts at escape.

After a few minutes, while Morgan paced nearby, the Raiders' artillery on Cemetery Hill barked, and great puffs of brick-colored dust began to spout from the sides of the buildings that sheltered the Yankees. The fire was not altogether accurate, and some rounds of solid shot fell on private homes. The artillery spotter was James Montgomery, a native of Elizabethtown, who pointed out targets below but carefully avoided sending fire toward his own family's home. Bed sheets and petticoats appeared from the rooftops and upstairs windows of the homes of Southern sympathizers so that Morgan's artillery would not fire on them.

Small-arms fire crackled from the buildings where the Yankees had taken cover, but they had no artillery of their own, and the contest was an uneven one. Great holes were being punched in the walls of buildings all around the square. In the space of about 20 minutes, 107 rounds were lobbed into Elizabethtown. Men were being wounded and killed. Lieutenant Colonel Smith was wounded in the face by a flying splinter.

Injured though he was, Smith still had plenty of fight left. Such was not the case with his men. White flags of various descriptions now began to flutter from the damaged buildings around the square. On their own initiative, the soldiers had surrendered Elizabethtown.

Morgan's men relieved the paroled Federals of their overcoats and boots, and shopped in the downtown stores for whatever other winter clothes they needed, paying for their purchases in Confederate money. Morgan bought $1,200 worth of finery for his new wife in Tennessee, then went for an arm-in-arm stroll around the square with Miss Belle McDowell, a celebrated Southern beauty down from Louisville. As he walked and quietly chatted with Miss McDowell, other ladies clustered around the general and pestered him for souvenirs of his visit until he had not a button left on his blue overcoat.

There was more to the aftermath of the fight than a shopping spree and an innocent flirtation, though. The Raiders burned the railroad bridge and the depot, along with 3,500 bushels of wheat. They burned the unfinished stockades, and they took every local horse that was fit for hard riding.

The men camped around town that night while Morgan stayed in the comfortable stagecoach inn of Aunt Beck Hill. Early the next morning, December 28, the men saddled up and, looking sharp in their new clothes and riding fresh mounts, rode north toward Muldraugh Hill.

The great trestles on Muldraugh Hill were a mile apart. Their size has been variously estimated. Morgan scholar James A. Ramage states that both were 500 feet long and 80 feet above the valley floor, and that is as reliable a set of figures as any. The trestles were long and they were high. Protecting them, theoretically, were two unfinished complexes of earthworks and gun platforms. They were manned by the 71st Indiana and the

78th Illinois, both under the command of Lieutenant Colonel Courtland Matson. Matson had no artillery within his works and could not respond when Morgan launched simultaneous attacks on both forts, dropping shells among the unlucky Yankees from above. After two hours, the garrisons both surrendered.

The log quarters of the defenders, the stockades, and the trestles were put to the torch. The flames against the dark hills and the leaden winter sky made a memorable sight, described by young James Allan Wyeth as, "the most brilliant display of fireworks I have ever seen."[21]

Wyeth added, "This was the second time that Morgan had captured the Indiana regiment, and he directed Ellsworth to telegraph Governor Morton of the Hoosier State, thanking him for again sending the regiment down and suggesting that the next time he could send the oil-cloths and overcoats without the men, as he was tired of paroling them." It was not just the clothes that Morgan treasured, though. The Yankees stacked more than 700 new Enfield rifles when they surrendered.[22]

The great object of the raid was accomplished. Morgan moved off several miles to the Rolling Fork River. The Raiders might have crossed, except that the river was high from the recent heavy rains. So, they settled down for the night on the west bank near Hamilton's Ford. There would be plenty of time to cross in the morning.

• • •

While Morgan had been breaking up railroad and stealing horses, the Federals had not been loafing around the Christmas hearth. On December 26, Colonel John Harlan left Gallatin by train, three trains in fact, with five regiments of infantry and an artillery battery. His orders were to drive the Thunderbolt from the railroad. General Rosecrans felt that he had Morgan in a box, this time. If Harlan could beat Morgan away from the L&N, Morgan would have no choice but to return to Tennessee, but he would have to avoid strong Federal forces along his probable escape routes at Bowling Green and at Glasgow. In addition, Colonel William A. Hoskins was at Lebanon with 1,300 men, soon to be increased by reinforcements to 3,300. Morgan would have to thread his way through a deadly maze if he were ever to return to Tennessee with his division intact.

Colonel Harlan had trouble from the start. The railroad was in a bad state of repair from the recent rains, and the cars "were barely sufficient to contain the men, horses, and guns of the brigade," but it was the locomotives that gave the colonel his worst headaches. The engine of the rear

10—Return of the Thunderbolt

train broke down at Big South Tunnel near Gallatin, and it was hours before a replacement from Nashville came up. The last train did not reach Bowling Green until late in the night of the 26th.[23]

The reunited convoy left Bowling Green for Munfordville early the next morning. Ten miles out, the replacement locomotive pulling the rear train broke down, causing another delay of several hours while the men waited for another replacement to pull in from Bowling Green. Once again, it was late at night before the last train arrived at Munfordville.

Harlan wrote that, at Munfordville, his command "disembarked immediately.... The battery and other horses of the brigade had been in the cars for nearly forty hours without a drop of water or a pound of forage. They were fed as well as supplies would permit; nothing but corn could be obtained at Munfordville to feed them." While some men tended the stock, the others lay down to sleep, so weary that they took no notice of the lack of tents.[24]

The brigade left Munfordville on foot at 3:00 A.M. on December 28, reinforced by the 13th Kentucky Infantry under Major E. H. Hobson and the 12th Kentucky Cavalry under Colonel Quintus Cincinnatus Shanks. Harlan now had nearly 3,000 men behind him.

The Federal strike force arrived in Elizabethtown on the morning of December 29 and learned that Morgan was only ten miles ahead at Hamilton's Ford on the Rolling Fork River. Harlan moved immediately, with Shanks' cavalry and a section of artillery leading the way.

Shortly before noon, from the crest of the tall ridge a mile from the river crossing, Shanks observed Morgan's cavalry. The artillery crews went to work and began firing down into the Rebels while a rider galloped back to hurry the infantry forward. When Colonel Harlan came on the scene, he could see some of the graybacks forming a battle line while others crossed the river.

• • •

For Morgan and his men, the morning of December 29 was a busy one. The bulk of the division was preparing to cross the Rolling Fork, but there were detachments getting ready to go off on their own missions. Colonel D. W. Chenault was going to destroy the railroad trestle at Boston. Colonel W. C. P. Breckinridge was sending three companies and one artillery piece to destroy Fort Allen guarding the railroad bridge at New Haven. And Major Robert Bullock was leaving with two artillery pieces to attack the garrison guarding the railroad bridge at Colesburg, about four miles below Hamilton's Ford. Also, there was a matter of military justice to attend to, the court-martial of Lieutenant Colonel J. W. Huffman for mistreating the soldiers captured at Bacon Creek.

About 11:00 A.M., Lieutenant Colonel Huffman was acquitted. Those sitting in judgment were just leaving the Hamilton house when they heard the sound of artillery fire from about a mile back. It was Colonel John M. Harlan's artillery announcing the arrival of 2,900 Yankees, ready to give battle.

Three hundred men under Basil Duke hurried into line to hold the ford until Major Bullock could return. The Rebel cavalrymen were in a good position. There were thick woods on both flanks and a large meadow between, with a depression running across it. Duke thought his men could not have been better protected if they had built fieldworks with the intention of fighting here.

The Federals had more men and more artillery, but they approached timidly. The Rebel skirmishers at the Hamilton house kept the enemy intimidated, but as the bluecoats continued piling in and pushing forward, the skirmishers fell back. The Yankees brought up four or five Parrott guns and began to fire.

Just then, Major Bullock arrived. His two artillery pieces were dragged into position, and his 500 men were added to the 300 already in line while the rest of Morgan's men continued crossing the river.

At last, Morgan sent word for Duke to withdraw, but it was not so easily done now. The Union artillery, called by Duke "the best served of any, I think, that I ever saw in action," was pounding the ford and killing the horses these cavalrymen needed for their retreat. One man counted ten dead horses in a 20-foot square; four horses were killed by a single shell. The enemy infantry was pushing forward, bayonets fixed, supported by the fieldpieces in their rear and the cavalry swinging around on their right.[25]

Suddenly, the enemy line was drawn back. Duke could not understand it, but he quickly reacted. He ordered Captain Virgil Pendleton to counterattack with 300 men while the rest of the rear guard crossed the river. Crossing the river, Duke was wounded by what was perhaps the final artillery round fired in the skirmish at the Rolling Fork. A fragment struck him behind his right ear, tearing away flesh and a small chunk of bone. The force of the blow hurled him from his horse into the river.

While Captain Tom Quirk pulled Duke to safety, Colonel Breckinridge took command and completed the withdrawal to the Nelson County side of the river. The Yankees did not pursue. Morgan's men camped that night in Bardstown, catching up to Colonel Chenault and destroying the stockade at Boston on the way.

The wet and wounded Duke was moved in a carriage filled with mattresses to the home of a Bardstown doctor where his wound was bandaged. It was widely held in the Federal Army that Duke was the real strategist of the Morgan organization. Colonel Harlan even alluded to Duke's importance in his account of the action of December 29; he reported the wounding of Duke and said that he was "believed to be the life and soul of all the movements" of the Raiders.[26]

While both of these evaluations might have been overstated, Duke did seem to be a moderating force in Morgan's loosely constituted command. The proof of his influence came the night after his wounding, when the Raiders went on a small rampage in Bardstown. They opened the jail and robbed the post office, taking the money and trampling the mail in the muddy street. They looted the stores, of course, with no pretense this time of paying even in worthless Confederate money. It was ugly behavior, and to quote James A. Ramage, was "the first plunder of private businesses by Morgan's men."[27]

• • •

Colonel Harlan had called off his attack on Morgan when it appeared to him that the Confederates were breaking up like a covey of quail and flying off in all directions. His losses were slight at only two killed and three wounded, but Harlan cited in his report the absolute weariness of his men after a long hard trip. That was no doubt true, but the next morning they were on the march again, heading toward New Haven. There, they drove off a detachment of Confederates who were besieging Colonel William H. Benneson and 80 men of Company H, 78th Illinois Infantry. Said Harlan, "The firing by my advance ... notified them that an enemy was near at hand. They immediately commenced a rapid movement back to their camp [and] abandoned the attack upon our forces at the bridge."[28]

Harlan's men rested at New Haven until the next morning when they moved to Lebanon Junction to stop and wait for further orders. In his report, Colonel Harlan wrote, "I claim for my command that it saved the Rolling Fork Bridge and most probably prevented any attempt to destroy the bridge at Shepherdsville, thus saving from destruction property of immense value, and preventing the utter destruction of the line of railway by which our army, near Nashville, was mainly supplied." Harlan would go on to become a justice of the U.S. Supreme Court. Some of his opinions, especially touching upon the subject of race, were memorable. But it is doubtful whether, for pure excitement, for that out-of-body rush of exhaustion blended with the wire-edge of danger, anything in Harlan's life was the equal of the maneuvers against John Morgan in December of 1862.[29]

Harlan's role on the Union side of the Christmas Raid was at an end. Now, Colonel William A. Hoskins at Lebanon would have a turn.

At Lebanon, Hoskins had 1,333 men, but reinforcements were on their way and his number would finally top out at more than twice that. In addition, he had 3,000 horses and mules; 300 wagons and draft animals; 200,000 rations; 1,600 small arms; and ample ammunition. What Hoskins did not have was a good position to defend. Lebanon was vulnerable because it was lower than the surrounding ground, so Hoskins moved his men two miles out of town to meet Morgan. Some of his skirmishers soon clashed with Morgan's, and reports came in that the Rebels might be 11,000 strong. Hoskins' men said their prayers and braced themselves for a difficult fight.

Then, on the morning of December 31, Hoskins discovered that Morgan was gone. He had bypassed Lebanon during a sleet storm in the night. Reconnaissance parties kept track of Morgan through the day, and late in the afternoon Hoskins set out in pursuit. The men followed Morgan to New Market where they learned that their quarry was in camp on the Rolling Fork River, only two miles ahead.

Hoskins deployed his men but did not move forward until the next morning, by which time Morgan was gone again. Hoskins followed at a respectful distance.

At Campbellsville, the sluggish Federals could see by the burning piles of Union stores that they were still on Morgan's trail but learned that the Thunderbolt had a five-hour lead. Hoskins boldly sent out a detachment forward to the Green River Bridge near Columbia, but they arrived after the bridge was burned.

The end of the chase was near. General Joseph J. Reynolds had marched out of Glasgow on December 31 and joined the pursuit at Campbellsville. They crossed the Green and followed Morgan, hoping to trap him against the Cumberland River. Through a long New Year's Day the Federals kept after Morgan but once again Morgan was too quick, and the manhunt was called off on January 2, 1863.

Reynolds apparently left no report of the last leg of the chase in which

10—Return of the Thunderbolt

his men took part. Colonel Hoskins' report of his efforts to prevent Morgan's escape was a litany of excuses and unverified fears:

> I labored under great disadvantage, from the fact that I could get no definite information of Morgan's force. I had been officially notified that Morgan, at the time of his attack on Elizabethtown, had less than 3000 men, and certainly but two pieces of artillery. I had also been officially notified that simultaneously with his attack on that place an attack was made on Munfordville supposed to be led by Kirby Smith, whose force was unknown. When I learned that the force advancing on Lebanon certainly had ten pieces of artillery, I inferred that a junction ... had been effected, the whole force being reported by citizens and scouts at 11,000.[30]

What had the Christmas Raid accomplished? Morgan's men had killed or wounded 150 Yankees and had paroled 1,800 of them. They had burned their stockades and several small L&N bridges. They had torn up miles of track and telegraph, and they had destroyed some water tanks and depot buildings. Most notable of all, they had achieved their main purpose in burning the two great trestles on Muldraugh Hill.

However, the list was not as impressive as it appeared. For all of the destruction wrought by Morgan's men, the railroad was closed for only five weeks. Moreover, it was not a critically important five weeks. General Rosecrans had accumulated months' worth of stores at Nashville before the Christmas Raid began and was not prevented from initiating a winter campaign against General Bragg at Murfreesboro, culminating in the Battle of Stones River.

In short, the Christmas Raid was long on style, but rather short in substance, and had little effect on the larger strategic picture.

• • •

The Louisville and Nashville Railroad had never had, and never again would have, a calendar year as contentious as 1862. Since spring the railroad had been under almost constant attack and the main stem had rarely been completely open. The railroad had been the special target of Morgan's cavalry. But the railroad's president was not at war with Morgan alone. James Guthrie was also continuing his never-ending fight with the military authorities in both Washington and in Tennessee. The complaints about Guthrie's preference for hauling private freight have been noted. It was, for obvious reasons, an objectionable practice on the part of Guthrie, but he did not reform his behavior, and the same accusation of putting profits over patriotism continued to be charged against him through the months ahead.

Another sore point between Guthrie and the government had to do with the mail contract. In July, Guthrie complained to Washington that the government, though it had paid for the through mail "for the quarter ending March 31, 1862," had not paid for the same service on either the Lebanon Branch or the Memphis Branch during that quarter. "The Department has not accepted or rejected our bid for the service since the 30 June yet we are carrying the mail," James Guthrie wrote.[31]

By December, the matter still had not been resolved. On December 5, Guthrie sent to George W. McLellan, second assistant postmaster, a letter stating, "This is to give the Department notice the Company will refuse to receive and transport the mails from and after the last day of this month."[32]

McLellan wrote to Secretary of War Stanton, "This Department has been in communication with Mr. Guthrie for some time past, endeavoring to arrange a mutually satisfactory compensation to be paid for the conveyance of the U.S. mails over his road and its branches; *but he demands more for the service than the law authorizes the Department to give*" (italics added for emphasis).[33]

"Under the circumstances," McLellan continued, "the Department deems it proper to inform you of the determination of the Rail Road Company, that you may take such steps as may be called for, to secure the continuation of the quickest means of mail communication with the army in Tennessee."[34]

Stanton referred the letter to President Lincoln, who soon received some advice from Postmaster General Montgomery Blair. In a letter dated December 31, 1862, Blair wrote, "As the mail in question is to a very great extent, 'a soldiers' mail,' there is a manifest propriety in its being taken charge of by the Quartermaster at Louisville. The company will scarcely undertake to discriminate as to what freight the Quartermaster shall send; and if the freight is put on board the train by a file of soldiers, they can only protest." Blair ended by saying that both he and the public would be gratified if Guthrie and his board exhibited "some harmless wrath."[35]

The records are spotty and incomplete, so it can only be presumed, by the determination of both Guthrie and Blair, that the L&N did lose its mail contract. But, no matter. Despite all of the troubles of 1862, the L&N was not hurting financially. The government was paying the railroad 25 percent more for its services than any other railroad and, on top of that, had shouldered the expense of repairing damages to the road. Its soldiers had done much of the physical labor needed to get the trains running again.

10—Return of the Thunderbolt

In the fiscal year 1861 (July 1, 1860–June 30, 1861), the L&N had earned a net profit of $461,970. When the books closed on the fiscal year 1862 (the first full year of war), the figures showed that the L&N had paid off all of its debts and still turned a net profit of $508,591. However, Morgan's Gallatin Raid, the Battle of Perryville, and the Christmas Raid had all occurred after the beginning of the new fiscal year. In addition, there were smaller incidents of destruction that ate into the railroad's reserves. Normal operating costs barely entered into the calculations now. The L&N was caught in a violent maelstrom, and unless things turned around, it looked as if the L&N accountants might have to write the final report of 1863 in red ink.

11

Guerrillas and the Great Raid

Mars, the god of war, did not approve of the L&N's refusal to carry soldiers' letters and parcels from home. Only days after Guthrie announced an end to his company's connection to army mail, a freakishly heavy snowfall collapsed the roof of the L&N shops in Louisville where rolling stock was manufactured and where the superstructures for bridges and trestles were prefabricated.

In spite of the setback, work continued on rebuilding the trestles on Muldraugh Hill. Until the work was done, L&N passengers were inconvenienced by having to detrain at Colesburg, thence travel by stagecoach to Elizabethtown, where they continued their journey by rail to points south. Simultaneous with the work on the Muldraugh Hill trestles, the army was constructing more formidable works to defend them.

For the army high command, winter was a time to shuffle troops. The general-in-chief emphasized the need to guard well the L&N, and by the abstracts from January 1863, his subordinates complied. The numbers at the principal points:

Louisville — 480 effectives present for duty
Muldraugh Hill — 328 present
Elizabethtown — 236 present
Lebanon — 985 present
Munfordville — 2,372 present
Bowling Green —1,843 present
Gallatin — 3,474 present
Nashville —1,325 present.

The numbers were even greater when the small garrisons at outposts, such as Bacon Creek and Nolin, and those troops along the branch lines were included.

The railroad was fully operational after February 1 and struggled to supply Rosecrans' army in winter quarters at Murfreesboro. The need was critical. According to Henry M. Cist, in *The Army of the Cumberland*, rations were in such short supply after the Battle of Stones River that "the whole army was threatened with scurvy."[1]

Luckily, winter was not the time for military operations, and the L&N had a few months during which it could make its deliveries, barely sufficient though they were, and could perform its repair and maintenance duties unmolested. The garrisons along the railroad struggled more against the weather than with the Confederates. There was not much to break the tedium of camp life. The men spent their time performing picket duty, chopping firewood, and resuming the despised routine of drill, inspection, and dress parade. For those who had been active campaigners at Shiloh or Perryville, the return to these last duties was especially irksome. A lucky few men of the garrison were assigned to be train guards (as per General Rosecrans' orders; every train had an armed guard now), or were chosen to go on small scouting missions in the vicinity of the camp.

With the budding of the trees, the Confederates became more active again, but in this spring of 1863, the Rebel threat was of a different character. General Bragg and his army were in southern Tennessee, far away from the main stem of the L&N. Until the Confederate Army could return and lay claim to Middle Tennessee and West Central Kentucky, young men with Southern leanings were on their own, and it was their determination to hold those areas until they were redeemed by the army proper. Campaigns and set-piece battles, and even large scale raids, such as those led by John Morgan, were mostly consigned to the past. Guerrilla warfare was the new threat to the L&N.

There had been small insurgent incidents in late 1862. During the second week in November, a guerrilla gang cut the telegraph below Munfordville, and in December there had been enough hit-and-run activity around Cave City that Rosecrans had to calm General Boyle's nerves with a reassuring message that read, "It is only small guerrilla parties.... They can be destroyed or driven away by combined movement from Columbia, Bowling Green, and Munfordville."[2]

There were sporadic outbreaks of guerrilla activity after the start of the new year. One minor episode occurred near Richland, Tennessee, on the last day of January 1863, when a partisan leader named Peddicord and

40 men disguised in Federal overcoats ripped up some railroad tracks (a poor effort — they only unspiked about five rails) and were about to destroy a cattle guard when a squad of the 129th Illinois chased them away. Brigadier General E. A. Paine had 350 men out patrolling for them. Paine was going to "make an example" of some of the civilians who had looked on while Peddicord's men did their mischief. As for the guerrillas themselves, Paine euphemistically wrote, "I expect to hear that the rebels fell off their horses and broke their necks."[3]

Harsh measures against vandals were in perfect accord with General Rosecrans' thinking. Using almost the same language as Paine, he expressed the opinion that it was all right to make examples of captured irregulars, but he cautioned, "do not want a report. Let them fall off a log and break their necks, for instance." If the language was vague, the meaning was clear: with neither official sanction nor specific instructions from headquarters to do so, Union soldiers were to give the guerrillas no quarter.[4]

A second late-winter strike against the L&N occurred in February when a band of 50 guerrillas destroyed a freight train of 21 cars at Woodburn, Kentucky, a few miles south of Bowling Green. They broke loose a locomotive and a freight car, which they fired and sent screaming southward. The roaring firebrand raced through Franklin and other stations at full speed and stopped only when it ran out of steam. The quick decision of a conductor on a northbound passenger train prevented a head-on collision when, hearing rumors of trouble ahead, he ordered his train to return to Nashville.

General Gordon Granger at Bowling Green dispatched both cavalry and infantry to chase and corner the Rebels, but they could not do it. The bushwhackers escaped justice for the time being, riding away on U.S. government mules.

The Rebels declined to hit the more powerfully defended targets — never Bowling Green or Munfordville or even the forts on Muldraugh Hill. Once they had been tempting prizes, but they had been rebuilt to be stronger than before under the direction of Captain Wickliffe Cooper. Fort Sands, for example, was now called, "the best fortification ... in Kentucky," with a campsite which was "almost ideal, high and dry and surrounded with the wonders of nature." The soldiers were comfortably housed in cabins with shelter-tent roofs.[5]

However, there were an abundance of weaker targets from which to choose. One was Richland, which the bushwhackers hit again during the third week in March. A group of Morgan acolytes got after a train on

11—Guerrillas and the Great Raid

March 19. The passengers traded fire with the bushwhackers, but the locomotive was finally derailed and the guerrillas came pouring aboard to rob the passengers as well as the mail car. Somehow, the conductor escaped and ran back to a nearby stockade. The guerrillas had made a mistake attacking a train so near a guard post. About 100 men of the 129th Illinois hurried to the scene before the raiders were finished and opened fire on them. The guerrillas fled, leaving behind four men who were captured, as well as 28 horses. Worse, perhaps, from their point of view, the Southerners had also left behind most of the mail and $9,000.

March continued to be a hot month. The Federals stayed constantly on the move, responding to incidents at Mitchellville, Tennessee, and Lebanon, Kentucky, and checking into reports of the bloody-handed Champ Ferguson, who was rumored to be skulking around Bardstown. Naturally, with the greening of the grass, the regularly enrolled Confederate commanders became more active as well. One was Fighting Joe Wheeler, now a major general and Braxton Bragg's chief of cavalry. Wheeler opened the new campaign year with an attack on the L&N northeast of Nashville.

On the afternoon of April 10, Wheeler discreetly moved between two Federal stockades overlooking the L&N a few miles northeast of the Tennessee capital. He took position on the left bank of the Cumberland with 2,000 men and three artillery pieces. A long, quiet wait followed. About four o'clock, a long train of 18 stock cars approached. Wheeler's artillery opened fire and disabled the locomotive while a regiment of dismounted cavalry poured out of the brush. They drove off the train guards, who offered only a symbolic defense before they retreated up the track on foot and warned a passenger train behind that the railroad was under attack. Some of Wheeler's cavalrymen now turned their attention to the two stockades and kept the garrisons pinned down, while the War Child led another group of graybacks to try and find a river crossing. He failed, but the three field pieces (E. A. Paine thought that they were Parrott guns) continued pounding the train into scrap. Since the guards had run away, the loss of human life was minimal — only two men were killed — but 35 rounds of 12-pound shot destroyed almost all of the horses and cattle on the cars. Wheeler demolished the train and its cargo and could do no more. He led his men off toward Lebanon.

This is how the spring of 1863 progressed. The Confederate raids were persistent, but they amounted to little more than a dangerous nuisance. Even Wheeler's use of artillery, dramatic though it was, delayed railroad traffic for no more than a few hours. By midnight on the day of the attack on the stock cars, trains were pulling into the Nashville depot.

The raids did keep the Federals stirred up, though. General Paine at Gallatin had his men out and also took the precaution of increasing the guards on northbound trains. His dispatches revealed an apprehension of more and larger attacks to come. All of the local commanders were nervous. Activities such as Wheeler's convinced the authorities that even Nashville was soon to be attacked. A reporter for the *Louisville Daily Journal* noticed the increased tension among the Federals in Nashville and told his readers, "From all appearances ... an engagement is soon to take place." Walter T. Durham, in *Nashville: The Occupied City*, observed, "Rosecrans must have expected [an attack] to be made on Nashville as he sent orders to General [Robert B.] Mitchell on April 19 to prepare for a surprise attack by putting up street barricades, manning the line of defense with well-armed troops, and preparing the batteries at the forts."[6]

In Kentucky, too, the troops were on full alert. General Jeremiah Boyle had inspectors out, checking the readiness of the garrisons at all of the important points along the railroad. Major J. H. Simpson was generally well-pleased with the condition of the forts and stockades, and praised the work of Captain Miles D. McAlester of the Corps of Engineers. He had designed the defenses, including a new one at Bowling Green. The Rebels had built five in 1861 and left one unfinished. The Federals later completed it, making six forts at Bowling Green.

From these strong positions along the L&N, the local commanders sent out patrols to maneuver against the guerrillas. General Henry Judah at Bowling Green also issued rifles to Union citizens in outlying communities so that they could defend themselves against irregulars. In a report to Boyle, Judah noted especially the efforts of the Unionists at Hickory Flat, saying, "They are doing good service. The guerrillas have ceased troubling them." If the combined efforts of soldiers and armed citizens could not prevent every guerrilla outrage, at least they gave the bushwhackers little opportunity to rest. Besides, the civilians no doubt benefited by the chance to perfect their skills as scouts and marksmen.[7]

They were going to need those skills soon, for John Hunt Morgan was coming back to the Bluegrass.

• • •

On or about June 13, Morgan sent a dispatch to General Wheeler in which he claimed that the Federal garrison at Louisville numbered no more than 300 men. He wanted permission to march against the City at the Falls. Wheeler kicked the matter up to Bragg, who agreed to the plan. Wheeler informed Morgan on June 14 that he was authorized to take 1,500 men and such artillery as his own discretion directed north to capture Louisville. However, Bragg anticipated a Federal advance against Tullahoma, and through Wheeler, he urged Morgan to pay attention to events in Tennessee. He said, "Should you hear that the enemy is advancing for a general engagement, General Bragg wishes you to turn rapidly and fall upon his rear."[8]

Morgan was not altogether happy with the reduced force of 1,500 that he was permitted. He pressed Wheeler to allow him an additional 500 horsemen. Once again, Wheeler approached Bragg, who agreed. The final orders were cut on June 18 and read, "General Morgan will proceed to Kentucky with a force of 2,000 officers and men, including such artillery as he may deem most expedient. In addition to accomplishing the work which he has proposed, he will, as far as possible, break up and destroy the Louisville and Nashville Railroad." In the flurry of letters that followed, Wheeler later remembered, "Not one word was said about his crossing the Ohio River; but, on the contrary, he was urged by me to observe the importance of his returning to our army as rapidly as possible."[9]

Yet, crossing the Ohio River was exactly what Morgan had in mind. Morgan habitually exaggerated and shaded the truth to suit himself, but this "Great Raid" that he proposed was based on an outright lie. His plan had been deceptive from the start, and he continued to mislead and disobey his superiors. Authorized to attack Louisville, Morgan intended all along to cross the Ohio River and to do so with more men than he was officially allowed. Given permission to lead 2,000 men, he rode out of Alexandria, Tennessee, with 2,500 behind him. James Ramage noted in *Rebel Raider* that General Bragg, "never forgave Morgan for the deception and never trusted him again."[10]

Morgan had intended to leave for Kentucky in late June, and had actually started on June 20, when the advance of General Ambrose Burnside's vanguard into East Tennessee caused Bragg to recall the Thunderbolt. It was not until July 1 that Morgan's raid actually got under way.

Even though harrassing the L&N was, theoretically, one of the great goals of the raid, Morgan showed little inclination to attack the railroad. From the beginning, he roamed far east of the main stem. He passed through Albany and Burkesville, skirmishing already with Yankee patrols, and then on July 3, he bumped into newly constructed defensive works at

Tebb's Bend on the Green River. They were manned by Colonel Orlando H. Moore and a detachment of the 25th Michigan Infantry. Morgan might have whistled around the fortification. He was mounted and the entrenched infantrymen were not. But, instead, he foolishly decided to attack. In a 30 minute fight on July 4, Morgan lost 75 men killed and wounded. He had no choice but to break off the attack. The raid was off to a bloody start.

It was not until Morgan arrived at Lebanon on July 5 that he even touched the L&N — and then only the terminus of a spur line. The defeat and capture of the target was not calculated to cause any serious interruption of General Rosecrans' flow of supplies. Six months earlier, Morgan had crept by Lebanon in the night; today he would attack.

Lebanon was protected by the 20th Kentucky Infantry, under Lieutenant Colonel Charles S. Hanson. The 8th and 9th Michigan Cavalry regiments, plus the 11th Michigan battery were reportedly on their way to reinforce the garrison, but they had not arrived and would not before the fight was over. The fight commenced with an artillery attack upon some earthworks south of the town. As Morgan's front line advanced, the pickets retreated to join their fellows in town at the large railroad depot. It was a substantial building. The fighting there went on for the next several hours. Finally, Morgan ordered an assault. The Union defenders were defeated, but 19-year-old Thomas Morgan, the general's brother, was killed just as the enemy surrendered. He died gasping in his brother Calvin's arms. Afterward, Morgan's men went on a little rampage. One of the Raiders, Henry C. Magruder, wrote about how the town was looted and burned. Magruder said that after Thomas Morgan was killed, "[General] Morgan did not care much what the boys did." The "boys" torched the depot and 20 other buildings, some of them private homes. They looted the stores and burned all the county and circuit court records, which included indictments of some of Morgan's men for various crimes, including treason. One of these indictments might have been for Ben F. Bowman, a Lebanon native, who was with Morgan on this 1863 raid. Bowman remembered many years later, "I never stole a horse the entire time I was with Morgan. All I ever stole was ropes. It just happened that each rope had a horse on the other end of it."[11]

Explaining his surrender, Lieutenant Colonel Hanson wrote, "I had only 350 men.... I held out until about 1 o'clock, when our ammunition became exhausted, and the rebels commenced burning the town, and my men wearied, quite a number wounded, and despairing of receiving reinforcements, I deemed it wise to give up."[12]

11—Guerrillas and the Great Raid 131

The surviving Morgan brothers blamed Hanson for Thomas' death. John Hunt Morgan verbally assaulted him and Captain Charleton H. Morgan grabbed the Yankee's long, dark beard and shouted, "I will blow your brains out, you damned rascal." Charleton Morgan did not follow through on his threat to murder Hanson; in fact, he later apologized. The captured Yankees were marched in the rain to Springfield, and if their testimony is to be believed, they were badly treated on the march. They were all robbed of their money and valuables, and some who had survived the fight in Lebanon died on the march afterward. A sergeant named Joseph Slaughter collapsed in the muddy road and was clubbed in the head and killed. Another fell beneath the wheels of a caisson and later died of his injuries.[13]

Altogether, fewer than ten Rebels were killed and another 258 or 30 wounded in Lebanon. Supplies of new rifles and ammunition and medicine and wagons were captured and Morgan's men moved away toward Springfield with their prisoners just as the slow Michiganders began, at last, to move up. Within hours, Brigadier General E. H. Hobson arrived in Lebanon at the head of two cavalry regiments, the 9th and 12th Kentucky. Brigadier General James M. Shackelford rode in with the 8th Kentucky Cavalry and a battalion of the 3rd Kentucky Cavalry and a section of the 22nd Indiana Artillery Battery. Colonel Frank Wolford was on his way with five more cavalry regiments. At Lebanon, Hobson was ordered to combine Shackelford's and Wolford's commands with his own and to lead the chase after Morgan. General Henry Judah was farther behind, but he, too, was moving north with 1,200 cavalry.

The end game had started. Morgan had far to go before his Great Raid was done and the powerful Federal forces approaching from behind him did not forecast a successful end for the Thunderbolt and his Raiders.

From Springfield, the Rebels rode all night and reached Bardstown at four o'clock the next morning. There, the Raiders drove in the pickets and had a little fight with Lieutenant Thomas W. Sullivan and 25 troopers who were holed up in a stable, protected by a barricade of planks and manure. The Rebels attacked from three directions, and two of Sullivan's men were killed. Small-arms fire was one thing, but the sight of Morgan's artillery moving into position was persuasive in a way that 58 caliber-rifle fire was not. Sullivan surrendered and was surprised when the chivalric Southerners took his and his men's boots and hats. The Bardstown stockade was put to the torch before the Raiders rode on, wearing their new head- and footgear, following the branch line to Bardstown Junction on the main stem. Lightning Ellsworth went straight to the telegraph office and settled down to play his usual tricks.

He had played the trick too often, and not all of the Federals were deceived. Colonel Charles D. Pennebaker, commanding the post of Munfordville, saw through the ruse almost immediately. The next day, he wired Major General Ambrose Burnside at department headquarters in Cincinnati, "The two dispatches received in your name yesterday inquiring for the whereabouts of General Judah and yours this morning inquiring news from this point, I am doubtful of. I answered the first of yours yesterday, but declined the second. Communicate in cipher." Later the same day he wired, "Has not Morgan swung a thief on the wires? Too many inquiries for General Judah."[14]

Pennebaker, whose regiment was the 27th Kentucky Infantry, was a competent young officer. Since the first reports of Morgan's foray into Kentucky, he had been ready to receive the Confederate, should he dare to attack the Green River town. General Boyle ordered Pennebaker to be ready to destroy his stores if Morgan approached, but the colonel was made of sterner stuff and seemed inclined to fight Morgan. In his reply to Boyle, Pennebaker said, "I am prepared for the work. Where is he and in what direction is he going?" He sent scouting parties out to Green and LaRue Counties, but they were unable to make contact with Morgan's cavalry and it was soon clear that Munfordville was going to be spared another battle.[15]

Ellsworth learned in the Bardstown Junction telegraph office that a train was coming up from Nashville. In no time at all, the train pulled into the junction and was captured. The passengers and the express car were robbed. The Raiders emptied the mail pouches and used the letters to start fires. After Morgan chatted with some of the female passengers, he permitted the train to reverse direction and back down the track to Elizabethtown.

Morgan's proximity to Louisville threw the city and its commanding general into an unaccountable panic. He had never attacked the city in any of his previous raids, but Morgan undeniably held the psychological upper hand, and the citizens there seem to have lived in constant dread that Louisville was about to be stormed. A steadier commander than Boyle might have been able to reassure the people of the city, but Boyle himself was convinced that an attack was imminent. The city was placed under martial law. General Burnside, relying on the reports of his Louisville subordinate, advised him to "remove all public stores and cross the river to

Jeffersonville," but also tried to buck him up by saying, "If the place is attacked, you must defend it to the last."[16]

Boyle's fears were unfounded. He had about 3,600 men behind all those miles of earthworks from 1862. Robert E. McDowell, historian of Civil War Louisville, pointed out that there were many more defenders able and ready to fight, as was proven on July 8 when a call went out and the city raised 40 companies in two days.

Morgan had no intention of attacking Louisville. He did not even attack Shepherdsville, whose defenders numbered only about 150 men. His mind was on flight. When Hobson's men rode out of the mist at Bardstown Junction on the morning of July 7, Morgan spurred away to the west. He crossed the railroad north of Elizabethtown and hurried toward Brandenburg, on the Ohio River in Meade County. According to James Ramage, "Guards at Muldraugh's Hill and other stockades on the L&N were mystified that Morgan did not wreak more destruction on the main line. 'Much excitement exists along the whole line of Railroad for his intention is no doubt to try and destroy portions of it,' observed an officer in Bowling Green." Destruction of the L&N had been one of Morgan's stated aims for going on the Great Raid; yet, he had barely touched it and now had ridden away from the railroad entirely.[17]

Hobson reported from Bardstown Junction, "I am in pursuit of Morgan, who will either move toward Brandenburg or Elizabethtown.... He is hard pressed. He has been damaged more this trip than either of his former raids. He lost ten or fifteen of his officers and a number of men.... Railroad all safe; but one small bridge burned; can be repaired in two days." A trainload of supplies was sent down from Louisville to sustain Hobson's men, and they picked up Morgan's trail again the next day.[18]

Morgan's scouts arrived at Brandenburg on the night of July 7; the general led the rest of his men into town on the 8th. The scouts had captured two river steamers, so Morgan did not have to linger on the southern bank. He began ferrying men across to the Indiana shore, an operation that took most of the day. A gunboat appeared and lobbed a few rounds in the direction of Morgan's men. It caused some confusion, but the men continued crossing. The next morning, July 9, Morgan's men struck for Corydon.

Boyle believed that Morgan would attack Jeffersonville and New Albany, and cross the river to strike Louisville from behind. He urgently requested, and received, reinforcements from Munfordville and Lebanon. Others believed that Morgan had doubled back and was heading for Big

Spring, on the Hardin-Meade-Breckinridge County line, or for Leitchfield. He might try to exit the state through Bowling Green. To block the back door, General Judah stopped in Elizabethtown, where he rested his men and requisitioned horses, before riding off to Leitchfield. General Hobson led his strike force to Brandenburg, several hours behind Morgan, and crossed the river on July 10. Between the Kentucky cavalrymen and the Northern militiamen, Morgan had his hands full for the next week.

There was fighting at Corydon, which cost Morgan 42 men killed and wounded. He captured the small town, and word spread quickly through Indiana that Morgan was across the Ohio River. Shelby Foote wrote that an exaggerated report of 10,000 graycoat cavalrymen under Morgan on Hoosier soil reached Indianapolis while the city was celebrating the Union victories at Vicksburg and Gettysburg. It was said that he was "on his way even now to capture and sack the city." The celebration came to "an abrupt and woeful end.... Church bells and fire bells rang the alarm, and a crowd turned out in front of the Bates House to hear Governor Morton read the latest dispatches. More than sixty thousand citizens responded throughout the state to his appeal for militia volunteers." These 60,000 swarmed out into the countryside to hinder Morgan in ways more commonly associated with the Confederates: sniping, felling trees to block the road, and generally behaving like bushwhackers in an effort to slow Morgan down for the Union cavalry.[19]

Conversely, the Union horse soldiers were receiving a gratifying reception north of the Ohio. Relations between Indiana and Kentucky had not always been of the warmest kind, but Hobson's cavalrymen were greeted as heroes by the Hoosiers. General Shackelford later reported, "The kindness, hospitality and patriotism of the noble State, as exhibited on the passage of the Federal forces, was sufficient to convince the most consummate traitor of the impossibility of severing this great Union. Ohio seemed to vie with her sister, Indiana, in facilitation our pursuit after the great Rebel raider. In each of these two great States, our troops were fed and furnished with water from the hands of men, women and children; from the palace and hut alike, we shared their hospitality."[20]

Morgan led his men northeast, roughly parallel to the right bank of the Ohio, through Salem, Vernon, Versailles, and Sunman, toward the Ohio state line. All along the way his men lived off of the locals. He crossed on July 13 and turned southeast, still following the river toward Cincinnati. If he had hoped to escape into a safer environment, he was disappointed, for more than 50,000 Ohio militamen were mobilized to oppose his advance. The Buckeyes took over for their Hoosier counterparts. Morgan was now down to fewer than 2,000 men, who seemed to share their leaders' nonchalance about the peril they were in. All along the way they had stolen horses from the local farmers and had looted the stores of necessities, but also of such useless encumbrances as birdcages, ice skates, and ladies' garments. In Ohio, they stole ceremonial devices from a Masonic temple — and all the while the enemy swirled around and behind them.

Morgan bypassed Cincinnati and, on July 19, tried to cross the Ohio River at Buffington Island. By this time, General Judah had moved up to the Ohio, taking the L&N Railroad to Louisville and then a river packet to Cincinnati, thence to Portsmouth. From there, he rode hard to surprise Morgan and block his way to the river. A regiment of Ohio militia with a complement of two fieldpieces was also on the scene. In addition, a flotilla of six well-armed steamers was on the Ohio. Buffington Island was usually an easy place to ford, but the river was a little higher than normal because of recent heavy rains, and the steamboats were able to draw near. As Morgan and his men appeared on the bank, the boats' guns fired; both General Judah and the Ohio militia attacked and, with wonderful good luck in timing, General Hobson arrived to charge Morgan from behind.

Morgan found a way out of the trap in the broken country of north bank ravines, but the attack had cost him his artillery and 700 men, including among those captured the indispensable Basil Duke and brothers Richard and Charleton Morgan. The killed and wounded numbered 120.

When news of Morgan's disaster at Buffington Island came to Louisville, the *Daily Journal* gazed into the future and saw that Morgan's end was near. The newspaper crowed, "John Morgan announced himself long ago 'Superintendent of the L&N RR.' We suggest that the depots at both ends of the road and all along the route be draped in mourning on account of their melancholy bereavement." The newspaper's funereal editorializing was premature — but not by much.[21]

Fourteen miles upriver from Buffington, Morgan tried to cross again when one of the armed riverboats showed up. In addition to its big guns, the boat had several regiments of West Virginia infantrymen lining the rails of the texas deck. Three hundred of Morgan's men got across, but the pounding and peppering from the boat drove the rest back to the Ohio bank again. Things had suddenly become much more serious. There was no other choice; they headed north.

Shackelford led a 500-man detachment of Hobson's command in hot pursuit. They were mounted on the best horses and were reinforced by

The L&N Railroad Yard at Nashville. Library of Congress.

local militiamen along the way, but, even so, Morgan skillfully eluded them for another week.

It was a memorable flight that Morgan and his exhausted men made, but on July 26, the crippling fatigue and broken-down horses defeated them. Near the village of West Point, Ohio, Morgan and his remaining 400 men were cornered. The raid was done.

The through-the-looking-glass nature of the Great Raid continued even into its final moments. Thinking quickly, Morgan surrendered to one of his own prisoners, a Buckeye militia captain named James Burbick, and demanded from him an immediate parole. Morgan believed he could get terms from Burbick more easily than he could from Shackelford, and he was right. In a moment, Burbick the prisoner became Morgan's captor and protector. When Shackelford rode up, Morgan informed him of the terms of his surrender. Shackelford had done what no one else had been able to do, he had run the Thunderbolt to ground, and he was not about to lose his prize now on a technicality. He ignored Morgan's claim of parole and Burbick's authority to grant it. Departmental commander Ambrose Burnside took the same position, and within a week, John Hunt Morgan and his men were in the Ohio State Penitentiary. General Hobson returned to Louisville and was serenaded by the post band.

John Morgan and some of his men would escape from the penitentiary on November 27. He would make his way south and cobble together a new command, but the rest of Morgan's military career — and the rest of his life — were a sad denouement to what had gone before. Morgan and his Raiders would never be seen again on the L&N Railroad.

12

A World without Morgan

About the time that John Hunt Morgan began his Great Raid, the fiscal year 1863 ended. The railroad had earned a net profit of $1,062,165. It was a phenomenal rebound in the company's fortunes, explicable, in part, not only by an interlude of several months in which there were few, if any, crippling acts of vandalism (nothing even approaching the terrible collapse of Big South Tunnel) but also by the continuing, aggressive policy of the L&N to haul private freight at greater profits, rather than military freight for lesser gains. To this last unsavory practice, both military and political observers had raised, and would continue to raise, constant objections, which the management of the railroad brazenly ignored. Of this, more later.

The company was in such a state of financial good health that James Guthrie and his board of directors undertook to plan some monumental projects for the future. One was the 14th Street railroad bridge, which would cross the Ohio River and connect the L&N in Louisville to the extensive rail system of the North.

Another proposal was to extend the Lebanon Branch to Danville and eventually to Somerset. Sending a tendril toward the foothills of the coal-rich Appalachians was a costly enterprise for a railroad whose president continually presented a bleak picture of imminent bankruptcy, but Guthrie and his executives wanted it and so did the military. As usual, they would act as partners in the endeavor. The railroad put up $1,000,000 in cash for seed money, but the government bore the brunt of the cost. It was agreed that the government would furnish "subsistence stores and quartermasters to furnish the quartermasters' supplies, wagons, tents, and teams, to pay the employees, and to furnish materials to work upon." In addition,

12 — A World without Morgan

General Boyle was authorized to impress as many as 8,000 Negroes as laborers.[1]

The plan would benefit the L&N in a number of ways: increased revenues on account of freight and passenger business, access to a fuel source to replace standing timber (of which there was now a sharp shortage), and, most attractive of all, when the project was complete, the extension would be the exclusive property of the L&N, even though the government had provided the materials and labor.

The L&N president's happy acceptance of government labor, material, protection, and payrolls represented a contradiction in Guthrie's political philosophy. As a Jacksonian Democrat, he had always been a financial conservative and opposed the use of government funds for internal improvements, but as president of the L&N, a private business endeavor which had a weaker claim to federal resources than the states did, he was quick to ask for government aid and was glad to receive it. Guthrie appears not to have been a man who was given to contemplation of self. Perhaps he never perceived the disconnect between his past and present thinking. Perhaps it was purely a matter of self-interest. He was not responsible for the well-being of the states and had no reason to approve of their receiving a portion of the national treasury, but he was responsible for the well-being of the L&N and, as its president, was eager to grasp all he could in order to further its profits. A more generous interpretation of Guthrie's change of opinion is that it was not a contradiction but rather an evolution in his thinking. Perhaps the urgent demands of national defense shaped Guthrie's new attitude toward the proper use of federal monies. It seems unlikely, but it may be so. The war forced a recalibration of many people's thinking.

• • •

In the midst of his responsibilities as president of the L&N, James Guthrie found time to be an advocate for his friends, even those with strong Southern sympathies. It was lucky for them that Guthrie continued to have influence with President Lincoln.

One case in which Guthrie intervened was that of Samuel B. Churchill. Back in October 1861, Churchill, who was a descendant of a prominent Central Kentucky family and a former Louisvillian, had been arrested in St. Louis for aiding and abetting the enemy, and his property assessed. One of Kentucky's U.S. senators, Lazarus W. Powell, wrote to Lincoln on Churchill's behalf, but the president turned him down, saying, "I cannot now interfere with the case."[2]

More than a year passed. When Churchill was judged to be such a threat to the Union cause that he should be banished to the Deep South, Guthrie wrote the president directly. On May 16, Guthrie sent a wire reading:

> Colonel Samuel B. Churchill, of St. Louis, formerly of this city, has been banished South with his wife and seven children, five of them very small. Colonel Churchill is a man of intelligence and high character, of moderate fortune. It will utterly ruin him to have to go South. I respectfully request that his sentence to be commuted. He will take the oath and give bond if allowed. I ask this because I know him and rely on his honor, and he is a cousin of my children.[3]

On May 16, 1863, Abraham Lincoln had a tangle of troubles on his mind. Only a few days before, General Joseph Hooker had been defeated by Robert E. Lee's smaller army at Chancellorsville and had retreated in confusion. U. S. Grant was fighting in Mississippi, trying to find the key to the capture of Vicksburg, and General Rosecrans was stubbornly refusing to budge from winter quarters at Tullahoma, though the year was so advanced that his men were planting shade trees along their company streets. It speaks to the important place that Guthrie held in Lincoln's thoughts that the busy commander-in-chief answered him the same day in the insignificant matter of an unrepentant Rebel's rights:

> Your dispatch of today is received. I personally know nothing of Colonel Churchill, but some months ago and more than once he has been represented to me as exerting a mischievous influence at St. Louis for which reason I am unwilling to force his continuance there against the judgment of our friends on the ground. But if it will oblige you he may come to and remain at Louisville upon taking the oath of allegiance and your pledge for his good behavior.[4]

Guthrie replied the next day, "I am assured Colonel Churchill will take the oath of allegiance and pledge myself he will be of good behavior and feel greatly obliged by your decision."[5] On May 19, by Special Orders No. 223, Secretary of War Stanton instructed General Samuel Curtis at St. Louis to pass Churchill and his family on to Louisville.

The case of Samuel B. Churchill was not quite closed. On March 7, 1865, President Lincoln wrote a query to Major General John Pope, now in command of the Department of the Missouri, with his headquarters at St. Louis. The president's telegram read: "Please state briefly what you concluded about the assessments in St. Louis. Early in the war one Samuel B. Churchill was sent from St. Louis to Louisville, where I have quite satisfactory evidence that he has not misbehaved; still, I am told his property at St. Louis is subjected to the assessment, which I think it ought not to be. Still, I wish to know what you think."[6]

General Pope seemed disinclined to be generous in the matter of assessments in general. He explained in his reply that the policy had been set in Washington, and in the particular case of Churchill, the order had been issued before he came to command. Pope referred Lincoln to an earlier letter to the War Department in which he explained in more detail the reasons for the Churchill assessment.

It is reasonable to assume that James Guthrie had once again interceded on Churchill's behalf, but the secessionist's name does not appear again in the *Official Records*, and the final decision on the matter of the assessment is not known.

• • •

That James Guthrie had any sway at all with President Lincoln from 1863 until the war's end is remarkable, considering that the complaints about the service provided the army by the L&N were incessant. During the forward movement toward Georgia, while General Bragg was being maneuvered out of Middle Tennessee, Rosecrans wired Guthrie, "We must have by your road at least twenty cars daily for commissary stores, beside what might be wanted for Quartermaster stores. Requisitions will be made by officers at Louisville."[7]

Guthrie apparently did not comply, for nine days later, on September 16, Charles A. Dana, who was Secretary of War Stanton's observer traveling with the Army of the Cumberland, wired his boss, "Though the L&N Railroad is paid by the Government for transportation at its own rate of charge, these rates being some twenty-five percent higher than are charged by the other roads, it persists in preferring private freight over that of the Government. It will be impossible to maintain this army without a complete change in the management of that road. The Government is its great customer, and should control its movements." Dana dismissed the excuse that 50 units of the L&N's rolling stock had been transferred over to the Nashville and Chattanooga Railroad, saying, that was "no reason why it should carry private freight rather than our supplies."[8]

The same day, Rosecrans wrote directly to Guthrie again. He said, "It will be absolutely necessary for your road to furnish us more transportation. The general impression is that private freight and express goods have preference over all others. I trust you will have this remedied at once."

Then, after the appeal came the threat: "This transportation is a military necessity, and we must have it, even if we have to press the whole road into service, which I shall not hesitate to do unless things are remedied."[9]

If Rosecrans had remained in command, he might have carried out his threat to nationalize the L&N, but the general's fortunes were about to take a disastrous plunge. He was whipped out of his boots at Chickamauga on September 20, and allowed himself to become besieged at Chattanooga. It was during this time that two corps were detached from the Army of the Potomac and sent west by rail with unprecedented speed to reinforce the Army of the Cumberland. Their arrival was too late for Rosecrans, who was unnerved by his defeat at Chickamauga and seemed unable to plan a breakout from Chattanooga. Rosecrans was replaced by General George H. Thomas, the "Rock of Chickamauga," on October 19.

The L&N had helped speed the "Potomacs" to Chattanooga, proving the efficient service it could provide, but soon the railroad was back to its old habits. On November 3, a new voice was added to the chorus of critics. General U. S. Grant, whose reward for the victory at Vicksburg was promotion to supreme command in the Western Theater, and who had come to Chattanooga to engineer the defeat of General Bragg's army on those surrounding precipitous ridges, added his own lament about the poor L&N service. Even when the very survival of a besieged army relied on its service, the L&N was falling short. Grant wrote, "Complaints are made of the stores not being [sent] fast enough over Louisville & Nashville Railroad. If stores do not come up the Cumberland on steamers, the Louisville road must send at least forty car-loads of provisions daily besides quartermaster's stores."[10]

Short of nationalizing the L&N, the U.S. government and its commanders in the field did what they could to improve the railroad's service to the army. The military authorities prohibited citizen travel on the L&N. In addition, a military supervisor of the western railroads was appointed. His name was John B. Anderson, a Kentuckian and a former employee of the L&N. Since that was the very line that was most objectionable in its behavior, Anderson was not a universally popular choice. Governor Andrew Johnson did not approve of his appointment, and U. S. Grant soon came to share the opinion that Anderson was not the man for the job. Anderson could not keep the Nashville and Chattanooga Railroad in good working order and could not find a way to compel better service out of the L&N. Criticized for the road's performance during the siege of Chattanooga and in the months after, Anderson was nudged out by General William T. Sherman before the Atlanta campaign began.

James Guthrie and his board of directors may have been too smart by half in trying to balance on the saber's edge of keeping the government sufficiently satisfied to prevent government seizure of the L&N and, at the same time, hauling enough private freight and civilian passengers to pay their own salaries as well as the stockholders' dividends. Duplicity might be too strong a word for what the L&N was up to, but the railroad's managers were certainly trying to serve two masters, and the more powerful of those masters decided to take an unexpected action.

In September 1863 work began to complete a new railroad between Nashville and Johnsonville, a village 76 miles due west on the Tennessee River. The government agreed to back the railroad's completion along the same terms, essentially, that it had in the extension of the Lebanon Branch of the L&N. That is, it would provide materials, slaves to do the labor, and soldiers to guard the construction crews. Governor Andrew Johnson was responsible for co-ordinating the effort to finish the Nashville & Northwestern Railroad, a job he undertook gladly, for as he later remarked, it would blunt the "exacting extortions of the Louisville and Nashville Road."[11]

As of November 10, Major General Lovell Harrison Rousseau became the military authority in the district through which the Nashville & Northwestern would run. By Special Field Orders No. 310, Rousseau was assigned to command the District of Tennessee, "including the defenses of the Louisville and Nashville Railroad to the Kentucky line, the Northwestern Railroad from Nashville to the Tennessee River, the Nashville and Chattanooga Railroad to Duck River, the Nashville and Decatur Railroad to Columbia, and the posts of McMinnville, Clarksville, Fort Donelson, and Nashville."[12]

It was a nearly impossible job to protect every mile of four railroads against every bit of mischief the bushwhackers could think of, and they were always thinking. Inevitably, there were some incidents. Guerrillas harassed the N&NW work gangs during the winter of 1863–64, but work went on at a rate of not quite a mile a day. A locomotive and cars arrived for use on the N&NW in February 1864. The railroad became operational in May 1864, and the L&N lost its monopoly on Nashville.

• • •

The absence of John Hunt Morgan did not mean a shortage of mischief in the L&N corridor. Even before he had crossed the Ohio, there were incidents in his wake. A typical incident was the one that happened at Woodburn and Rocky Hill, near Bowling Green. At about noon on July 4, 50 to 100 guerrillas led by a captain named Umber attacked Rocky Hill. They robbed the store of a merchant named Dickinson and then went for the railroad depot. A clerk from Dickinson's store tried to talk them out of torching it, explaining that it was filled with citizens' property and was not used by the government. The guerrillas paid him no attention. They set the depot on fire and tore down all the telegraph wires and robbed the telegrapher. Fifty citizens gathered to watch the depot burn but did not try to douse the flames as the guerrillas rode out of town, headed south.

The irregulars made a wide swing around Bowling Green and hit the L&N again at Woodburn, near the Warren-Simpson County line. Cavalry were dispatched to cut off the guerrillas' escape, and Major Ignatius Mattingly and the men of the 26th Kentucky Infantry boarded a special train and rolled down to Woodburn. They found the Rebels in an encore of their Rocky Hill performance. They were firing the depot and destroying the telegraph, but they fled when the Yankee-filled train arrived. The riflemen of the 26th sent two or three volleys in their direction and wounded several. They chased the guerrillas about a mile before the cavalry took over. The vandals got away to the south, leaving behind four prisoners, 11 or 12 horses, and about 12 guns.

Colonel Cicero Maxwell, post commander at Bowling Green, in keeping with General Boyle's policy, began assessing the suspected disloyal citizens of Rocky Hill; their money would rebuild the depot whose arson they had done nothing to prevent. When Maxwell went on furlough, the duty devolved on Lieutenant Colonel Thomas B. Fairleigh. He completed the accounting and sent to Boyle's headquarters a summary, saying, "I enclose you a paper showing you the value of the property of the leading citizens in that neighborhood and the amount proposed to be levied on each.... With the approval of General Boyle, I will at once by order direct the citizens named in that paper to pay to any agent whom the railroad company may direct the amount assessed on each.... In the event one fails to comply with the order, I propose to take property worth the full amount."[13]

He added, "The depot cost $1040 several years ago. The levy amounts to $1221 and it is not more than sufficient to rebuild the depot now, even if every cent is collected."[14]

In a later bit of correspondence, Fairleigh explained that, in idly watching the depot burn, the citizens of Rocky Hill (a "peculiarly disloyal" community) were guilty of "passive disloyalty." He continued, "By making the proposed assessment it is thought the citizen will soon learn that he is pecuniarily interested in the protection of the road and property on it, and to that extent made actively loyal."[15]

Boyle endorsed the order to assess the citizens of Rocky Hill, but the theory that the citizens of Kentucky were made "actively loyal" by Boyle's policies and the example set by the treatment of the citizens of Rocky Hill is not easily proven. So numerous were bushwhacker raids on the L&N during the late summer and fall of 1863 that the *Louisville Daily Journal* opined, "It would seem that a regular system of guerrilla warfare has been inaugurated in Kentucky." There were guerrilla raids at Nolin; at Dripping Springs, just north of Bowling Green; at New Haven on the Bardstown Branch; and at New Hope on the Lebanon Branch; where it was reported that Captain Littleton Richardson and his band of 250 marauders had placed obstructions on the track to throw the train. After the train wrecked, they fired into the cars and forced the passengers' surrender. "After the surrender, all the passengers were robbed of their clothing, money, and other valuables, the cars were all set on fire and destroyed, the locomotive disabled, and the track torn up for a short distance," the *Daily Journal* reported.[16]

Richardson liked the rich pickings of this newest hunting ground, and he remained for several weeks, during which time he also hit Bardstown. There, he and his band burned the depot, along with a locomotive and rail cars. They also went on a robbing spree, emptying store shelves and also citizens' pockets.

Southern Kentucky was not spared. A soldier in Bowling Green complained, "The guerrillas ply some devilment every day or two. We run out after them. They are too fast and get out of the way." The boldest of the guerrillas even came near Louisville where a group of saboteurs called the Sons of Liberty gave them continuing aid. Robert McDowell, in his excellent book *City of Conflict*, wrote, "Around Louisville, scarcely a night passed that guerrillas did not strike.... The eastern suburbs, providing richer pickings, were particularly subjected to the horrors of these raids."[17]

General Boyle himself admitted that guerrilla outrages continued despite his efforts. In late October 1863 he wrote, "The guerrillas overrun the border and rob banks, sack towns, and pillage the people." He felt the situation could be turned around if only he had the horses to mount more Federals to oppose the guerrillas, but others seemed to agree that a more drastic solution was needed—a different commander.[18]

The officer the government chose to replace Boyle was Stephen Gano

Burbridge, a 32-year-old native of the Bluegrass, whose educational resumé included both Georgetown College in Scott County and the Kentucky Military Institute near Frankfort. Admitted to the bar after graduation, the sharp-eyed Burbridge moved to Logan County and was living on his plantation there when the war began. He was commissioned a colonel in August 1861. The next month, he began gathering his regiment, the 26th Kentucky Infantry, at Owensboro. Period photographs of Burbridge show an intense, dark-haired man with a satanic goatee and an eager gleam in his eye, as if he could not wait for the work ahead.

Burbridge commanded his regiment through the early western campaigns but left them during Buell's 1862 march across northern Alabama in order to serve with William Tecumseh Sherman. He fought at Vicksburg, Chickasaw Bayou, and Arkansas Post, and performed up to the demanding standards of "Uncle Billy." Sherman liked Burbridge and approved of his appointment to handle matters in the District of Kentucky.

Jeremiah Boyle was officially relieved on January 12, 1864. The interim successor to Boyle was Brigadier General Jacob Ammen, who was followed after one month by Burbridge, who was now a brigadier himself.

The people thought that Boyle's policies had been harsh and often unfair, but Burbridge was going to make Boyle look like a Sunday School teacher by comparison. Burbridge's tenure was so brutal that he would earn the nickname by which people in Kentucky still remember him, "Burbridge the Butcher."

13

The Uneasy Interlude, 1864

In January 1864, Kentucky governor Thomas E. Bramlette authorized the imprisonment of five secessionists for every loyal citizen the guerrillas kidnapped. The actions of the commonwealth's chief executive seemed to foreshadow the plans of the district's new military commander, Stephen G. Burbridge, to proceed with a harsher brand of justice in suppressing the guerrillas. After taking command, Burbridge continued Boyle's policy of assessment, once considered to be so cruel, but he went even further. He confiscated objectionable books from shops and threatened to seize entire inventories. He decreed that Southern sympathizers who lived in a five-mile radius of the site of a guerrilla raid might be arrested and banished from the county. He announced that anyone traveling after dark would be considered a thief. He struck candidates he disliked from the ballot and proclaimed a shoot-to-kill order; henceforth no guerrillas would be taken alive. Worse still, Burbridge ordered the execution of four prisoners for every Union man killed. Under the man who the people soon began calling "Burbridge the Butcher," 50 Kentucky men were killed by firing squads, many of them not guerrillas and some of them not guilty of any offense greater than patronizing a shop where guerrillas might have done business.

However, there was a way to escape Burbridge's bloody decrees. When two sons of the wealthy Duke family were ordered to be executed, Burbridge informed their parents through private channels that the boys' lives could be redeemed for $2,000. The bribe was paid, and two other Confederate boys, sons of less affluent families, were chosen to die in place of Charlton and John Duke.

A few months after Burbridge took over from Boyle, a report to Secretary of War Stanton from Judge Advocate General Joseph Holt summarized the guerrilla problem in Kentucky and examined the new commander's remedies. Holt concluded that they "cannot fail to produce the happiest effect in mitigating these atrocities.... These executions have inspired a most wholesome terror, and it is to be hoped that the stern but necessary policy thus inaugurated will be in nothing relaxed." The report predicted that Burbridge's approach would ultimately "be hailed with universal satisfaction."[1]

Wherever it was that Holt hoped to discover the "happiest effect" and "universal satisfaction" of which he spoke, it was not in Kentucky. The people were horrified. What Bramlette, Burbridge, and Holt failed to recognize was that holding ground and protecting corporate property was not quite the same as winning the war. In their calculations, the lives and occupations of the ordinary people seemed not to signify, and the fact was, they were losing the hearts and minds of Kentuckians everywhere. Kentucky was becoming Southern because the men in uniform came to be more of a comprehensive threat than the guerrillas themselves. Kentuckians could not abide the imprisonment, the voter suppression and restraint of trade, the censorship, the restriction on free travel, and the promiscuous bloodletting they were suffering at the hands of the agents of the government to which they had once been loyal.

The growing disgust with the federal government was not confined to the farmers and small-town merchants. In Louisville, too, the citizens could see a great many negative changes that had come over their city during the war. Louisville was fast becoming the refugee center of the central regions of the state, and destitute families crowed its streets and alleys. So dire was their need that the army was forced to distribute daily rations to the beggars.

Not that the army was strictly a charitable and benevolent presence. Louisville had been occupied by soldiers since 1861, and their welcome was wearing thin. The sheer number of boys in blue was intimidating; the city was cramped and filled beyond its comfortable capacity. If their behavior had been professional, they would no doubt have found the city more hospitable, but they were not professional. They were volunteers, rough farm boys and boys from the North's urban slums, and they were often disorderly. Robert McDowell wrote that they "felt that the territory south of the Ohio River was enemy territory, and behaved accordingly. And in all fairness, their feelings were not entirely unjustified." In addition, the army's presence attracted the predatory underclass: gamblers, whores, and grifters.[2]

• • •

13 — The Uneasy Interlude, 1864

At the extreme southern end of the L&N, the situation was different in some ways, but similar in others. The anti-government sentiment in Nashville had burst from the surface in 1861— Tennessee, unlike Kentucky, had seceded — and the Federal garrison of nearly 6,000 soldiers was still a hated reality. The prisons, the hospitals, and the barracks, with their unpleasant odors and sounds and grim facades, the street barricades and the forts bristling with cannon were constant reminders that Nashville was, indeed, occupied. Union officers were in the habit of seizing dwelling houses for their own and for military use, a practice to which Major General Lovell H. Rousseau objected, saying that it was "bad for the Government and unjust to the people."[3]

Governor Andrew Johnson was despised for his personality and his policies. Even so, increasing numbers of Nashvillians were finding it to their advantage to pledge their allegiance to the federal government, like the child who grudgingly behaves, not because he wants to, but because it's easier than taking the punishment. Walter Durham acknowledged that Johnson's "approach to winning converts to the Union cause by threats, intimidation, and banishment was beginning to be successful. Reluctantly, citizens had come forth to take the loyalty oath; the names of hundreds of them had been published." The contemporary records bear Durham out. District commander Rousseau stated in a report dated January 30, 1864, "The disposition of the people to return to their allegiance is general and apparent."[4]

However, Durham explained, "Everyone knew that many who took the oath did so with reservations that were great but not articulated" and were motivated to take the oath to avoid Johnson's assessments and his "ready disposition to imprison citizens on trumped up charges, or even with no charges at all."[5]

Like its sister city to the north, Nashville had a refugee problem. Major General Rousseau wrote, "The negro population is giving much trouble to the military, as well as to the people. Slavery is virtually dead in Tennessee, although the State is exempted from the emancipation proclamation. Negroes leave their homes and stroll over the country uncontrolled. Hundreds of them are supported by the Government who neither work nor are able to work. Many straggling negroes have arms obtained from soldiers, and by their insolence and threats greatly alarm and intimidate white families, who are not allowed to keep arms" The blacks tended to move into abandoned residences of the city, and with no means of support, their suffering was great. When the Western Freedman's Association pointed out the problem and recommended to Governor Johnson that refugee camps be established, he opposed the idea on the grounds that government camps would only attract more refugees. But General Rousseau oversaw the establishment of such a camp in February 1864, even without the governor's support.[6]

It was not just plantation blacks that fled as refugees to the city. The dispossessed mountaineers of East Tennessee also found their way to Nashville and had as hard a time of it there as the contrabands did. Colonel William D. Hamilton of the 9th Ohio Cavalry remembered:

> One day while in camp some of the boys told me that in a house near by were some refugees who were sick and starving. I went and found an old man and wife with two married daughters, two daughters-in-law, and eight grandchildren. They had traveled on foot from one of the mountain counties of East Tennessee. The old man said, "Our men-folks had to leave home and sleep in the woods to keep from being forced into the Southern army; and now they have gone to jine you 'uns. It wasn't safe for men and women-folks to stay, and we tuck all our truck and victuals and started six days ago to come here. When we had nothing left to eat some good folks helped us. But some of the young 'uns tuck sick and we had to leave most of our truck and carry 'em. We had nothing to give 'em to eat and they grew worse. We got here yesterday and went into this empty house, but we've been up most of the night with the children."
>
> A young woman was sitting on a stool in a corner of the room beside what appeared to be a bundle of old clothes on the floor. She turned them down and I saw the wasted form of a little girl—the child was dead.
>
> Another mother showed me her little son lying in a corner weak and delirious. All were suffering from starvation.[7]

Hamilton went back to his camp and had coffee and rations sent over to the mountain refugees and then visited the Nashville post commander, General Robert S. Granger, who provided ongoing relief for them, including, presumably, medical attention and more suitable quarters.

So sharp was the refugee problem at Nashville in the first quarter of 1864 that 3,000 indigent persons were transported to Louisville, which was only theoretically better able to accommodate them. Those that stayed in Nashville did what they must in order to survive. Some of the women became prostitutes.

Like Louisville, Nashville had a thriving red-light district. It was called Smoky Row and was the scene of frequent disturbances that strained the resources of General Granger and alarmed the law-abiding citizens. The number of prostitutes was a health threat as well. Many young soldiers had their health permanently undermined by a visit to the row, and the

13 — The Uneasy Interlude, 1864

volume of syphilis and gonorrhea cases was so great that special hospitals were set aside for the treatment of venereal disease. It was only after the whores were made to pay a fee for a license to practice their trade and to submit to regular medical examinations that the problem even began to come under control.

However, under the grim and seedy surface, there were hopeful signs that Nashville would be poised to become a major Southern city after the war. The soon-to-be completed Nashville & Northwestern Railroad would remain to be a permanent source of income and, like the L&N, would be the center of a web of related economic activity. The government had established a massive complex of railroad repair facilities in Nashville. Durham wrote, "By the spring of 1864, the principal shops of the U.S. Military Railroads, Division of the Mississippi, had consolidated at Nashville. There, routine services and maintenance were performed on all of the 221 locomotives of the division. At times as many as one hundred might be found in the city.... Rail cars were also repaired and refurbished in the shops."[8]

Moreover, the facilities for the storing of freight and the required transportation services that were now used for the military would transition over to civilian use once the cruel war was over. Nashville was, and would be, the handler of monstrous quantities of freight. Durham continued, "From November 1, 1863, to September 1, 1864, ... 41,122 horses, 38,724 mules, 3,795 wagons, 445,355 pairs of shoes, 182,300 woolen blankets, 107,715 waterproof blankets, 131,848 shelter tents, and 397,112 infantry tents passed through the Nashville depot." And this did not even include the 108,000 pounds of hay and grain. And this did not take into consideration the quantities of weaponry and human foodstuffs that also passed through Nashville to the army farther south. The storage facilities for such a voluminous inventory were colossal; one of the new warehouses was over 1,000 feet long.[9]

• • •

One change to which the people of Louisville and Nashville had to become accustomed was not logistical but political. The language of the Emancipation Proclamation permitted it, and the idea had been accepted with some talk but little trouble in the North. However, it was slow in coming to Kentucky and Tennessee, and when it did, it tore at the roots of Southern belief, and it was a sight that rocked even Southern Unionists: African American soldiers.

Enrollment of Negro soldiers came first to Tennessee. General Eleazer Paine began enlisting blacks in Gallatin in July 1863 and dispatched the new recruits to Nashville. But recruitment in the capital was a more delicate question and had to be approached more slowly if the small but important coterie of pro-Unionists was not to be antagonized.

A recruiting station was opened in the Tennessee capital in September 1863, but enlistees were slow in coming, partly because of the stipulation in the Emancipation Proclamation that blacks were henceforth free only in those areas in active insurrection against the government. Union troops had occupied Middle Tennessee in 1862, and the region was not technically in rebellion. Therefore, many of the local blacks were not free and could not, of their own volition, enlist. The same situation prevailed in Kentucky.

To help make clear their way to military service, Union Major George L. Stevens addressed a black audience in Nashville and encouraged the men to join, explaining to them that "free persons of color would enter the army and be discharged as free men. Slaves of disloyal masters could volunteer and would be free men at the expiration of their enlistments. Slaves whose loyal master consented to joining the army would [also] be free men at the expiration of their enlistments." Loyal masters would not suffer a dead loss by letting their male slaves enlist; they would be paid $300 for each slave who made his mark on the sign-up paper.[10]

Major Stephens' powers of persuasion must have been formidable, for by October 2, there were regiments of blacks in blue parading through Nashville's streets. The black soldiers were not initially combat troops but were assigned fatigue duty. A great many of them reinforced the garrisons in towns guarding the railroads.

Ironically, the situation in Kentucky was even more delicate than in Tennessee. Lincoln had always been very cautious of causing offense in the Border States, and Kentucky, in the center of that line of states and also the starting point of the western armies' supply line, had to be treated with special care. Tennessee was under the thumb of occupying Union forces, and protest was naturally muted. In Kentucky, a loyal state from the start, the people felt less restraint, except for fear of Burbridge. In spite of the Butcher, Kentuckians, from the governor down to the private in the ranks, voiced their opposition to the enlistment of those they had been taught to consider inferior.

In January 1864, Governor Thomas E. Bramlette vowed that no recruiting of black soldiers would be tolerated in Kentucky. The next month, the General Assembly protested against the enlistment of blacks and requested directly of the president that the camps for Negro soldiers be relocated outside of the state.

Their concerns were ignored. According to the WPA's *Military History of Kentucky*, on February 29, the federal government, "ordered James B. Fry, U.S. Provost Marshall General, to cause the immediate enrollment of all male Negroes in Kentucky between eighteen and forty-five year of age.... Five days later General Burbridge ordered all impressed Negroes released from their work and sent home to their masters so that the enrollment might be accurate."[11]

"Louisville became one of the state's primary induction centers for U.S. Colored Troops," wrote J. Blaine Hudson in *The Encyclopedia of Louisville*. "Black soldiers were concentrated in barracks at Third and Oak Streets, and a ten-acre refugee camp for their families was located at Eighteenth and Broadway, then the outskirts of town."[12]

Eventually, the number of black Kentuckians who enlisted was nearly 24,000. This was second only to Louisiana and 13 percent of the national total. It was not accomplished, though, with the consent or approval of their white comrades-in-arms. Robert Winn, a Kentuckian in Co. E, 3rd Kentucky Cavalry, which was stationed at that time in Gallatin, Tennessee, wrote his sister, "In Gallatin our boys had more of the Nigger than they could bear. There are hundreds of Contrabands and Refugees there, and in some cases in the same house — there has been one full Regiment raised there of U.S. Colored and one company pretty filled now."[13]

Another Kentuckian who had objections to campaigning alongside blacks was Lieutenant Colonel John H. Ward of the 27th Kentucky Infantry, then serving in East Tennessee. In January 1864, he wrote a lengthy diatribe protesting an order for him to help enlist blacks for an artillery regiment. Ward wrote to Major General John G. Foster, his commanding officer:

> I consider this a wide departure from the legitimate cause for which we fight, an insult to every true soldier, an attempt to pervert this war to party purposes, a great ... an irreparable injury to the cause. I cannot endure the sight of my flag ... carried by such hands. These are the sentiments of my Regiment. It would be impossible to restrain them if ever brought in contact with a negro Regt., and, as I would not permit individual disorderly and mob-like attacks I would lead the Regiment and rescue our flag from such disgraceful custody. My spirit of open and fair dealing demands that you should know what our sentiments and intentions are. If such soldiers suit your purpose you can retain us and not be surprised if

we do as I have said. If not then I demand that we be mustered out in a body, for whatever is our fate, we intend to share it together. It is true we knew of laws and orders, making negro soldiers, before, but it was never brought to our own doors before, and we were content to put off any action, as long as we could hope that something might occur that would render it unnecessary.[14]

Lieutenant Colonel Ward's letter edged dangerously close to mutiny. Through the intervention of his alarmed father, General William T. Ward, and also of Major General Lovell H. Rousseau, he was persuaded to recall his letter. If young Ward did not reconsider his views, he did at least continue to serve with his regiment in East Tennessee, through the Atlanta Campaign, and until their return to Kentucky as guerrilla hunters near the end of the war.

The best-known Bluegrass critic of the enlistment of black soldiers was Colonel Frank Wolford, the rough-cut cavalryman who was known affectionately to his men as Old Meat Ax. Wolford was one of those who had helped run John Hunt Morgan to ground. On March 10, 1864, the people of Lexington hosted a gala to honor Colonel Wolford. They presented to him a fine sword and scabbard, as well as a pistol, sash, and a pair of elegant spurs. When the time came for Wolford to make his remarks, he unwisely turned to the subject of black enlistment. The colonel said that the order to enlist Negroes was unconstitutional and unjust and that it was "the duty of the people of Kentucky to resist it as a violation of their guaranteed rights.... The people of Kentucky did not want to keep step to the music of the Union, alongside of negro soldiers." Wolford called the policy "startling," an "insult," and a "degradation." For an incredible three hours he continued in this same vein. One would think that he had, perhaps, had too much to drink, but Wolford claimed never to drink intoxicating liquors. Still, one could not characterize him as intemperate.[15]

Within the week, Wolford was arrested by General Burbridge on orders of Major General John M. Schofield, commander of the Department of the Ohio. He might have faced a court-martial and imprisonment, but he had advocates in Washington. Congressman Robert Mallory and Senator Lazarus W. Powell went to Lincoln to appeal on Wolford's behalf. Lincoln listened to them, but was not entirely won over by their arguments. He said, "I have understood that on his position of loyalty, he had ifs and buts."[16]

The discussion became somewhat heated. Lincoln tried to defuse the tension by means of a distracting story, a common strategy of the president's, but Senator Powell interrupted and told the president that it was "no fit occasion to indulge in an anecdote."[17]

Lincoln could not have been pleased with the tone of Mallory and Powell's visit, but he did not move to clap Wolford in prison. However, the colonel's criticism of administration policy was too loud and too public to be entirely ignored. On March 25, he was removed from the U.S. service by President Lincoln.

There the matter rested and might have continued to rest, except that Wolford would not leave it alone. He went on the stump. He spoke all over Kentucky and persisted in his pet themes. He called Lincoln "a tyrant, a usurper, and a fool," and denounced the enlistment of Negroes as "against the law, contrary to the usages of war, and disgraceful."[18]

On June 27, Wolford was arrested in Lebanon by order of General Burbridge and was ordered to report to Washington, D.C., under guard. He may have met with the president. If he did, his oratory failed him for once, and he returned to Louisville during the second week in July, paroled but still awaiting trial with 13 charges hanging over his head.

Wolford remained in this legal limbo for the next five months, until the fall. It is not surprising that during the presidential campaign he stumped around the state for General George B. McClellan, who was Lincoln's Democratic opponent in the 1864 election. Lincoln lost Kentucky, but he won the election, and perhaps thinking that the danger was passed, the president released Wolford from arrest during the last week in November. The end of the story came on January 5, when it was reported in the *Louisville Daily Journal* that Wolford was "unconditionally released from his imprisonment and arrest." It was an ugly and undignified conclusion to what had been a useful military career, but it goes to illustrate the passions that were aroused by the subject of black enlistment. Men were willing to throw away their livelihood and their freedom, and to skirt the very edge of treason because of it. Lincoln did not retreat from the policy, however, and the people of Kentucky and Tennessee had no choice but to accept it as a new reality. In their minds, though, one question remained open: when the time came, would black soldiers fight? The answer to that question would be known before the end of the year.[19]

• • •

Attacks on the L&N were not focused on the taking of life, usually. The object was simply to disrupt the schedule, tear up the railroad, and to gather up whatever plunder the express car and the passengers were carrying.

However, one attempt to sabotage the L&N in 1864 grew out of the practice of black enlistment and had as its specific target a troop train moving African American troops from Louisville to Nashville.

Louisville had a cell of a clandestine group called the Sons of Liberty, whose purpose was to sabotage the Union effort in whatever way was practical. One of its leading members was Judge Joshua Fry Bullitt. When it became known that a troop train filled with blacks would be leaving Louisville on June 27, the Sons quickly went into action. The idea was to derail the train at Muldraugh Hill. In *City of Conflict*, Robert E. McDowell quoted Judge Bullitt's remarks, "You know where the track goes around Muldraugh's Hill, south of town, with a steep drop-off on one side? There's a blind curve at the highest point. We'll put rocks and ties on the track where the engineer can't see them in time to stop and throw the whole train into the gorge. It ought to kill a good ninety percent of those bastards."[20]

What Bullitt and the others did not know was that there was an informer in their midst. His name was Felix Stidger. When he heard what was planned, he went straight to Colonel Thomas B. Fairleigh of the 26th Kentucky Infantry. Fairleigh had briefly been the post commander at Bowling Green and was the one who had imposed an assessment on the people of Rocky Hill, Kentucky, to punish them for the passive crime of standing idle while guerrillas burned their L&N depot in 1863. In April 1864, Fairleigh was detached from his regiment for duty in the adjutant general's office in Louisville. Fairleigh liked Louisville. He often attended the plays and socialized a good deal, but he was somewhat disdainful of the rundown and dirty condition of the city. (He wrote in his diary on April 2, "It rained last evening and the streets were flooded.... There is one consolation in it — it will wash off some of the mud and filth.")[21]

Fairleigh found the work in the AG's office to be more than ample, but he became even busier in May, when he was named post commander of Louisville. As the man responsible for civil and military security, he evidently cultivated a small ring of spies, including Stidger. His solution to the impending attack by the Sons of Liberty was elegant in its simplicity. He quietly loaded the Negro troops on board a river packet and sent them to Nashville by water. Then, he equipped two flatcars of a small train with fieldpieces and riflemen and sent it down the track to Muldraugh Hill where the unsuspecting Sons were waiting in the woods to spring their trap. The train stopped short of the blind curve, the troops detrained and rushed forward — some of them to clear the track while others splattered the hillside with rifle fire — and the artillery began lobbing shells into where the Sons were thought to be. The plot was cruel in its intent but almost comic in its climax. Less humorous was the arson of two bulging government warehouses in Louisville the following month, a loss of $1,500,000 — an act for which the Sons might have been responsible.

• • •

There were relatively few incidents along the L&N during the spring and summer of 1864. In March, guerrillas burned a train near New Hope, Kentucky. In April, they removed some rails from the line just south of Gallatin, and a crew of construction workers was attacked by Ellis Harper and his bushwhackers near Mitchellville, but most of the attacks came on the branch lines, not on the main stem. The most potentially dangerous raid was in Bardstown in June, when the guerrilla leader George M. Jessee led an unusually large band of 300 irregulars from their usual stomping grounds in Owen, Henry, and Shelby Counties for the fresh territory of Nelson. Jessee divided his men into two equal units. While the first demonstrated toward the main line, Jessee led the other into Bardstown, where 25 well-armed men of Company I, 48th Kentucky Mounted Infantry, led by Lieutenant Turney G. Driskell were barricaded inside the courthouse.

The 48th Kentucky was a new regiment, raised in October 1863 for the express purpose of contending with roaming bands of guerrillas. The regiment was scattered by company along the length of the L&N from Louisville to Cave City by order of General Burbridge. Now it looked as if Company I was going to get its chance to fight. Driskell wired Colonel Fairleigh in Louisville that the guerrillas were on their way but that he was determined to resist. Fairleigh dispatched a detachment of the 9th Michigan Cavalry to Bardstown and ordered Driskell to hang on.

Instead, at the first sight of Jessee and his desperadoes, Driskell's backbone turned to water, and he surrendered without ever having fired a shot. Jessee paroled Driskell and his timorous defenders of Bardstown and went on a looting spree until the Michigan cavalry approached from the direction of Louisville. Jessee and his men galloped away toward Boston where they destroyed a railroad trestle, the water tank, and the stockade. The guerrillas crossed the L&N north of Elizabethtown and proceeded southwest through Stephensburg, where they enlisted some volunteers, and on toward Grayson County. The 9th Pennsylvania Cavalry was after them, and Colonel J. W. Weatherford and the 13th Kentucky Cavalry out of Lebanon mobilized to cut them off, but Jessee's men broke up into smaller groups and doubled back to the east, eluding with ease all the Federal cavalry on their trail. By July 4, Jessee was back in Henry County.

Through the spring and summer, there were guerrilla sightings and occasional gunfire at Fountain Head, Tennessee, and at Glendale, Kentucky, also at New Haven, at Auburn, and near Guthrie on the Memphis Branch. But removing a couple of rails and firing pistols at a passing train were love taps compared to the sledgehammer blows of 1862, when tunnels were collapsed and great bridges and trestles burned. In 1864, when the guerrillas showed up in an L&N town, they were more likely to rob private citizens and attack the stores rather than the railroad itself.

It may well have been that the blockhouses were simply too formidable to challenge now, in the fourth year of war. At the conclusion of an inspection tour in July 1863, Captain O. M. Poe, chief engineer, 23rd Army Corps, found that the defensive works along the L&N were "advanced well-nigh toward completion." Poe added, "It only remains for the same system of artillery administration which I recommended on the fortifications of Covington and Newport, and which I have by letter urged on the chief of artillery for fortifications (Brigadier General [Davis] Tillson), to be established on the fortifications of the Louisville and Nashville Railroad, to insure, with the full complement of guns ... a very secure defense."[22]

General Tillson, who was chief of artillery in the Department of the Ohio, must have come through, for by the end of spring 1864, the artillery frowning down on the L&N was impressive: three 12-pounders at Fort DeWolff at Shepherdsville; one 12-pounder and two six-pounders at Fort Sands; two 12-pounders, two six-pounders, and one three-inch rifled gun at Fort Boyle; two 30-pounder Parrotts and two 12-pounders at Fort Terrill at Munfordville; one ten-pounder Parrot, one 3.8-inch rifled James, two 12-pounders, two six-pounders and two 24-pound Howitzers at Fort Willich, also at Munfordville, two 12-pounders at each of Munfordville's batteries, Hale and Dayton; and so on, through Bowling Green and down into Tennessee, where General Rousseau said, "Against guerrillas and small bodies of cavalry without artillery, these blockhouses are impregnable." He warned that in between the works the railroad needed, "a sufficient mounted force to destroy the roving bands of the enemy." Rousseau, commanding what was now styled the Department of Nashville, and Brigadier General Hugh Ewing, commanding the Western District of Kentucky (also known as the 2nd Division, District of Kentucky), seemed to have enough cavalry and mounted infantry scouring the countryside to deter even the most reckless guerrillas. In addition, there was a complement of soldiers riding as guards on every north- or southbound train on the L&N. There were usually other soldiers on board, as well, men who had "veteranized" and were returning south from the furlough each man got as partial reward for re-enlisting. Often, they had so little to do that they livened up the trip with a little bit of target practice on the livestock grazing along the route. There were complaints.[23]

Still not quite satisfied as to the question of protection, James Guthrie petitioned the government to supply 300 Henry rifles with which to arm the L&N employees. As usual, Guthrie was not entirely candid, insisting that "the increase of guerrilla bands has been such that unless those engaged in running the trains are armed it will not be possible much longer to retain them in the service," and citing the number of trains, "which have lately been frequently stopped." In fact, the summer and fall were remarkably free of violence against the L&N. The government rejected Guthrie's request for repeating rifles to arm what would have become a private L&N army.[24]

• • •

James Guthrie's actions during the late summer and fall of 1864 belied his vocal concerns about the safety of the L&N. His concentration was often redirected toward other matters. There were wholesale arrests in Louisville beginning in the last week in July and continuing through the first half of August. Judge Joshua Fry Bullitt, one of the leaders of the Sons of Liberty, and 21 other opponents of the Union cause were taken into custody. Guthrie wrote in protest to General William T. Sherman in the field near Atlanta. Although Guthrie's letter is lost (as are most of his papers from the war years), what he wrote can be inferred by Sherman's long answer, dated August 14, 1864. Sherman wrote, "I regret exceedingly the arrest of many gentlemen and persons in Kentucky, and still more that they should give causes of arrest. I cannot in person inquire into these matters, but must leave them to the officer who is commissioned and held responsible by [the] Government for the peace and safety of Kentucky."[25]

Sherman was polite but blunt. He let Guthrie know from the start that he did not agree that the arrests of Bullitt and the others were unjust, but now that he had laid that question to rest, Uncle Billy went on to give the L&N president a little lecture about patriotism, as well as the cause of the war and its remedy. In one long, breathless paragraph, as if he could not pause in his rush to educate Guthrie, Sherman wrote, "I notice in Kentucky a disposition to cry against the tyranny and oppression of our

Government. Now, were it not for war you know tyranny could not exist in our Government; therefore any acts of late partaking of that aspect are the result of war; and who made this war?" He said:

> You know and I know that long before the North, or the Federal Government, dreamed of war the South had seized the U.S. arsenals, forts, mints, and custom houses, and had made prisoners of war of the garrisons sent at their urgent demand.... You also remember well who first burned the bridges of your railroad, who forced Union men to give up their slaves to work on the rebel forts at Bowling Green, who took wagons and horses and burned houses of persons differing with them honestly in opinion.... The rebels first introduced terror as a part of their system, and forced contributions to diminish their wagon trains and thereby increase the mobility and efficiency of their columns.... They dared us to war, and you remember how tauntingly they defied us to the contest. We have accepted the issue and it must be fought out. You might as well reason with a thunderstorm. War is the remedy our enemies have chosen. Other simple remedies were within their choice. You know it and they know it, but they wanted war, and I say let us give them all they want; not a word of argument, not a sign of let up, no cave in till we are whipped or they are. Those side issues of niggers, State rights, conciliation, outrages, cruelty, barbarity, bankruptcy, subjugation, etc., are all idle and nonsensical. The only principle in this war is, which party can whip.... I hope the question will soon resolve itself into "Shall we have a government that must be obeyed, and will you fight for it?" and if the answer be affirmative they are friends, if in the negative or doubtful, then they are enemies or mere denizens of the land, stript of the right of suffrage, debarred from speaking or writing, yea even from marrying, for I would stop the breed.[26]

Having schooled Guthrie on the beginning, prosecution, and hoped-for resolution of the war on the national scale, Sherman now drew a breath and began a new paragraph. For his conclusion, he returned to the subject of Kentucky:

> I surely wish you all in Kentucky well. I want to push the main rebel army far from you, and to root out that other class, who, under the plea of being soldiers, are regarded by us all as common vagabonds and thieves. Joe Johnston would never sanction such dogs as call themselves guerrillas in Kentucky, nor would Lee or Bragg, or any other man who thinks he is fighting to establish a new and independent government better suited to their interests and honor. I will, therefore, sustain General Burbridge if satisfied he is not influenced by mere personal motives, and nothing has occurred to evince anything of the kind. Bullitt and the rest must therefore spend some years abroad and take time to study and reflect on the great theory of self-government which began with old Adam and has made precious little progress since. I should like Governor Bramlette and the real

13 — The Uneasy Interlude, 1864

thinking men of Kentucky to know the kindly feelings I entertain toward them, and how earnest is my with to insure to them tranquility and peace.[27]

Bullitt and the 21 others were imprisoned in Memphis until November, when they were paroled. Bullitt, at least, returned to Kentucky. Shortly after, fearing rearrest, the judge made his way to Canada where he had all the time necessary to "take time to study and reflect on the great theory of self-government." He did not come back to his home state until after the end of the war.

• • •

The sudden arrests of Judge Bullitt and his fellow conspirators at this particular time seem to have been a result of the declaration of martial law and the suspension of the writ of habeas corpus imposed on Kentucky in the summer of 1864. The interruption of civil liberties was certainly a response to the many guerrilla raids that went on far to the east and far to the west of the L&N corridor, but its timing shows that it also had to do with the fall elections; a similar suspension had occurred the previous year, right before the state and local elections. The stakes were higher now. There was a presidential election in 1864, and naturally, Guthrie took an active interest. He traveled to the Democratic Convention in Chicago in September.

The Democrats saw an opportunity to make a one-term president of Abraham Lincoln, for the war was bloodier than ever in the East and seemed to be stalled in the West. The country was tired and discouraged. However, as is often the case, opportunity threw the opportunists into confusion. The Democrats were badly fragmented. One faction, the War Democrats, wanted to prosecute the war to a military conclusion, no matter what the cost in time or treasure. The Peace Democrats believed that the time was right for a negotiated peace. Each faction was further divided into splinter groups of extremists. The two blocs cobbled together a rickety campaign that was destined to squander the chance to put a Democrat in the White House.

Former commander of the Army of the Potomac, General George B. McClellan, was the Democrats' choice for their presidential nominee. The most notorious "Copperhead" in the nation, Clement Vallandigham, was the moving force behind the convention and wrote much of the 1864 platform. It was Vallandigham who moved that McClellan's nomination be declared unanimous, and the convention delegates agreed. The matter of

McClellan's running mate remained. Going in, the nomination for the vice-presidency seemed to belong to Peace Democrat James Guthrie. In the first ballot, he had 65½ votes to 55½ for his nearest opponent, the Ohio congressman George H. Pendleton, another Peace Democrat.

The *New York Times* reported, "Mr. Guthrie led on the first ballot, but as the bargain was that Pendleton, who is [Clement] Vallandigham's 'right bower,' should be the coming man, there was a general skedaddling to him on the second, and he was nominated."[28]

When the second ballot was taken, the New York delegation defected to Pendleton, who quickly went on to receive 226 votes to Guthrie's 65½. The ticket would be McClellan-Pendleton, and Guthrie returned to Louisville and the job he knew best how to do.

• • •

In the fiscal year ending on June 30, 1864, the accounts showed that the L&N had enjoyed its best year to date. The railroad had earned a net profit of $1,803,953. The guerrillas had been quieter than usual, and the war had shifted far to the south. It looked as if the Union was bringing the Rebellion to an end on battlefields so far away from the L&N that the railroad could soon begin to operate in something like a normal business climate. Things looked more promising than they had for years, heading into fall.

Complacency was premature, however. Whether anyone knew it or not, hell was about to boil over.

14

Hell Boils Over

General William T. Sherman came closest to nationalizing the L&N. As he was planning his Atlanta campaign, he met in Nashville with his transportation officials and made it plain to them exactly what he expected. He called in Colonel J. B. Anderson, General J. L. Donaldson, and General Amos Beckwith for the discussion. He had already restricted the railroads to military use only. Now he needed more. As Sherman recalled it in his *Memoirs:*

> I assumed the strength of the army to move from Chattanooga into Georgia at 100,000 men, and the number of animals to be fed ... at 35,000; then, allowing for occasional wrecks of trains, which were very common, and for the interruption of the road itself by guerrillas and regular raids, we estimated it would require 130 cars, of ten tons each, to reach Chattanooga daily, to be reasonable certain of an adequate supply.... Colonel Anderson promptly explained that he did not possess cars or locomotives enough to do this work. I then instructed him to hold on to all trains that arrived at Nashville from Louisville, and to allow none to go back until he had secured enough to fill the requirements of our problem.[1]

It did not take Guthrie long to realize that something was wrong, and that something was that Sherman was seizing all of his rolling stock and refusing to allow its return. Guthrie wrote to Sherman and complained that it would be impossible for him to forward the required supplies if the general would not release the cars and locomotives to come back to Louisville. Sherman remembered:

> I wrote to him, frankly telling him exactly how we were placed, appealed to his patriotism to stand by us, and advised him in like manner to hold on to all trains coming into Jeffersonville, Indiana. He and General Robert Allen, then quartermaster at Louisville, arranged a ferry-boat to transfer

the trains over the Ohio River from Jeffersonville and in a short time we had cars and locomotives from almost every road at the North.... To this fact [railroad co-operation] as much as to any other simple fact, I attribute the perfect success which afterward attended our campaigns; and I have always felt grateful to Mr. Guthrie, of Louisville, who had sense enough and patriotism enough to subordinate the interests of his railroad company to the cause of his country.[2]

Considering the continual complaints about the poor service provided the army by the L&N, and considering that Guthrie was mollified only when he was authorized to confiscate the engines and cars of another railroad, one wonders if Sherman wrote tongue-in-cheek this last observation praising Guthrie's sense and patriotism.

Sherman stepped off from Chattanooga on May 6 and 7. From then until July 9, his columns pushed forward against the Army of Tennessee, General Joseph E. Johnston commanding. It was essentially a running skirmish. Johnston has been praised by historians (and was praised by his soldiers at the time) for the skill with which he fell back, never losing equipment nor ordnance to the enemy, and continually punishing the Yankees as they were forced to move against his entrenched positions. At the one genuine battle of the campaign, at Kennesaw Mountain on June 27, he slaughtered Sherman's men who were thrown forward in an ill-considered frontal attack.

Johnston has also been condemned by historians (as he was by the man of his time who really counted, President Jefferson Davis) for giving up so much ground. When Johnston failed to stop Sherman's advance at the Chattahoochee River, he was relieved of command and replaced by General John Bell Hood. The change came on July 17.

Hood threw his men at Sherman in furious attacks at Peachtree Creek, then again at what was called the Battle of Atlanta, and finally at Ezra Church, and lost each battle He sacrificed more men in the space of a week than Johnston had in two and a half months, but he killed a lot of Yankees, too. Trains loaded with the bodies of soldiers killed around Atlanta rumbled up the Western & Atlantic Railroad to Chattanooga where the somber cargo was transferred to other trains going on to Nashville. From there the honored dead made their way on the L&N or other railroads to home and the family burial ground.

The irreplaceable Confederate soldiers who were killed outside of Atlanta made their way home in different directions. The grief must have grown even sharper for their families, for these boys that John Bell Hood

14 — Hell Boils Over

lost died for nothing. Atlanta was besieged through the month of August and fell to the Federals on September 2. It was this victory, as much as any other factor, that secured the re-election of Abraham Lincoln.

Hood reformed his army outside of Atlanta while he pondered his next move.

• • •

During the time that Atlanta was under siege and afterward, Hood sent raiders north into Tennessee to operate along Sherman's long, taut supply line. The first raid was led by Fighting Joe Wheeler, who rampaged with 4,500 men through East and Middle Tennessee from August 10 until September 12, when Major General Rousseau succeeded in throwing him out of the state.

Close on the heels of Wheeler's raid was another, led by Nathan Bedford Forrest. Forrest was a man to be dreaded. Already, he had performed feats of such martial brilliance that his rhythmic name would canter ever after through Southern mythology. His 4,000 men and the fieldpieces they dragged into Middle Tennessee were more of a threat than Wheeler, but Rousseau contended with Forrest too, kept him away from Nashville, and forced him south, and on October 5, the "Wizard of the Saddle" led his men across the state line into Alabama.

Neither Forrest's raid nor Wheeler's had done Sherman's supply line any serious damage, but what they did seem to do was to inspire a renewed vigor among the guerrillas in the corridor of the Louisville & Nashville Railroad. They thought they saw the dawn of a new day for the Confederacy, and operating behind the front, along the lines of communication and transportation, they did what they could to hold the Upper South until the regulars could come to redeem it for the CSA.

On October 10, Ellis Harper cut the railroad near Big South Tunnel and murdered two railroad workers and four soldiers of the 40th USCT. Five of them had their heads split open with an ax; why the sixth victim was spared this gruesome treatment was a mystery. Guerrillas and Confederate regulars alike treated with particular brutality any blacks who opposed them. Perhaps the body without the ax wound was that of a white man.

Two black soldiers escaped Harper and his gang and ran to Gallatin where they told the post commander, Captain Benjamin S. Nicklin (13th Indiana Artillery), of the attack. Nicklin dispatched a detachment of 40 men of the 1st Tennessee Mounted Infantry, followed an hour later by a squad of men from the 101st USCT, with orders to chase and kill Harper's guerrillas. Three hours later, at 7:00 P.M., Nicklin sent a third small group, six artillerymen of his own regiment, by handcar up to the tunnel. Harper and his gang escaped, of course. On October 21, the same band of irregulars destroyed two locomotives and 13 cars near Woodburn, Kentucky. On November 2, a band of guerrillas under an unnamed leader hit Cave City. On November 7, two Negro cooks were locked in a freight car at the Rocky Hill station and burned alive. The same month a hospital train was attacked near Gallatin.

And so it went. There is a sameness to the many guerrilla attacks that makes a reciting of the details of each one a redundancy. It is enough to say that in the fall of 1864 they came in bunches. James Guthrie demanded of the furiously busy commanders farther south that greater numbers of guards be placed along the L&N and was assured that more troops would be placed on the L&N as soon as they could be spared. General Burbridge issued General Orders Number 8, which took the fight against the guerrillas to a new level: "The irregular bands of armed men within our lines, disconnected from the rebel army ... are guerrillas, and will be treated as such.... Hereafter no guerrillas will be received as prisoners; and any officer who may capture such, and extend to them the courtesies due to prisoners of war, will be held accountable for disobedience of orders." Burbridge's ill-considered order only served to make the bushwhackers more desperate, for what did they have to lose now? If they were killed in a pistol fight with the Federals or if they were captured alive—either way, they were just as dead. They agreed among themselves that they might as well die fighting.[3]

Likewise, General Orders Number 8 increased the blood thirst of the Union patrol leaders. What was in it for them to spare the life of a suspected guerrilla? Burbridge had threatened to punish them for disobedience of orders if they showed military courtesy to prisoners. It was easier by far to kill them all and take no prisoners.

Kentuckians had as much to fear from their protectors as from the bold horsemen who followed the black flag.

• • •

John Bell Hood was a Kentucky-born graduate of West Point. His courage was a proven quality and, to some, so was his lack of prudence. He had fought in Longstreet's Corps of the Army of Northern Virginia earlier in the war, leading a unit made up of Texans mostly. He had attacked the nearly unassailable Little Round Top across a field of boulders at Gettysburg and had taken a shell fragment that destroyed the use of his left arm. Recuperating in Richmond, he had enjoyed a hero's welcome. While socializing with the capital's elite, Hood met and impressed President Jefferson Davis.

Later that same year, having come west with Longstreet, Hood was shot in the upper thigh at the Battle of Chickamauga and endured an amputation of his right leg. Hood survived and eventually returned to active service, but when he began his day's duties each morning, an orderly had to strap him in the saddle. And he took huge doses of laudanum to dull the relentless pain; Hood's questionable judgment of 1863 was even more impaired in 1864 by drugs.

During the Atlanta Campaign, Hood had shown the kind of aggressiveness that Jefferson Davis liked, and to make sure the president noticed it, Hood remained in contact with him, trumpeting his desire to fight Sherman and criticizing Johnston for giving up ground without a good fight. Hood had cultivated Davis' favor in the city on the James River, and now he reaped his reward on the south bank of the Chattahoochee. Hood led the Army of the Tennessee.

After the unsuccessful fights to save Atlanta, he still had 40,000 men left. It was a dangerous army. The question was how best to use it.

The plan that Hood developed could not have caught Sherman more off guard. Indeed, it seemed to annoy him as a military professional. He said, "I cannot guess his movements as I could those of Johnston, who was a sensible man and only did sensible things."[4]

The nonsensical theory that motivated Hood was this: If he abandoned Georgia and drove north for Tennessee and Kentucky, Sherman would be forced to follow in order to protect his supply line. Sherman's army would become strung out and loose, as Hood imagined it, and he would be able to attack the weak spots. With luck, he could defeat Sherman in detail. With perfect luck, Nashville would fall, Hood would reoufit his army with captured Yankee stores and enroll thousands of recruits. He would drive inexorably north, up the L&N, across the breadth of Kentucky to Louisville. There he would decide on the next move.

Hood's army broke camp in late September 1864 and tramped north, moving with a skill born of practice. The Confederates moved so quickly behind their cavalry screen that several days passed before Sherman knew that Hood was on the move. The crippled Kentuckian was across the Chattahoochee by October 1.

On October 4, Hood struck the Western & Atlantic Railroad at Big Shanty and Acworth. Sherman's supply line had suffered its first break. The next target was the large Union supply depot at Allatoona. Hood knew now that Sherman was after him, had been since the 3rd, but so far, everything was working as planned.

Of course, such luck could not last. By October 5, Sherman was at Kennesaw Mountain and could see to the north the snaking gray and butternut column of Confederate soldiers. He could also see the rising smoke of a small but spirited fight at Allatoona between one of his advance units under General John Corse and the Rebel rear guard under General Samuel G. French. The fight had been going on since 7:00 A.M., when the Confederates opened up with artillery fire from the direction of the Acworth Road. The Federals responded in kind. For the next hour and a half, the cannon roared, but at 8:30, a Rebel courier carrying a white flag approached the Yankees. The courier had a demand from French that Corse surrender. Corse refused. About a quarter of an hour later, the bluecoats came under attack from three directions at once: north, east, and west. Corse's men held for two hours before they were driven back to their works. The fighting continued into the afternoon when French, aware that more of Sherman's force was coming up, broke off the attack. He hurried north to join those Rebels who had gone on ahead to New Hope Church and Dallas, leaving behind 150 dead for Corse's men to bury. For Corse, it was worse; he reported that he had lost 600 killed, wounded, and missing, and Corse himself suffered a wound in his cheek and in one ear. This was what the northbound Rebels were capable of when they turned to fight.

Hood was reeling up the same ribbon of road and rails that Sherman had unwound in his advance the previous summer. The Confederates hit Resaca on October 12 and tore up the tracks between there and Hood's next destination, Dalton.

Sherman was pressing Hood hard now. At LaFayette, the graybacks dug in, but when Sherman arrived on October 17, they were gone. Hood had slipped his army across the state boundary on the unanimous advice of his subordinate generals and vanished into the rugged country of northeast Alabama. Sherman pursued a short distance farther, but soon called off the chase. He dismissed Hood, saying, "Damn him.... If he will go to the Ohio River, I will give him rations.... Let him go north. My business is down South."[5]

On November 19, Hood pushed forward from Florence, Alabama, toward the Tennessee line. He arrived in Middle Tennessee to find that his

14 — Hell Boils Over

small army had been given a great gift. General John Schofield at Pulaski was separated from General George H. Thomas at Nashville by 60 miles. Sherman had sent Thomas to Nashville on September 26 while Forrest was on his raid, but now there was a greater threat to counter, and the "Rock of Chickamauga" was busy gathering units from all over Missouri and Kentucky to supplement the number of Nashville's defenders. But all of his units were not up and Schofield was at Pulaski.

Hood quickly got his army between Schofield and Thomas at Spring Hill. He had them! His army would deliver Armageddon unto Schofield's Yankees tomorrow and then he would attend to Thomas.

The crippled general's men bivouacked to rest for the hard work coming tomorrow, but somehow a fatal mistake was made. Hood's generals failed to block one of the possible escape routes, Columbia Pike, and Schofield's Army of the Ohio was able to slip by the Confederates in the night.

Hood ripped into his generals at dawn when the blunder was discovered, and he was still in an evil mood when, on November 30, he found the Yankees at Franklin. Schofield gladly would have gone on to Nashville, but the bridge over the Harpeth River had been burned, and he had no choice but to entrench and wait with his back to the river while his engineers constructed another bridge. Now, here they were, dug in and waiting.

Hood appraised the situation at a glance and ordered a frontal assault. His generals were shocked. The numerical odds were about even, but Schofield's infantry was behind fieldworks and was strengthened by the support of big guns. A minor objection was raised by the Confederate generals, a suggestion or two put forward, but these men had been on the sharp end of a furious dressing down after Spring Hill, and no one was in the mood to say what each man thought, that this was an ill-considered, even a suicidal plan.

The attack began about four o'clock on the afternoon of November 30. The Rebels advanced over two miles of open ground. Artillery rounds began to fall among them; then they were in range of the Yankee rifles and suddenly the town and the river and everything beyond disappeared in an impenetrable cloud of black-powder smoke, and the sounds of tramping feet and of flags flapping in the autumn breeze disappeared in a roar of musketry and cannon fire that could be heard in Nashville.

The first volley shredded the neat ranks of advancing Rebel infantry, but they kept coming, right into the center of the Federal line. They scrambled over the works and beat the Yankees back. The Rebel infantry had carried the day. This was the moment! They were turning the Yankees' own cannons against them and then discovered too late that they had no way to fire them; the Yankees had carried away all of the friction primers and the Confederates had not brought any of their own.

In his insightful article, "For Want of a Primer" (*North and South*, September 2008), Daniel L. Mallock made the persuasive argument that it was this simple oversight that cost the Confederates a possible victory at Franklin, and he placed the blame squarely on the commanding general's shoulders. Hood had hurried his generals into this attack. Mallock wrote, "How easy it would have been for the Confederate commanders to have foreseen this moment and planned for it — if given the requisite amount of time to do so!"[6]

While the Rebels tried to find a solution to their fatal mistake, the Yankees rallied and crashed into the men who had punched a hole in their line. The Confederates could not hold on to what they had won. They hurried out of this awful trap, back toward their own lines where they reformed and tried again. They tried a dozen times, but they never again had the success of that first charge when it looked for a glorious moment as if they were actually going to win the fight.

The battle ended after dark. Hood had lost more than 6,200 men, three times the number of Union casualties. Five Confederate generals were dead, including Patrick Cleburne, the "Stonewall of the West," whose loss would be keenly felt in the days to come. Schofield got safely across the Harpeth River and joined Thomas on December 1. General Hood arrived two days later and began the siege of Nashville.

• • •

Hood was thinking ahead when, on November 21, he sent an order to Brigadier General Hylan B. Lyon at Corinth to cross over into Tennessee and move up the Tennessee and Cumberland Rivers toward Kentucky. Hood wanted Lyon to tear up the northern rail approaches to Nashville and to cut the telegraph lines. Also, Hood wanted all the gristmills for scores of miles around to be put into good working order so that his army could use them during the liberation of Tennessee.

Lyon was 28 years old, a native of Eddyville, Kentucky, and a graduate of West Point, class of 1856. He was commissioned as a lieutenant of artillery and saw service in Florida and in the Pacific Northwest. In April 1861, Lyon resigned his commission and joined the newly formed Confederate Army, continuing as an artillery officer. At Fort Donelson, he was captured and spent the next six months as a prisoner of war at Johnson's Island. Exchanged, he went on to fight at Vicksburg, at Chattanooga, and at Brice's Crossroads. At this last battle he attracted the favorable attention of General Nathan Bedford Forrest.

Lyon was promoted to brigadier general in June 1864 and was given a division under Forrest. Now, General Hood was calling on him to achieve an important but difficult goal in his home state, and all Hood could spare him were 800 men and two artillery pieces with which to do it.

Lyon moved north from Corinth on December 6. At the Cumberland River, he captured a steamboat and began ferrying his men over. While in the process, he was able to capture six other boats and 50 prisoners.

Clarksville, Tennessee, was too well defended for his small force to attack, but he did destroy the nearby rail and telegraph lines with one of his brigades while the other pushed on toward Hopkinsville, Kentucky. There were no longer any Federals in Hopkinsville when Lyon arrived. The USCT garrison had run away.

The pugnacious Lyon burned the Christian County courthouse and clothed and shod about 400 of his men out of the local stores. With the town safely under control, Lyon decided to continue operations, for a while anyway, with a divided command. Colonel J. Q. Chenoweth's 2nd Brigade would remain in Hopkinsville, while Lyon went with Colonel J. J. Turner's 1st Brigade toward Cadiz, Princeton, and Eddyville. Like Hopkinsville, those towns were known to have garrisons of Negro troops.

As the 1st Brigade approached, the defenders of each of these three towns fled and abandoned them to the Rebels. Lyon procured more supplies for his men, then burned the courthouses at Cadiz and Princeton before turning back toward Hopkinsville, where he found Colonel Chenoweth retreating from a brisk skirmish with the 1st Cavalry Division, USA. General Edward M. McCook and his horsemen had surprised the Rebels and scattered them. The returning Lyon brought order to the confusion, reunited his two brigades, and advanced again to Hopkinsville. Now it was McCook's turn to be surprised. The Rebels pushed the Federal cavalry out of the way and hurried to Madisonville where they burned the courthouse. Beyond there was Ashbysburg, where they crossed the Green River. In a skirmish at the crossing, Lyon lost 19 killed or captured.

On December 20, Lyon reached Hartford where he found a small garrison of 48 officers and enlisted men. They were easily captured and were paroled while Lyon prepared to burn yet another courthouse. At the request of Doctor Samuel O. Peyton, General Lyon spared the records in the county clerk's office, but the courthouse was torched.

There were six inches of snow on the ground when Lyon moved out of Hartford and the temperature was estimated at minus 20 degrees. To make matters worse, Rough River was in flood. Still, Lyon's men could take warm comfort in the fact that they had burned five courthouses, torn up miles of railroad and telegraph, had escaped their one serious encounter with the enemy and had consistently stayed ahead of them since. Moreover, they were better mounted and better supplied now than they had been at the beginning of their mission, and young men were coming in bunches to join them. The WPA's *Military History of Kentucky* said that 578 men from Hardin, Breckinridge, and Meade Counties went west to join Lyon.

The eager recruits might as well have been patient and waited, for Lyon was headed in their direction. At Leitchfield, to no one's surprise, Lyon's men set fire to the courthouse. They made two local boys chop up the courthouse benches for kindling. From Leitchfield, Lyon's men rode to Elizabethtown. A detachment of 50 Rebels won a small skirmish with Elizabethtown's garrison of 45 men. Then they destroyed the L&N depot (which contained $500,000 worth of military supplies), a rail car loaded with lumber, the nearby trestles, and the stockade where the town's Federal garrison was quartered. That they were not quartered in the courthouse seems to explain why Lyon's men did not burn it.

While this one detachment went about its mischief in Elizabethtown, Lyon took the rest of his men toward Glendale where they destroyed the depot. The Rebels also paid a visit to old Camp Nevin where they captured the small garrison of the blockhouse that guarded the L&N bridge over the Nolin River and captured a trainful of Union soldiers. The soldiers, Lyon paroled; the train, bridge, and blockhouse, he burned.

It looked to the people of Bullitt County and Jefferson County as if Lyon was on his way to Muldraugh Hill and Lebanon Junction and then Louisville itself. Reinforcements were hurried to Forts Sands and Boyle, and an extra guard put over the trestle at Colesburg. The militia was called out at Louisville, and the defensive works on the southern outskirts of the city were strengthened and improved.

But the Rebels were not coming. At Nolin, Lyon learned that his raid was no longer part of a larger strategy; General Hood's army had been badly beaten by General George Thomas at Nashville. In fact, the Army of Tennessee had effectively ceased to exist. What remained of it was in headlong retreat out of Tennessee. The effect of this news was devastating to morale. Lyon estimated that after hearing the news of Hood's defeat, 500 of his men deserted.

All of Lyon's success amounted to little without a great victory by John Bell Hood's army to make the gains permanent. There was nothing left but to get out. Lyon led his diminished force south from Kentucky as quickly as he could, wondering, no doubt, what exactly had gone wrong at Nashville.

• • •

Everything had gone wrong at Nashville. Because of Franklin, Hood had a badly reduced army and an anemic officers' corps. The numerical odds against him were at least two to one, and maybe greater. Shelby Foote observed, "He was too weak to have any realistic hopes of taking the city, but too proud to go back. So, he hunkered down to wait and see what mistake Thomas might make."[7]

Hood's army, after what they had been through, might have benefited from a breathing spell in which to rest and possibly to receive reinforcements (Hood continually hoped for reinforcements from Texas), if the weather had been soft. But the weather turned as sharp as an icicle, and the Confederates, exposed in their curving lines on the outskirts of Nashville, suffered greatly. They were hungry, too, and later claimed that they survived on four ears of corn per man per day. But they were used to hunger pangs. It was this arctic weather that caused Southern boys the most agony. Sam Watkins, 1st Tennessee Infantry, later recalled in the strange mix of past and present tense he used in his memoirs:

> The earth is crusted with snow, and the wind from the northwest is piercing our very bones.... A few raw-boned horses stood shivering under the ice-covered trees, nibbling the short, scanty grass. Being in range of the Federal guns from Fort Negley, we were not allowed to have fires at night, and our thin and ragged blankets were but poor protection against the cold, raw blasts of December weather — the coldest ever known.[8]

Their fellow Southerners, the citizens of Nashville, were slightly better off. There was a shortage of firewood, but they were sheltered, at least. They joked that "the Yankees had brought their weather with them."[9]

There might have been a trace of hysteria in their joking. The people of Nashville had been through a lot since 1862, but now it looked as if they might be caught in the crossfire of two great armies. The people were nervous, and the arriving Federal regiments hurrying between the L&N depot and the forts; the bursts of small-arms fire; and brief artillery duels kept their nerves drawn tight. Their shivers were not always because of the winter chills.

On the surface, the calmest man in Nashville might have seemed to be General George H. Thomas. It was a façade. Thomas' problems were manifold, but he was a stalwart man and not one given to letting his feelings show.

One of General Thomas' most pressing difficulties was that General Sherman had gone off on his Indian summer ramble from Atlanta to the sea, and had taken almost all of the fit cavalry mounts in the West. Thomas was left to scrounge up horses wherever he could find them in a wide circle whose circumference reached as far north as Louisville, where horses were unharnessed from public conveyances right in the street. No one's horses were safe. Governor (and Vice-President Elect) Andrew Johnson even lost his fine horses to the demands of Nashville's defense. The cavalryman James H. Wilson was ordered to Edgefield to try and cobble together a cavalry and to guard the L&N Railroad, which was the only supply line into the city, since the Southerners had blockaded the Cumberland River below Nashville.

Secondly, while it was true that the Federals outnumbered the Rebels, the boys in blue were not quite an army. Here again, Sherman had weakened Thomas by taking "the choice and pick of the Western troops" on his jaunt across Georgia. Thomas had to supplement his veterans with the garrisons he stripped from scattered posts, the walking wounded from Nashville's military hospitals, and from such unusual noncombatants as teamsters, cooks, clerks, and orderlies.[10]

Thirdly, Grant, who was campaigning against Robert E. Lee in faraway Virginia, was beginning to harangue Thomas to attack. He sent an urgent telegram on December 6 — attack, he said. Sherman believed that Hood presented little or no threat to the Ohio River, but Grant was worried. When no word of an attack came from Tennessee, Grant sent a second telegram on December 8. At the same time, he wired General Halleck that Thomas should be relieved if he had not attacked by the end of the day.

Halleck put the responsibility back on Grant's stooped shoulders. He said, "If you wish General Thomas relieved, give the order. No one here will interfere. The responsibility, however, will be yours, as no one here, so far as I am informed, wishes General Thomas to be removed."[11]

Unable to get Halleck to do his dirty work, Grant backed down. He tried to make nice with Thomas on December 9 when he wired a message that started, "I have as much confidence in your conducting a battle rightly as I have in any other officer," but then his frustration spilled over again and he said, "but it has seemed to me that you have been slow, and I have had no explanation of affairs to convince me otherwise."[12]

However, even while he was assuring Thomas of his confidence, Grant wrote a telegram to Halleck removing the Virginian from command in favor of Schofield. Grant did not know that an immobilizing ice storm had hit Nashville on the same day of his decision to relieve Thomas, December 9, and men could not stand, even on level ground. Obviously, an attack was out of the question. Halleck consulted with Grant, and the order to relieve Thomas was temporarily pocketed. Halleck warned Thomas that Grant was talking of his removal and that his job was in peril. In his reply, Thomas offered to "submit without a murmur." But a change in command would not change the weather; with Middle Tennessee locked in ice, there was nothing that Thomas nor Schofield nor any other general could do. Naturally, there was nothing that Hood could do either, but Grant fumed while the ice continued to fall.[13]

More than one historian has commented on the irony of Grant, stalemated for six months by Lee in the trenches at Petersburg, bullyragging Thomas about being a few days slow at Nashville. What explained Grant's prejudice against Thomas? Partly, it came from the 1862 march from Shiloh to Corinth when, on General Halleck's order, Thomas commanded what had been Grant's Army of the Tennessee. His disdain for Thomas grew even deeper after Thomas saved the day on the slopes of Missionary Ridge at Chattanooga in November 1863 and outshone Sherman. In his official reports of the battle, Grant threw the credit for the victory to Sherman and virtually slandered Thomas by his lack of praise.

But there was more. Someone in headquarters at Nashville was prodding Grant, feeding him relentlessly critical news of Thomas' performance. The whisperer was Major General John M. Schofield, who, though commander of the Army of the Ohio, was Thomas' unhappy inferior. Schofield's baby-face concealed a raging ambition that burned at his core, and no treachery was too great where his ambition was concerned. It was said, metaphorically, that no man's back was safe if Schofield was behind him, and that included Major General Thomas. Schofield had been sending telegrams to Grant, libeling Thomas for not attacking Hood. His motivation was simple. If Grant relieved Thomas, then Schofield would be the senior commander at Nashville.

When Thomas learned what was going on behind his back, he took no action against Schofield. There were more important matters to attend to, and if things turned out all right against Hood, then all of Schofield's treacheries would mean nothing at all. Regarding Grant's incessant, bullying telegrams, Thomas seems to have remarked on them only once. He said privately to his cavalry commander, James H. Wilson, at the end of a war council on December 10, "Wilson, the Washington authorities treat me as if I were a boy.... If they will just let me alone, I will show them what we can do."[14]

Grant had no idea of leaving him alone, and on the 11th, he could stand it no longer. He sent a communiqué to Thomas, saying, "If you delay the attack longer the mortifying spectacle will be witnessed of a rebel army moving for the Ohio River, and you will be forced to act.... Let there be no further delay." The storm was barely over, and the thaw had not even begun. There was nothing Thomas could do but delay.[15]

On December 13, the temperature rose slightly, the sleet turned to rain, and the ice on the ground melted into slush. It looked to Thomas as if the time had come. The final preparations were made on the 14th. He sent a force north to Big South Tunnel to protect the L&N. He reviewed the battle plan with his generals, and he ordered that the men in the ranks were to draw a larger than normal issue of 60 rounds of ammunition. At dawn on December 15, Thomas checked out of the St. Cloud Hotel and rode three miles out to the battle line.

Nashville nestled in a deep bend of the Cumberland River, which curved around the city on the north. It was an advantageous feature of the local geography that gave Thomas the benefit of anchoring both his left flank and his right flank on the river. General James B. Steedman, whose command included seven full regiments and a battalion of United States Colored Troops, occupied the left flank, east of Nashville. Next to him, proceeding west, was Schofield; next came General Thomas J. Wood; then General A. J. Smith; and finally, on the far right flank, was the cavalry of General James H. Wilson. It was a good strong position, made stronger by a line of inner works, the previously mentioned forts (such as Fort Negley), and by the gunboats trolling on the Cumberland River, adding extra protection to the flanks.

The plan was for General Steedman to make a demonstration against the Rebel right flank while generals Wilson and Smith, pivoting on Wood, swung around and slammed into the Rebel left. Schofield would march from near Fort Negley, pass behind Wood, and take position in the rear of Smith and Wood, behind but within supporting distance. The treacherous Schofield was unhappy with the secondary role assigned to his Army of the Ohio, but he obeyed.

14 — Hell Boils Over

The Confederate line stretched in a long curve between Murfreesboro Pike and Hillsboro Pike, from General B. F. Cheatham on the right, westward to Stephen D. Lee in the center, to A. P. Stewart on the left. Stewart's line was refused at Hillsboro Pike and turned southwest. Five redoubts helped strengthen Stewart's sector.

The morning was foggy. Colonel Thomas J. Morgan commanding the 1st Colored Brigade said the mist "lay like a winding sheet over the two armies." Steedman did not step off until 8:00 A.M.. The great wheel began half an hour later. En echelon, Generals Wilson, Smith, and Wood advanced and smashed into the Rebel left. From Nashville's rooftops and hillsides, the citizens watched the terrible contest. Most of them had never lost their Confederate sympathies, and they hoped for a Union defeat. "No army on the continent ever played on any field to so large and so sullen an audience," one Northern officer wrote. Some Nashvillians got too close to the Federal lines and were put to work, carrying ammunition forward and wounded to the rear. The overeager sightseers soon lost their desire for a front-row seat and returned to the city.[16]

When General A. J. Smith ran into heavier resistance than expected in his front, Schofield was sent into the fight. His orders were to slip two miles farther to the right flank and attack in support of Smith. Once in position, Schofield ended up in the middle between Smith's right flank and Wilson's left flank, and his well-rested and eager regiments were perfectly positioned to overlap General A. P. Stewart's tired Confederates. General Darius Couch advanced his Second Division of the Army of the Ohio across the Hillsboro Pike and across an open valley a half mile wide where the men came under both artillery and small-arms fire. The Yankees charged forward with a battle cry toward the artillery, pushed back some Rebel gunners and captured a few more, along with several fieldpieces. Stewart's line was bent southward at right angles to Lee in the center. By that time, the sun was sinking low and the battle sputtered to an end.

The Rebels had given up 16 cannon and over 2,000 soldiers. They had also been pushed back two miles. December 15 was a hard day, but the Rebels' day was not done. They worked all through the night erecting new fieldworks along a more compact line, only half as long as before. Their work was vital if they were to survive the fight of the coming day, but Hood interrupted it and wasted their time and energy by shifting his three corps around. On the morning of December 16, the second day, General Lee would be on the right, Stewart in the center, and Cheatham on the left. If retreat became inevitable, Franklin Pike and Granny White

Pike would be their way out. Hood seemed to expect it. He ordered his wagon train to return to Franklin.

General Thomas' plan for the second day was essentially the same as it had been on the first. Steedman and Wood would combine for a hard jab into the Rebel right and right-center, while Smith, Schofield, and Wilson swung around with a crushing, curving punch to the Confederate center and left.

At noon, the general attack opened. The Confederate artillery was well served this day, and it hurt the Yankees as they advanced. The Rebel defense was stiff, especially on the right flank, where the contest was for control of Overton's Hill. The 1st and 2nd Colored brigades fought alongside General Thomas J. Wood's 4th Corps and took a real pounding from General Stephen D. Lee's Confederates. Colonel Charles R. Thompson of the 2nd Colored Brigade reported later that he lost 25 percent of his numbers engaged in less than 30 minutes. However, on the other end of the Rebel line, the pressure of the Federal attack was too great. The gray line trembled, and then it shattered. Hood had no reserve to send in. The center collapsed, and the Army of Tennessee dissolved before Hood's eyes. General Stephen D. Lee had been holding his own on the right and was surprised at the sudden collapse of the left and center. He rode quickly over to the tangled mass fleeing down the Franklin Pike and tried to cut them off, crying, "Rally, men, rally! For God's sake, rally! This is the place for brave men to die!"[17]

Enough of the running men gathered around the inspiring Lee to stymie the Federals for the few minutes of daylight remaining. Eventually, Lee collected two divisions around him and they made up the rear guard for Hood's retreating army.

Sam Watkins wrote about the retreat:

> Nearly every man in the entire army had thrown away his guns and accoutrements. More than 10,000 had stopped and allowed themselves to be captured, while many, dreading the horrors of a Northern prison, kept on, and I saw man ... broken down from sheer exhaustion, with despair and pity written on their features. Wagon trains, cannon, artillery, cavalry, and infantry were all blended together in inextricable confusion. Broken down and jaded horses and mules refused to pull, and the badly-scared drivers looked like their eyes would pop out of their heads from fright. Wagon wheels, interlocking each other, soon clogged the road, and wagons, horses, and provisions were left indiscriminately.[18]

General Hood expressed it differently. He admitted the completeness of the rout and said, "For the first and only time a Confederate army abandoned the field in confusion."[19]

14 — Hell Boils Over

When the Confederate collapse came, it happened almost too fast for the Yankees to believe. As his men chased the Rebels down Franklin Pike, Thomas rode from his left flank to his right, over the field where the armies had contended, until he came to the ground where Steedman and Wood had fought Lee. There, Thomas saw black and white soldiers lying dead together where they fell. The sight moved him. "The issue is settled!" he said. "Negroes will fight!" They all could fight, those defenders of Nashville. "Oh, what a grand army I have," said Thomas.[20]

Thomas' grand army had bagged a total of 4,462 Rebels, captured 58 artillery pieces, and cost Hood 6,000 men killed, wounded, or missing. They had extinguished the Army of Tennessee, effectively ended the war in the West, and preserved the city of Nashville. Incidentally, they had also saved the L&N Railroad from the last, great Confederate threat it would face in the War of the Rebellion.

15

The Last Guerrilla

While the armies of Thomas and Hood maneuvered in Tennessee and finally came together in the terrific contest at Nashville, things had not been quiet in Kentucky. The guerrillas had begun a fall campaign, and General Burbridge's efforts against them were as inefficient and oppressive as ever. Finally, Burbridge overstepped his boundaries. Unexpectedly, it was an economic rather than a military controversy that ended Burbridge's brutal reign. In October 1864, Burbridge announced that out-of-state hog sales were prohibited except within certain narrow dictates. Henceforth, all Kentucky farmers were expected to sell their hogs to the U.S. government, particularly to certain meatpackers who Burbridge preferred. The smell of kickbacks began to outstink the hogs. Farmers, forced to sell at lower prices than they might have gotten in a free and open market, lost an estimated $300,000 in one month. Governor Thomas Bramlette protested to President Lincoln on November 14, 1864, and Burbridge was ordered to rescind the order. Now was the time to get rid of Burbridge for good, while he was out of favor with the president over the "Great Hog Swindle." A Kentucky delegation traveled to Washington to meet with the president. They must have argued their case against Burbridge persuasively, for the "Butcher" was relieved of command at the beginning of February 1865. "Thank God and Mr. Lincoln," the *Louisville Daily Journal* crowed.[1]

In Burbridge's place, President Lincoln appointed Major General John M. Palmer, another native Kentuckian (though transplanted to Illinois) and a veteran of Stones River, Chattanooga, and the Atlanta Campaign. The *Daily Journal* approved of the choice, saying, "The appointment of General Palmer brightens the prospect of Kentucky." He arrived in Louisville to set up his headquarters on February 20.[2]

15 — The Last Guerrilla

During this time, central Kentucky was infested with bands of guerrillas. "Old Reverend" Jim Cundiff led a gang in Hardin County, and Press Williams led another. It was reported that as many as 250 bushwhackers were hiding out in the region west of Elizabethtown. Nat Smith had a pack of 40 men in the area of Horse Cave. There were Bill Marion, flop-eared Samuel O. "One-Armed" Berry, and the long-haired legend, Jerome Clark, whose alias, "Sue Mundy," was a mockery bestowed upon him by George Prentice, the editor of the *Daily Journal*. It was Henry Magruder, though, who made a livelihood of attacking the L&N. He looked like an intense young poet, but he was a remorseless killer.

Magruder grew up on the Bullitt County farm of his grandfather. He recalled it as a happy boyhood until age 15, when he learned that he was born of an unwed mother. "A single word gloomed and shaded my future," he later said. "I knew that I would be banished from society, by some be scorned, by others pitied.... My life was darkened in its morning, and has had no sunshine since. At this early age I was ready for every desperate adventure, and only hoped for an early end."[3]

There was no more desperate adventure than the war, and Magruder entered it in 1861 as a Rebel soldier at age 19. At Bowling Green, he was chosen to be the Bullitt County representative in the "Buckner Guards," an escort for General Simon Bolivar Buckner.

When General Albert Sidney Johnston later reviewed the guards, he was so impressed that he made the elite company part of his own bodyguard. Magruder was near Johnston when he died on the first day at Shiloh and was one of those who accompanied the general's body to safety in Confederate-held Corinth.

His special service at an end, Magruder transferred to John Hunt Morgan's cavalry in time to go with him on the May 1862 raid to Cave City, where the southbound train was stopped and the express box was emptied of $6,000. Magruder was impressed by how lucrative the life of a raider could be when Morgan took the contents of the express box and divided it with his men. Naturally, Magruder stayed with the Thunderbolt through all of the subsequent raids, until the Great Raid in the summer of 1863. Magruder and a few others became separated from the main column when a gunboat fired on them while crossing the Ohio River from Brandenburg into Indiana. Magruder spent several days in the Hoosier State, trying to catch up to Morgan and, at the same time, to avoid the local militiamen and General Hobson's cavalry. Deciding it was hopeless, Magruder finally returned to the Kentucky shore by means of a highjacked skiff. He remembered, "When we reached the good old State, *we sat down and 'were glad'*"⁴ (emphasis in original).

The little band made their way by a circuitous route to the Cumberland River and into Tennessee. They attached themselves briefly to the 8th Tennessee (Magruder did not say whether it was an infantry or a cavalry regiment) and a colonel whose name Magruder remembered as Dibben. When an officer named Hamilton deserted, Magruder went with him. Hamilton and 25 of his men were later captured, and Magruder found himself, once again, without a commander.

It was about this time that Morgan, who had escaped from his Ohio prison cell, was coming into Kentucky for his last raid. Operating on the basis of rumor, Magruder moved north to Bardstown where he hoped to rejoin Morgan, but the Thunderbolt was not there. Magruder tried Harrodsburg next, but Morgan was not there either. Some of Morgan's men were, though, fresh from their defeat at Cynthiana. Their news was flatly disheartening. It was of no use to join Morgan now. Magruder rode with the men on their trek south toward Tennessee. A captain named Alexander led them across the Cumberland, but when he was killed, a lieutenant named Mitchell took command and brought the squad of fugitives back to Bloomfield in Kentucky.

Now, the day of the black flag dawned for Henry Magruder. On September 1, soon after the return to Kentucky, Magruder and a band of 15 followers stopped a passenger train at New Hope on the Lebanon Branch of the L&N. The train guard was paroled and sent back to Louisville while the guerrillas robbed the passengers and the train. The *Daily Journal* reported the attack and said, "McGruder [sic] as far as we can learn, is a new aspirant for guerrilla honors. We do not recollect of having ever heard of him and his band before. It is hoped that his career may be marked with disaster and speedily brought to an end."⁵

After this first train robbery, Magruder and his men hit Lebanon Junction, New Haven, and New Hope in quick sequence. They were strangely quiet in October, but when they went back to work, they attacked a train at Lebanon and then hit Bardstown Junction and Boston, all in a two-week span. By now, the *Nashville Daily Union* was calling Magruder the "rebel superintendent of the road." No one had had a similar appellation since John Hunt Morgan.⁶

Magruder's bushwhackers drifted off towards Campbellsville in late November, but then returned to their usual habitat to strike four more times before the end of the year. They hit the towns of Bloomfield, New

Haven, and Bardstown, and an isolated train on a lonely stretch of the Lebanon Branch.

Winter did not slow them down. In mid-January the most famous guerrilla of all came and joined them. William Quantrill, the Missourian, had led 40 bushwhackers to Kentucky in order to be far away from the scene of their crimes when the end of the war came. These were the men who had sacked Lawrence, Kansas. Old habits were hard to break, however, and a new state did not inspire a reform in their behavior. They left a trail of corpses behind them from Canton in western Kentucky to Nelson County, where they found a thriving population of their own kind.

Magruder, for one, was not overly impressed by the Missouri chieftain or his reputation. He referred to him as "this man Quantrell [sic] from Missouri." They did ride together over the next few weeks, but Magruder did not subordinate himself or his own band to Quantrill's command, except insofar as was appropriate since the Missouri gang was larger. Quantrill had little interest in spreading terror along the L&N, and they mostly robbed citizens, stores, and stagecoaches.[7]

Quantrill had gone his own way by the time of Magruder's last and most audacious raid. On February 18, 1865, the combined bands of Magruder and Jerome Clark attacked Lebanon Junction and Fort Jones near Colesburg. At Lebanon Junction, they killed three soldiers of the 12th U.S. Colored Artillery — men of the Fort Jones garrison — and captured a train. One of the soldiers ran and hid in a boxcar full of hay and was burned up when the train was torched. The marauders wrecked the telegraph office, robbed the stores, and went to the hotel where they "threw the dishes on the sidewalk, walked on the table with their feet, turned over the stove full of fire, and with a polite bow, rode away."[8]

They rode on to Fort Jones, which they boldly attacked until they were met with artillery fire. The brief attack on Fort Jones marked the end of the Civil War in Hardin County.

It was about this time that orders went out for the guerrillas in Kentucky to assemble in Paris, Tennessee, there to join General Hylan B. Lyon and become regular soldiers again. Magruder, Mundy, and a lesser-known bushwhacker named Henry Metcalf headed west in response to the call. They killed two Negro soldiers as they rode toward Meade County. Near Cloverport, they were joined by the guerrilla Bill Davison, who knew a hiding place. Magruder remembered, "Scouts of Yankees were all around us, and it was getting to be pretty close quarters." After resting two days, they proceeded down the Owensboro road, threading their way between the Federal patrols, and had gotten as far as Hawesville when they were attacked by a small squad of Hancock County Home Guards carrying .44 Ballard rifles. Davison was shot twice and later died of his wounds, and some accounts say that Magruder was hit in the arm. He and the other guerrillas doubled back toward Breckinridge County, where they ran into a larger party of Home Guards. This time, Magruder was shot in the lower back. The bullet ranged upward, punctured his left lung, and exited through his chest. He begged Clark and Metcalf to take him back to Meade County where he knew that Dr. J. P. Lewis would treat his wounds. Clark and Metcalf reluctantly agreed.

Nine days later, on March 12, Major Cyrus J. Wilson (formerly of the 26th Kentucky Infantry, but now a guerrilla hunter for Major General Palmer) and 50 men of the 30th Wisconsin Infantry surrounded Magruder, Clark, and Metcalf in a tobacco barn near Guston. Wilson demanded their surrender. Clark answered with some rounds from his pistols and wounded three soldiers. The bluecoats fell back while Dr. Lewis went in to negotiate their surrender. In a few moments, Major Wilson went in to parley. He explained truthfully to Clark that he was going to take them back dead or alive and that the three guerrillas' surrender would undoubtedly result in their execution. But, he promised, they would be treated fairly while in his custody and that, in surrendering, they would lengthen their lives by at least a few days.

In the end, the guerrillas did surrender. They returned with Wilson by steamboat to Louisville. Henry Metcalf seems to have had influential friends, for although he was sentenced at his military trial to hang, the sentence was commuted to five years in the state prison in Frankfort. Jerome Clark was not so lucky; he was convicted at the end of a brief trial and sentenced to hang. A crowd of at least 4,000 citizens and soldiers gathered to watch Clark die on March 15. The long-haired youngster — he was only 21— showed no fear as the noose was placed around his neck. He gave a little speech from the gallows proclaiming his status as a legally enrolled Confederate soldier. He said he was dying for the Southern cause, and then the trap was sprung. The executioner had misjudged the condemned man's weight, so the fall did not break his neck. Clark kicked and struggled at the end of the rope as he slowly choked to death. George Prentice of the *Louisville Daily Journal*, who had invented in his commentaries the persona of "Sue Mundy" for Clark, described the young guerrilla's death. Prentice wrote, "Never before did we witness such hard struggles and convulsions. It was feared for a time that he would break his lashings."[9]

Clark's body was claimed by his family. It was returned to them in a good metal coffin and carried south to Franklin, Kentucky, on the L&N.

Henry Magruder lingered near death from his wound in the Louisville Military Prison hospital. He was not well enough to either put on trial or to execute. It was expected that he would die and cheat the executioner out of a day's pay.

• • •

Magruder and Clark were not the only guerrillas operating along the L&N in the spring of 1865, just the ones closest to corporate headquarters. In the month that Magruder and Clark were captured, there were reports of guerrilla raiding parties in the area of Glasgow and Elizabethtown, in Lebanon, and a large concentration of as many as 1,200 was rumored to be near Russellville on the Memphis Branch. Bill Marion and Bill Hughes still rode, as did Ellis Harper, who raided between Nashville and the Kentucky line.

Their efforts were useless; their cause was lost. But they persisted and were a constant worry to the garrisons between Louisville and Nashville.

One person who was not so fretful seems to have been James Guthrie. In the final, frantic burst of guerrilla activity, he once again found time to pursue his political ambitions. His past few tries for public office were unsuccessful, but in January 1865, he ran for U.S. Senate and the seat of Lazarus W. Powell, who was stepping down. Guthrie's prime contender for the seat was General Lovell H. Rousseau, commander of the newly named District of Middle Tennessee. Rousseau had his allies, the influential Speeds of Louisville among them, but when the General Assembly met on January 11 to choose Kentucky's new senator, it was James Guthrie who won, 65 votes to 56.

Stephen G. Burbridge, in the final weeks of his turbulent tenure as commander of the District of Kentucky, sent Rousseau a letter of consolation that said, "Allow me to congratulate you upon the excellent race you made for U.S. Senate. I am truly sorry (and so are all Union men) that the Election could not have been postponed for a few days. You would undoubtedly have been elected."[10]

But Rousseau was not elected. In the March 2 session of the upper house, according to the Senate *Journal*, "Mr. Powell presented the credentials of the honorable James Guthrie, elected a senator by the legislature of the state of Kentucky for the term of six years, commencing on the 4th day of March, a.d. 1865."[11]

It was a hopeful time. The state had a new senator, the city of Louisville had a new mayor, Philip Tomppert, Sr., and the war was drawing down in the east. When the word came of Lee's surrender at Appomattox, Louisville celebrated with cannon fire from the forts and fieldworks surrounding the city, fireworks, and a grand illumination of the business district. It was said, "The L&N office at 3rd and Main was 'conspicuous for its brilliance.'"[12]

Nashville had a similar experience. The news from Appomattox arrived on the morning of April 10. Crowds gathered in the street outside the newspaper offices to hear the news and stayed to celebrate in a spontaneous street festival. Walter Durham wrote, "As downtown streets filled with citizens, soldiers, and freedman, flags appeared at every hand and, by noon, the big guns of the forts blasted salutes that shook the city." Nashville, too, was illuminated that night. Bands played, and the party lasted until daylight.[13]

Both Louisville and Nashville planned more elaborate celebrations for the following Saturday, April 15, but they were cut short when word arrived from Washington that John Wilkes Booth had shot President Lincoln.

• • •

When Lincoln died, Henry Magruder still lived. The *Daily Journal* reported frequently on his condition, and though it was up and down, the opinion of all who saw him was that he was bound to die. But he hung on. It may have cheered him to learn that Bill Marion killed Dr. J. P. Lewis, the Meade County physician whom Magruder had trusted to treat his wound and who had apparently betrayed him. It certainly would have cheered him to know that both Bill Marion and Bill Hughes vowed to take vengeance if Mundy, Magruder, or Metcalf hanged. "I will Shoot or hang fifty of your men you may think got them first but you will find that I will get them.... I haunt the city of Louisville until I have revenge," Marion said. But Munday hanged on March 15, and Marion had not begun to carry out his threat of 50 murders before he himself was cornered and killed near Lebanon on April 15.[14]

"If Capt. Medkiff [sic] and our brave companion Wm. [sic] Magruder are harmed, a hundred Yankee scalps shall be the just retribution," said Hughes. But he did not follow through. Hughes got initial credit for what was probably the last guerrilla attack on the L&N when, on April 26, a train was thrown from the track on the Memphis Branch near Allensville,

Kentucky. The guerrillas fired into the train. The guards and passengers fired back. The *Daily Journal* reported that the bushwhackers "were driven off without doing much damage. A wrecking train went down from Bowling Green to move the wreck and fix the road." It was later reported that this gang of badmen was led not by Hughes, but by a man named Tom Morrow, who was badly wounded before the irregulars returned to the thickets.[15]

Magruder was still in the infirmary on May 13 when the orderlies carried in the paralyzed body of William Quantrill. Three days earlier, Quantrill and his raiders had gone into a Spencer County barn to escape a little rain shower. Some of the boys were having a corncob fight when the sentries cried out that the Yankees were upon them. They scrambled for their horses at first fire, but Quantrill's horse was a new one, unused to the sound of gunfire. The horse shied and Quantrill could not get into the saddle. He ran to Clark Hockensmith who had mounted up and ridden away and could have escaped, except that he came back for Quantrill. As the guerrilla chieftain tried to climb up behind Hockensmith, he was shot in the back and fell paralyzed, a Yankee bullet pressing against his spine. As Quantrill lay helpless, face down in the barnyard mud, the Federals galloped past chasing Hockensmith, who they killed, and the other rough Missourians. One of the bluecoats fired down at Quantrill and shot off part of his right hand. He was transported to the Louisville Military Prison hospital in a Conestoga wagon filled with straw. On his deathbed, he converted to Catholicism, but he could not keep his mind on the hereafter. His thoughts kept returning to the war. On June 6, 1865, he called out for his boys to get ready. And then he died.

One wonders what may have passed through Magruder's mind as he watched and heard the delirious Missouri guerrilla die. His own flesh was wasting away, but he was still holding his own when the *Daily Democrat* reported on July 25, "We suppose there is not such a case on record of the wounded man. One day he wrestles playfully with life, the next he is struggling in the arms of death."[16]

Magruder came to have good relations with Major Cyrus Wilson, the man who had captured him. He presented to Wilson his brace of Remington army revolvers, the relics of a short, violent life. Also, after Magruder narrated his "confession" in a marathon session of talking on August 10, he entrusted the 50 pages of foolscap to Wilson for publication. General John M. Palmer refused to allow the small book to be published until after Magruder's trial. However, in the end, Major Wilson kept his word to the young killer and the confession was published. It was called *Three Years in the Saddle* and, being a rare look at war-time events from the irregular's point of view, it was one of the most interesting pieces of literature in the guerrilla canon.

Magruder's trial began on September 13 and was in session intermittently until mid–October. Part of the time Magruder was so weak that the trial was held in the infirmary. It was said that he had grown so thin that some of his old Bullitt County friends did not at first recognize him. On or about October 17, he was convicted and sentenced to hang. "It is hard, but I reckon it is fair," Magruder said to his attorney. Now time moved fast. On his last day, Friday, October 20, Magruder visited briefly in the infirmary with his mother, his aunt, and two cousins. At 3:15 P.M., the 125th Colored Infantry band began to play and the regiment formed into a hollow square. Twenty minutes later Magruder came out, smoking a cigar and dressed in a military jacket and gray trousers, with a white kerchief tied around his neck. The *Daily Journal* commented upon his "firm and dignified air," and described him as having "an intelligent, pleasing cast of countenance." He stopped at the foot of the gallows steps to throw his cigar away. Scavengers scrambled to pick it up as Henry Magruder took the last thirteen steps of his life, climbing toward the platform and the dangling noose. The charges against him were read, a task which took 20 minutes. The condemned boy looked calmly over the crowd below and searched the windows and rooftops of the surrounding buildings. Some thought that he signaled to someone in the distance, supposedly a sweetheart from happier days.[17]

When the reading was done, Magruder was asked if he had anything to say. "Not a word," he answered. A white hood was placed over his head, the noose slipped around his neck, his arms and legs were bound, and at ten minutes after four o'clock the world dropped out from under Henry Magruder.[18]

The last great guerrilla was dead. The war was over and the L&N had endured.

Afterword

Not only had the L&N endured, it thrived. In the fiscal year ending on June 30 1865, the books showed that the railroad earned a net profit of $2,172, 515 in the last year of the war. Not only that, but the railroad had $2,913,151 in assets, including 60 locomotives, 57 passenger cars, 321 boxcars, 114 flatcars, and other types of rolling stock. Part of that total was a half million dollars in various other kinds of resources, including $69,425 worth of lumber, axles, and wheels; $23,654 in iron and steel; over $18,000 in repair materials at shops in Louisville, Bowling Green, and Edgefield; almost $3,000 in coal, and so on. The L&N, including all branches, was now 286 miles long.

During the war, the L&N had suffered $688,372 in damages, but the net profit for the same period was $6,009,195. The railroad had come through in good shape.

Part of that was due to the heroic role played by Albert Fink. He and his repair crews were always quick to the scene of a break in the road and were often attacked by guerrillas. Yet, they remained committed to their hard and dangerous duties and kept the railroad open as much as humanly possible. For his efforts, Fink was promoted by the corporation to general superintendent at war's end.

It was good for the daily operation of the railroad to be in Fink's capable hands while James Guthrie attended to his duties as U.S. Senator. Guthrie's efforts on behalf of the railroad were tireless in the years 1861–1865, but it would be harder to characterize them as heroic. He was, by necessity, more involved in the political side of doing business in wartime, but his behavior was too shifty to be admired without reservation. He kept the army impoverished in one campaign after another while giving precedence to hauling private freight and civilian passengers. It was an ongoing practice for which he was repeatedly condemned by men who were in a position to know. Furthermore, he lied without hesitation when it was in the interest of the bottom line. In 1862, for instance, he told General Montgomery Meigs that $700,000 in destruction had been inflicted on the L&N, a figure that was greater than the actual total for the entire span of the war. By proclaiming loudly and frequently the calamitous condition of the L&N, Guthrie was able to persuade the government to rebuild downed bridges (like the one at Nashville in 1862), to bear the bulk of the expense in building the Lebanon Branch extension, and at the same time to pay a higher premium for services than was paid to any other railroad. It was not a swindle, but it was a predatory attitude against a government that was fighting for the nation's existence.

One wonders just how committed Guthrie really was to a Union victory. It has already been seen that, at the beginning of the war, he happily traded with both the federal government and the Confederacy. He championed the rights of Southern sympathizers whose actions were so egregious that they had been placed under arrest and imprisoned. In 1864, he was a Peace Democrat who wanted a negotiated peace with the South.

And, as if his known wartime behavior were not enough, there remains the question of his *unknown* behavior. The Filson Historical Society in Louisville houses a large collection of Guthrie-related papers, but there is a conspicuous lack of personal documents. Explaining this blank spot in the historical record, a note inside the collection quotes John Dugan, author of a 1952 master's thesis at the University of Florida, Gainesville. The thesis was titled "James Guthrie: His Interests in Internal Improvements in Kentucky from 1820 to 1869." In his thesis, Dugan wrote, "The vast bulk of the correspondence and personal manuscripts of James Guthrie was destroyed in error at the death of his son-in-law, Dr. William B. Caldwell." It was a suspicious error and one that seems to have erased forever the possibility of a careful examination of Guthrie's dealings during the war.[1]

U.S. Senator James Guthrie did not step down as president of the L&N. At the annual stockholders' meeting of October 2, 1865, a resolution was offered which read: "Resolved, that as a testimonial of our confidence in the skill and ability with which the Hon. James Guthrie has discharged the arduous duties devolving on him as President of the Louisville and Nashville Railroad, since he has been in office, we tender to him our sincere thanks, and request him, notwithstanding his larger sphere of action, to consent to act as President of the road for the coming year." Guthrie allowed his name to appear on the ballot and was elected. Well might the stockholders have been pleased with Guthrie — every year, he had made money for them.[2]

In addition to his continuing leadership of the L&N, Guthrie showed a vigorous interest in expanding his investments in new and exciting directions. He sensed that America's nascent oil industry had a promising future. Even before the close of the war, he was in correspondence with a Northern speculator named John Carpenter who was interested in acquiring an

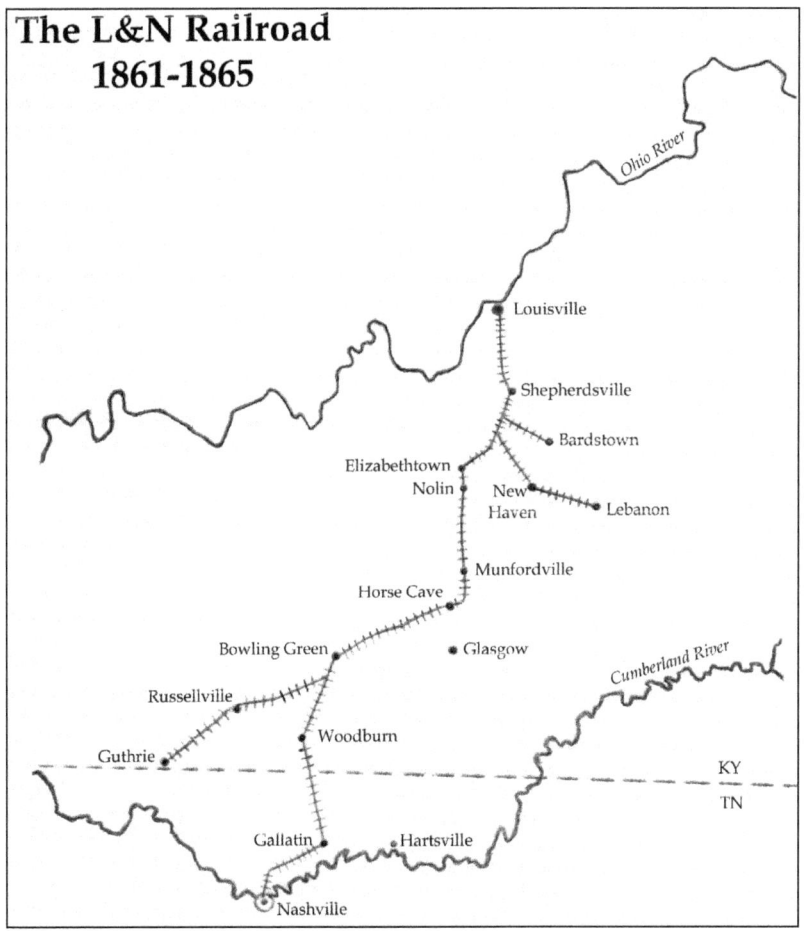

The L&N Railroad, 1861–1865. Map by the author.

option on some of Guthrie's acreage along the L&N. On February 15, 1865, Carpenter wrote Guthrie from the Metropolitan Hotel in New York City, "I find the Petroleum fever here very high and as I suppose there is some oil on your land on the Nashville Railroad, I think I can make a small speculation on it. Will you give me the refusal of the land for thirty days at $80,000. Please answer by telegraph."[3]

Guthrie answered, "You shall have my tract of land on the [illegible] of the Louisville and Nashville Railroad about eight miles from Louisville."[4]

If he had lived, Guthrie might have been a serious competitor to the robber baron John D. Rockefeller, but by 1868 the 76-year-old Guthrie was an ailing man. He resigned from the Senate halfway through his term and returned home to Louisville. Two months later, in April, he became bedfast and lingered in that condition until his death at his residence on Walnut Street in Louisville on March 13, 1869. His obituary in the *Courier-Journal* referred to him as a patriot and a statesman. It continued, "A marked feat in his history is that, during the war he blatantly and openly opposed all usurpations of power and individual persecutions on the part of the Federal authorities," and then drifted into a pale prevarication when it continued, "without at any time destroying the confidence of the Federal authorities in his fidelity to the vigorous prosecution of the war." In fact, there were many whose confidence Guthrie abused during the prosecution of the war. At times, it seemed, Guthrie's war was with the federal government.[5]

What could be said about Guthrie without fear of contradiction was that, by whatever means in a perilous time, he preserved the L&N and laid the footing for the postwar success of the company he served. In the twentieth century, the railroad owned over 7,000 miles of track in 13 states. It was one of the best known American corporations and became emblematic of the southland.

The Louisville and Nashville Railroad operated under its own name until 1983.

Chapter Notes

Introduction

1. U.S. War Department, *The War of the Rebellion: A Compilation of the Official Records of the Union and Confederate Armies*, 129 volumes (Washington, D.C.: Government Printing Office, 1880–1901), Volume 29, Part I, 149. (Hereafter referred to as *OR*.)
2. Shelby Foote, *The Civil War, A Narrative: From Fredericksburg to Meridian* (New York: Random House, 1974), 765.
3. John E. Clark, Jr., *Railroads in the Civil War: The Impact of Management on Victory and Defeat* (Baton Rouge: Louisiana State University Press, 2004), 167.
4. Foote, *Fredericksburg to Meridian*, 766.
5. Ibid., 765.
6. Robert C. Black, *The Railroads of the Confederacy* (Chapel Hill: University of North Carolina Press, 1998), 8.
7. Robert E. McDowell, *City of Conflict: Louisville in the Civil War, 1861–1865* (Louisville, KY: Louisville Civil War Roundtable, 1962), 122–123.

Chapter 1

1. John E. Clark, Jr., "The Importance of the Railroads in the Civil War," *North and South*, March 2008, 73.
2. Kinkaid A. Herr, *The Louisville and Nashville Railroad, 1850–1963* (Lexington: University Press of Kentucky, 2000), 4.
3. Ibid.
4. Maury Klein, *History of the Louisville and Nashville Railroad* (Lexington: University Press of Kentucky, 2003), 11.
5. James Barnett, "Munfordville in the Civil War," *The Register of the Kentucky Historical Society*, October 1971, 340.
6. Herr, 25.
7. "The Union Banquet," *Louisville Daily Journal*, 25 January 1860 (first quote), McDowell, 31, (second quote).
8. "The Union Banquet," *Louisville Daily Journal*, 25 January 1860.
9. Ibid.

Chapter 2

1. W.B.R., "Our Tennessee Correspondence," *New York Times*, 28 March 1862.
2. Klein, 17.
3. *Dictionary of American Biography, Volume VIII* (New York: Charles Scribner's Sons, 1932), 62.
4. Carl Sandburg, *Abraham Lincoln: The War Years, Volume I.* (New York: Charles Scribner's Sons, 1948), 94–97.
5. Klein, 27.
6. McDowell, 33
7. Pontiac. "Affairs in Kentucky," *New York Times*, July 12, 1861.
8. Sergeant E. Tarrant, *The Wild Riders of the First Kentucky Cavalry* (Lexington, KY: Henry Clay Press, 1969), 7.
9. *OR*, Volume 4, 249.
10. Josie Underwood, *Josie Underwood's Civil War Diary*, ed. Nancy Disher Baird (Lexington: University Press of Kentucky, 2009), 11.

Chapter 3

1. Underwood, 106.
2. *OR*, Volume 4, 415–16.
3. Ibid., 416.
4. William C. Davis, *The Orphan Brigade*

(Garden City, NJ: Doubleday and Co., 1980), 37.
5. *OR*, Volume 4, 414–15.
6. McDowell, 44
7. William T. Sherman, *Memoirs of General W.T. Sherman* (New York: Library of America, 1990), 215.
8. Co. C, 3rd Kentucky Regiment, "To the Editor of the *Daily Journal.*" *Louisville Daily Journal*, 5 October 1861.
9. Basil Duke, *The Civil War Reminiscences of General Basil W. Duke, CSA* (New York: Cooper Square Press, 2001), 74.
10. Ibid., 74.
11. Ibid., 74.
12. R.M. Kelly, "Holding Kentucky for the Union" in *Battles and Leaders of the Civil War: The Opening Battles,* eds. Robert Underwood Johnson and Clarence Clough (Edison, NJ: Castle Books, 1995), 381.
13. *OR*, Volume 4, 295.

Chapter 4

1. *OR*, Volume 4, 299.
2. William Sumner Dodge, *History of the Old Second Division, Army of the Cumberland* (Chicago: Church and Goodman, 1864), 69.
3. Steven L. Wright, ed., *Kentucky Soldiers and Their Regiments in the Civil War, Abstracted from the Pages of Contemporary Kentucky Newspapers*, 5 vols. (published by the editor, 2009): 106.
4. *OR*, Volume 4, 437.
5. *OR*, Volume 4, 444.
6. William C. Davis, *The Commanders of the Civil War* (London: Chrysalis Books, 2004), 21.
7. Ibid., 26.
8. Shelby Foote, *The Civil War, A Narrative: Fort Sumter to Perryville* (New York: Vintage Books, 1986), 169.
9. *OR*, Volume 4, 478.
10. Ibid., 502–03.
11. Ibid., 551.
12. Basil Duke, *A History of Morgan's Cavalry* (Bloomington: Indiana University Press, 1960), 94 (first quote); Dan Lee, *Kentuckian in Blue* (Jefferson, NC: McFarland, 2010), 51.
13. William C. Robinson, letter to Charlie, 13 October 1861, collection of the Abraham Lincoln Presidential Library, Springfield Illinois.
14. Alexander McDowell McCook, letter to Governor William P. Dennison, 15 November 1861, Collection of the Ohio Historical Society, Columbus, Ohio.
15. *OR*, Volume 4, 307 (first quote); Dodge, 74 (second quote).

16. Michael A. Peake, *Indiana's German Sons: A History of the 1st German 32nd Regiment, Indiana Volunteer Infantry* (Indianapolis: Max Kade German-American Center, Indiana University-Purdue University at Indianapolis and Indiana German Heritage Society, 1999), 8.
17. Lyman S. Widney, *Campaigning With Uncle Billy*, ed. Robert I. Girandi (Victoria, BC: Indiana University Press, 2008), 20.
18. "Redstick," "Army Correspondence," *Fremont Journal*, 22 November 1861, collection of the Ohio Historical Society, Columbus Ohio.
19. *Louisville Anzeiger*, 5 November 1861.
20. Pontiac, "James Guthrie Speaks Out Again," *New York Times*, 5 December 1861.

Chapter 5

1. Larry J. Daniel, *Days of Glory: The Army of the Cumberland, 1861–1865* (Baton Rouge: Louisiana State University Press, 2004), 21.
2. Alexander K. McClure, *Recollections of Half a Century* (Salem, MA: Salem Press, 1902), 332.
3. "Abraham Lincoln Papers," www.memory.loc.gov, accessed September 16, 2009.
4. John E. Tilford, "The Delicate Track — The L&N's Role in the Civil War," *Filson Club Historical Quarterly*, July 1962, 214.
5. *OR*, Volume 7, 480.
6. *OR*, Series II, Volume LII, Part II, 152.
7. *OR*, Volume 7, 16.
8. Ibid.
9. Pontiac. "The Campaign in Kentucky," *New York Times*, 27 December 1861.
10. *OR*, Volume 7, 17.
11. Ibid.
12. Ibid., 15.
13. Ibid., 20–21.
14. *OR*, Volume 7, 741.
15. Underwood, 142.
16. Ibid., 133.
17. *OR*, Volume 7, 934 (first quote); William C. Davis, *The Orphan Brigade*, 49 (second quote).
18. *OR*, Volume 7, 781.
19. Lyman S. Widney, Diary, collection of the Hart County Historical Society, Munfordville, Kentucky.
20. "Affair at Munfordville," *New York Times*, 20 January 1862.
21. John Beatty, *The Citizen-Soldier: The Memories of a Civil War Volunteer* (Lincoln, NE: Bison Books, 1998), 106.
22. Ibid. (first quote); Josephine Covington, letter to Judge Wells, March 2, 1862,

quoted in the introduction to Underwood, 17 (second quote).
23. Beatty, 106.
24. *OR*, Volume 7, 419–420.

Chapter 6

1. *OR*, Volume 7, 735–36.
2. Ibid., 626.
3. Ibid., 657.
4. Sergeant E. Tarrant, *The Wild Riders of the First Kentucky Cavalry* (Lexington, KY: Henry Clay Press, 1969), 75.
5. Spillard F. Horrall, *History of the 42nd Indiana Volunteers* (Chicago: published by the author, 1892), 113.
6. Ibid.
7. J.A. Brents, *The Patriots and Guerrillas of East Tennessee and Kentucky* (New York: published by the author, 1863), 108.
8. "Unionism in Tennessee," *New York Times*, 9 June 1862 (first quote); *OR*, Volume 10, Part II, 57–58 (second quote).
9. *OR*, Volume 10, Part II, 79.

Chapter 7

1. Jacob D. Cox, *Military Reminiscences of the Civil War, Volume I* (Teddington, Middlesex, England: Echo Library, 2008), 282.
2. *OR*, Volume 10, Part I, 32.
3. *OR*, Volume 16, Part II, 31. (first quote), 173 (second quote).
4. Lowell H. Harrison, *The Civil War in Kentucky* (Lexington: University Press of Kentucky, 1975), 38.
5. *OR*, Volume 16, Part I, 738.
6. McDowell, 67.
7. Ibid., 68.
8. *OR*, Volume 16, Part I, 736.
9. Ibid., 733 (first and second quotes), 737 (third quote).
10. Ibid., 780.
11. Ibid.
12. Ibid., 770.
13. *OR*, Volume 16, Part II, 155.
14. Ibid.
15. Ibid., 231.
16. Ibid., 241.
17. James A. Ramage, *Rebel Raider: The Life of General John Hunt Morgan* (Lexington: University Press of Kentucky, 1986), 116.
18. Ibid., 116.
19. *OR*, Volume 16, Part I, 872.
20. Ibid.
21. "Guerrillas in Tennessee," *New York Times*, 7 May 1862 (first quote); Southern folk rhyme (second quote).

Chapter 8

1. Daniel, 115.
2. *OR*, Volume 16, Part II, 451.
3. *OR*, Volume 16, Part I, 697.
4. Ibid., 166.
5. Ibid., 88.
6. Walter Durham, *Nashville: The Occupied City* (Nashville: Tennessee Historical Society, 1985), 125.
7. C.V.S., "Affairs in Tennessee: A Wharfless City/Nashville Square Business Houses/Berry & Co.'s Southern Methodist Publishing House/Private Residences/State House," *New York Times*, 7 August 1863 (first quote); C.L.B., "Nashville: The City Streets/Contrabands/Army Feeling Toward Them," *New York Times*, 21 August 1863.
8. *OR*, Volume 16, Part I, 88.
9. Francis B. Carpenter, *Six Months at the White House with Abraham Lincoln: The Story of a Portrait* (New York: Hurd and Houghton, 1866), 103.
10. *OR*, Volume 16, Part II, 513.
11. *OR*, Volume 16, Part I, 979.
12. Sam Watkins, *Company Aytch* (New York: Plume, 1999), 42.
13. *OR*, Volume 16, Part II, 822.
14. *OR*, Volume 16, Part I, 960.
15. Ibid., 961.
16. Ibid., 980.
17. Watkins, 43.
18. Harrison, 45–46.

Chapter 9

1. *OR*, Volume 16, Part I, 315.
2. Ibid., 207–208 (first quote), 213 (second quote).
3. *OR*, Volume 16, Part I, 48.
4. Ibid., 563 (first quote), 162 (second quote).
5. Joseph Wheeler, "Bragg's Invasion of Kentucky," in *Battles and Leaders: The Opening Battles*, 10.
6. *OR*, Volume 16, Part I, 1090.
7. *OR*, Volume 17, Part II, 713 (first quote); *OR*, Volume 16, Part I, 968.
8. *OR*, Volume 16, Part II, 843.
9. *OR*, Volume 16, Part I, 895.
10. Untitled, undated newspaper clipping from the *Louisville Daily Journal*.
11. *OR*, Volume 16, Part II, 536–37.
12. Tarrant, 113.

13. Tarrant, 113.
14. Tarrant, 115.
15. *OR*, Volume 16, Part I, 1016–17
16. *OR*, Volume 16, Part II, 564–65.
17. Curtius, "Gen. Buell's Department," *New York Times*, 5 October 1862.
18. Ibid.
19. McDowell, 96.
20. *OR*, Volume 16, Part II, 465 (first quote), 525 (second quote).
21. *OR*, Volume 16, Part II, 519
22. Ibid.
23. Letter of Joshua F. Speed to Abraham Lincoln, 17 September 1862, Abraham Lincoln Papers, www.memory.loc.gov, accessed September 17, 2009.
24. *OR*, Volume 16, Part II, 416.
25. McDowell, 87 (first quote); Foote, Fort Sumter to Perryville, 661 (second quote).
26. Curtius, " Department of the Ohio," *New York Times*, 6 October 1862.
27. Ibid.

Chapter 10

1. OR, Volume 20, Part II, 57
2. Ibid., 75
3. Ibid., 84 (first quote), 85 (second quote).
4. *OR*, Volume 16, Part II, 646–47.
5. Ibid., 647.
6. Ibid., 644.
7. Daniel, 182 (first quote); Horrall, 155 (second quote).
8. *OR*, Volume 20, Part II, 108.
9. Durham, *Occupied City*, 207 (first quote); B.C.T., "Affairs at Nashville," *New York Times*, 23 November 1862 (second quote).
10. "Gen. Rosecrans' Army," *New York Times*, 19 November 1862.
11. William Denison Bickham, *Rosecrans' Campaign with the Fourteenth Army Corps* (Ann Arbor: University of Michigan Library, 2006), 87.
12. *OR*, Volume 16, Part II, 340.
13. *OR*, Volume 20, Part II, 63–64.
14. *OR*, Volume 20, Part II, 208–09.
15. Duke, *Morgan's Cavalry*, 332.
16. Darrell Bird, "Morgan's Raid Remembered," *News-Enterprise* (Elizabethtown, KY), 28 December 1992–4 January 1993.
17. Ibid. (first quote); Jones, *Civil War in Hardin County*, 26 (second quote).
18. Mary Josephine Jones, *The Civil War in Hardin County, Kentucky* (Vine Grove, KY: Ancestral Trails Historical Society, 1995), 29.
19. Ibid.
20. Ibid.
21. Bird, "Morgan's Raid Remembered."

22. James Allan Wyeth, *With Sabre and Scalpel: The Autobiography of a Soldier and Surgeon* (New York: Harper and Brothers, 1914), 185.
23. *OR*, Volume 20, Part I, 137.
24. Ibid., 138.
25. Duke, *Morgan's Cavalry*, 338.
26. *OR*, Volume 20, Part I, 139.
27. Ramage, 143.
28. *OR*, Volume 20, Part I, 140
29. Ibid., 141.
30. Ibid., 147.
31. James Guthrie, letter to P.G. Washington, July 1862, Guthrie-Caperton Papers, collection of the Filson Historical Society, Louisville, Kentucky.
32. George W. McLellan, letter to Edwin M. Stanton, 5 December 1862, Abraham Lincoln Papers. www.memory.loc.gov, accessed September 16, 2009.
33. Ibid.
34. Ibid.
35. Montgomery Blair, letter to Abraham Lincoln, 31 December 1862. Abraham Lincoln Papers. www.memory.loc.gov. Accessed September 17, 2009.

Chapter 11

1. Henry M. Cist, *The Army of the Cumberland* (New York: Charles Scribner's Sons, 1882), 138.
2. *OR*, Volume 20, Part II, 191.
3. *OR*, Volume 23, Part II, 33.
4. Durham, *Occupied City*, 223–24.
5. Jones, 41.
6. Durham, *Occupied City*, 225.
7. *OR*, Volume 23, Part II, 201.
8. *OR*, Volume 23, Part I, 817.
9. Ibid., 817–818.
10. Ramage, 160.
11. Henry C. Magruder, Three *Years in the Saddle: The Life and Confession of Henry C. Magruder* (Utica, Kentucky: McDowell Publications, no date), 21 (first quote); "A Fond Recollection of Ben F. Bowman," *Lebanon Enterprise*, 27 June 1963 (second quote).
12. *OR*, Volume 23, Part I, 692.
13. Ramage, 164.
14. *OR*, Volume 23, Part I, 703.
15. Ibid., 689.
16. McDowell, 149.
17. Ramage, 166–167.
18. *OR*, Volume 23, Part I, 703.
19. Foote, *Fredericksburg to Meridian*, 680.
20. *OR*, Volume 23, Part I, 640.
21. Wright, *Kentucky* Soldiers, 3: 147.

Chapter 12

1. *OR*, Volume 30, Part III, 787.
2. Abraham Lincoln, *The Collected Works of Abraham Lincoln, Volume 5*, ed. Roy P. Basler (New Brunswick, New Jersey: Rutgers University Press, 1953), 127.
3. *OR*, Series II, Volume IV, 627.
4. Ibid.
5. Ibid., 631.
6. *OR*, Volume 48, Part I, 1113.
7. *OR*, Volume 30, Part II, 407
8. *OR,* Volume 30, Part I, 188.
9. *OR,* Volume 30, Part III, 667.
10. Ibid., 26.
11. Walter T. Durham, *Reluctant Partners: Nashville and the Union* (Nashville: Tennessee Historical Society, no date), 169.
12. *OR,* Volume 31, Part III, 109.
13. *OR,* Volume 30, Part III, 180.
14. Ibid., 181.
15. Ibid., 182.
16. Wright, *Kentucky Soldiers*, 3: 147.
17. Robert Winn to Thomas M. Wheatley, Winn-Cook Family Papers, collection of the Filson Historical Society, Louisville, Kentucky (first quote); McDowell, 156 (second quote).
18. *OR,* Volume 31, Part I, 750.

Chapter 13

1. *OR*, Volume 39, Part II, 213 (first quote), 214 (second quote).
2. McDowell, 125–26.
3. *OR*, Volume 32, Part II, 269.
4. Durham, *Occupied City,* 279 (first quote); *OR*, Volume 32, Part II, 267 (second quote).
5. Durham, *Occupied City*, 279.
6. *OR*, Volume 32, Part II, 268.
7. William Douglas Hamilton, *Recollections of a Cavalryman of the Civil War after Fifty Years, 1861–1865* (Columbus, Ohio: F.J. Hess Printing Company, 1915), 88–89.
8. Durham, *Reluctant Partners*, 120.
9. Ibid., 120–21.
10. Ibid., 55.
11. Works Progress Administration, *Military History of Kentucky* (Frankfort: Adjutant General of Kentucky, 1939), 205.
12. J. Blaine Hudson, "African Americans," in *The Encyclopedia of Louisville*, ed. John Kleber (Lexington: University Press of Kentucky, 2001), 15.
13. Robert Winn, letter to sister, 12 March 1864. Winn-Cook Family Papers, collection of the Filson Historical Society, Louisville, Kentucky.
14. John H. Ward, letter to John G. Foster, 19 January 1864, Speed Family Papers — Farmington Collection, collection of the Filson Historical Society, Louisville, Kentucky.
15. WPA, *Military History of Kentucky*, 205–206.
16. Carl Sandburg, *Abraham Lincoln: The War Years, Volume III*. (New York: Charles Scribner's Sons, 1948), 493.
17. Ibid., 494.
18. Wright, *Kentucky Soldiers,* 4: 229.
19. Wright, *Kentucky* Soldiers, 5:4.
20. McDowell, 164–65.
21. Thomas B. Fairleigh, Diary: January – June 7, 1864, collection of the Filson Historical Society, Louisville, Kentucky.
22. *OR*, Volume 23, Part II, 609–610.
23. *OR,* Volume 38, Part IV, 167.
24. *OR,* Volume 39, Part II, 198.
25. Ibid., 247.
26. Ibid., 247–48.
27. Ibid., 249.
28. "The Last Hours of the Chicago Convention," *New York Times*, 4 September 1864.

Chapter 14

1. Sherman, *Memoirs*, 468.
2. Ibid., 469.
3. McDowell, 181.
4. Shelby Foote, *The Civil War, A Narrative: Red River to Appomattox* (New York: Random House, 1974), 612–13.
5. Ibid., 613.
6. Daniel Mallock, "For Want of a Primer," *North and South*, September 2008, 60.
7. Foote, *Red River to Appomattox*, 674.
8. Watkins, *Company Aytch,* 205.
9. Henry Stone, "Repelling Hood's Invasion of Tennessee" in *Battles and Leaders of the Civil War: Retreat With Honor,* eds. Robert Underwood Johnson and Clarence Clough (Edison, NJ: Castle Books, 1995), 456.
10. Benson Bobrick, *Master of War: The Life of General George H. Thomas* (New York: Simon and Schuster, 2009), 284.
11. Sandburg, War Years, 3: 636.
12. Ibid.
13. *OR*, Volume 45, Part II, 114.
14. Bobrick, 284.
15. *OR*, Volume 45, Part II, 143.
16. *OR*, Volume 45, Part I, 536 (first quote); *OR*, Volume 45, Part II, 143 (second quote).
17. Foote, *Red River to Appomattox*, 703.
18. Watkins, 208.
19. Bobrick, 296.
20. Ibid., 297.

Chapter 15

1. Wright, *Kentucky Soldiers*, 5: 42.
2. Ibid.
3. Magruder, 3–4.
4. Ibid., 24.
5. Wright, *Kentucky Soldiers*, 4: 211.
6. Ibid., 290.
7. Magruder, *Confession*, 55.
8. Carolyn Wimp, ed., *Hardin County, Kentucky Newspaper Abstracts, 1905 to 1907* (Vine Grove, KY: Ancestral Trails Historical Society, 2002), 39.
9. Wright, *Kentucky Soldiers*, 5: 76.
10. Stephen G. Burbridge, letter to Lovell H. Rousseau, 13 February 1865, John A. McAllister Collection, collection of the Library Company of Philadelphia, Philadelphia, Pennsylvania.
11. *Journal* of the U.S. Senate, 2 March 1865, Century of Lawmaking, memory.loc.gov.
12. McDowell, 197.
13. Durham, *Reluctant Partners*, 286–87.
14. Wright, *Kentucky Soldiers*, 5: 86.
15. Ibid., 98 (first quote), 119 (second quote).
16. Wright, *Kentucky Soldiers*, 5: 184.
17. "Execution of Henry C. Magruder," *Louisville Daily Journal*, 21 October 1865.
18. Ibid.

Afterword

1. John Dugan, "James Guthrie: His Interests in Internal Improvements in Kentucky from 1820–1869." (master's thesis, University of Florida, Gainesville, 1952), excerpt in the Guthrie-Caperton Family Papers, collection of the Filson Historical Society, Louisville, Kentucky.
2. Louisville and Nashville Railroad Company Records (1865), University of Louisville Archives and Records Center, Louisville, Kentucky.
3. John Carpenter to James Guthrie, 15 February 1865, Guthrie-Caperton Family Papers, collection of the Filson Historical Society, Louisville, Kentucky.
4. James Guthrie to John Carpenter 15 February 1865, Guthrie-Caperton Family Papers, collection of the Filson Historical Society, Louisville, Kentucky.
5. "James Guthrie Obituary," *Courier-Journal* (Louisville, KY), 14–15 March 1869.

Bibliography

"Abraham Lincoln Papers." www.memory.loc.gov. Accessed September 16, 2009.

B.C.T. "Affairs at Nashville." *New York Times*, November 23, 1862.

Barnett, James. "Munfordville in the Civil War." *Register of the Kentucky Historical Society*. October 1971.

Barton, Lon Carter. "The 'Reign of Terror' in Graves County." In *Kentucky's Civil War, 1861–1865*. Edited by Jerlene Rose. Clay City: Back Home in Kentucky, 2005.

Beatty, John. *The Citizen-Soldier: The Memoirs of a Civil War Volunteer*. Lincoln: Bison Books, 1998.

Bennett, Samuel Winston. Diary. Owensboro Area Museum of Science and History, Owensboro, Kentucky.

Bickham, William Denison. *Rosecrans' Campaign with the Fourteenth Army Corps*. Ann Arbor: University of Michigan Library, 2006.

Bird, Darrell. "Morgan's Raid Remembered." *News-Enterprise* (Elizabethtown, KY). December 28, 1992–January 4, 1993.

Black, Robert C. *The Railroads of the Confederacy*. Chapel Hill: University of North Carolina Press, 1998.

Bobrick, Benson. *Master of War: The Life of General George H. Thomas*. New York: Simon & Schuster, 2009.

Bohn, Gustav. "Camp Nolin." *Louisville Anzeiger*. November 5, 1861.

Brents, J. A. *The Patriots and Guerrillas of East Tennessee and Kentucky*. New York: J. A. Brents, 1863.

Burbridge, Stephen G. Letter to Lovell H. Rousseau. February 13, 1865. John A. McAllister Collection. Library Company of Philadelphia, Philadelphia, Pennsylvania.

C.L.B. "Nashville: The City Streets/Contrabands/Army Feeling Toward Them." *New York Times*. August 21, 1863.

C.V.S. "Affairs in Tennessee: A Wharfless City/Nashville Square Business Houses/Berry&Co.'s Southern Methodist Publishing House/Private Residences/State House." *New York Times*. August 7, 1863.

"Camp Nevin, Kentucky." *Harper's Weekly*. December 7, 1861.

Campbell, D. A. "The Battle of Munfordville." Civil War Accounts File. Hart County Historical Society, Munfordville, Kentucky.

Carpenter, Francis B. *Six Months at the White House with Abraham Lincoln: The Story of a Portrait*. New York: Hurd and Houghton, 1866.

Carpenter, John. Letter to James Guthrie. February 15, 1865. Filson Historical Society, Louisville, Kentucky.

Catton, Bruce. *Grant Takes Command*. Boston: Little, Brown, 1969.

"Chicago Convention." *New York Times*. September 1, 1864.

Cist, Henry M. *The Army of the Cumberland*. New York: Charles Scribner's Sons, 1882.

Civilian Accounts File. Hart County Historical Society, Munfordville, Kentucky.

Clark, John E. "The Importance of the Railroads in the Civil War." *North and South*. March 2008.

_____. *Railroads in the Civil War: The Impact of Management on Victory and Defeat*. Baton Rouge: Louisiana State University Press, 2004.

Clark, William T. Diary. Lancaster County Historical Society, Lancaster, Pennsylvania.

Cox, Jacob D. *Military Reminiscences of the Civil War, Volume I*. Teddinton, Middlesex, England: The Echo Library, 2008.

Cunningham, O. Edward. *Shiloh and the Western Campaign of 1862*. Eds. Gary D. Joiner and Timothy B. Smith. New York: SAvas Beatie, 2007.

Curtius. "Department of the Ohio." *New York Times*, October 6, 1862.

Daniel, Larry J. *Days of Glory: The Army of the Cumberland, 1861–1865*. Baton Rouge: Louisiana State University Press, 2004.

Davis, William C. *The Battlefields of the Civil War*. London: Salamander Books, 2003.

_____. *Breckinridge: Statesman, Soldier, Symbol*. Baton Rouge: Louisiana State University Press, 1974.

_____. *The Commanders of the Civil War*. London: Chrysalis Books, 2004.

_____. *The Orphan Brigade*. Garden City, NJ: Doubleday and Company, 1980.

Denney, Robert E. *Civil War Medicine: Care and Comfort of the Wounded*. New York: Sterling Publishing Company, 1994.

"Department of the Cumberland: Affairs at Nashville." *New York Times*. December 18, 1862.

"Department of the Cumberland ... How Nashville Impresses a Stranger." *New York Times*. June 1, 1863.

Dictionary of American Biography, Volume VIII. New York: Charles Scribner's Sons, 1932.

Dodge, William Sumner. *History of the Old Second Division, Army of the Cumberland*. Chicago: Church and Goodman, 1864.

Dugan, John. "James Guthrie: His Interests in Internal Improvements in Kentucky from 1820–1869." Master's Thesis, University of Florida, Gainesville, 1952. Excerpt in the Guthrie-Caperton Family Papers, 1780–1939. Filson Historical Society, Louisville, Kentucky.

Duke, Basil. *The Civil War Reminiscences of General Basil W. Duke, CSA*. New York: Cooper Square Press, 2001.

_____. *A History of Morgan's Cavalry*. Bloomington: Indiana University Press, 1960.

Durham, Walter T. *Nashville, The Occupied City: The First Seventeen Months, February 16, 1862 to June 30, 1863*. Nashville: Tennessee Historical Society, 1985.

_____. *Reluctant Partners: Nashville and the Union, July 1, 1863 to June 30, 1865*. Nashville: Tennessee Historical Society, n.d.

Eisenschiml, Otto, and Ralph Newman. *The Civil War, Volume I: The American Iliad*. New York: Grosset and Dunlap, 1956.

Engerud, Hall. "Morgan's Christmas Raid." *Glasgow Times.* December 11, 1931.

Engle, Stephen D. *Don Carlos Buell: Most Promising of All.* Chapel Hill: University of North Carolina Press, 1999.

Esposito, Vincent J., ed. *The West Point Atlas of American Wars.* New York: Praeger Publishers, 1978.

"Execution of Henry C. Magruder." *Louisville Daily Journal.* October 21, 1865.

Fairleigh, Thomas B. Diary: January 1–June 7, 1864. Filson Historical Society, Louisville, Kentucky.

Fogle, McDowell A. *Fogle's Papers: A History of Ohio County, Kentucky.* Utica, KY: McDowell Publications, 1981.

"A Fond Recollection of Ben F. Bowman." *Lebanon Enterprise.* June 27, 1963.

Foote, Shelby. *The Civil War, A Narrative: Fort Sumter to Perryville.* New York: Random House, 1974.

———. *The Civil War, A Narrative: Fredericksburg to Meridian.* New York: Random House, 1974.

———. *The Civil War, A Narrative: Red River to Appomattox.* New York: Random House, 1974.

Gardiner, Florence Edwards. *Cyrus Edwards' Stories of Early Days.* Scottsville, KY: South Central Historical and Genealogical Society, 1959.

"Gen. Buell's Department." *New York Times.* October 2, 1862.

"Gen. John Hunt Morgan Called 'Great Raider of Confederacy.'" *Lebanon Enterprise*, June 27, 1963.

Glover, Amos. "Diary of Amos Glover." Edited by Harry J. Carmen. http://publications.ohiohistory.org/ohstemplate.cfm?action=dated&page=0044258.html&s. Accessed January 29, 2008.

"Gov. Johnson and the Clergymen of Nashville." *New York Times.* July 4, 1862.

"Gov. Johnston [sic] Among the Nashville Clergymen." *New York Times.* June 30, 1862.

"Guerrillas in Tennessee." *New York Times.* May 7, 1862.

Guthrie, James, et al. *Report of the Kentucky Commissioners to the Late Peace Conference Held at Washington City.* Frankfort, KY: Jno. B. Major, State Printer, 1861.

Guthrie-Caperton Family Papers, 1780–1939. Filson Historical Society, Louisville, Kentucky.

Hall, Eliza Calvert. "Bowling Green and the Civil War." *Filson Club Historical Quarterly.* October 1937.

Hamilton, William Douglas. *Recollections of a Cavalryman of the Civil War after Fifty Years, 1861–1865.* Columbus, Ohio: F.J. Hess Printing Company, 1915.

Hardin County Historical Society. *Who Was Who in Hardin County.* Elizabethtown, KY: Hardin County Historical Society, n.d.

Harp, Beth Chinn. *Torn Asunder: Civil War in Ohio County and the Green River Country.* Georgetown, KY: Kinnersley Press, 2003.

Harp, Lucille. "The L&N Depot at Munfordville." *Hart County Historical Quarterly.* April 1982.

Harrison, Lowell H. *The Civil War in Kentucky.* Lexington: University Press of Kentucky, 1995.

Harrison, Lowell H., and James C. Klotter. *A New History of Kentucky.* Lexington: The University Press of Kentucky, 1997.

"Hart County Landmark Certificates Presentation." *Hart County Historical Quarterly.* October 1974.

Hawkins, Nadin G. "John Hunt Morgan: The Original Hart County Raider." *Hart County Historical Quarterly.* April 1993.

Hess, Earl J. *Banners to the Breeze.* Lincoln: University of Nebraska Press, 2000.

Hibbs, Dixie. *Nelson County: A Portrait of the Civil War.* Charleston, SC: Arcadia Publishing, 1999.

Hood, John Bell. "The Invasion of Tennessee." In *Battles and Leaders of the Civil War: Retreat With Honor.* Edited by Robert Underwood Johnson and Clarence Clough Buel. Edison, NJ: Castle Books, 1995.

Hood, Sam. "General John Bell Hood." *Kentucky's Civil War, 1861–1865.* Edited by Jerlene Rose. Clay City, Kentucky: Back Home in Kentucky, 2005.

Horrall, Spillard F. *History of the 42nd Indiana Volunteers.* Chicago: by the author, 1892.

"James Guthrie Obituary." *Courier-Journal* (Louisville, KY). March 14–15, 1869.

"John Hunt Morgan's Men Called Robbers." *Lebanon Enterprise.* June 27, 1963.

Johnson, Mark W. *That Body of Brave Men: The U.S. Regular Infantry and the Civil War in the West.* Cambridge, MA: Da Capo Press, 2003.

Jones, James B. "A Tale of Two Cities." *North and South.* March 2008.

Jones, Lewis H. Letters. Lancaster County Historical Society, Lancaster, Pennsylvania.

Jones, Mary Josephine. *The Civil War in Hardin County, Kentucky.* Vine Grove, KY: Ancestral Trails Historical Society, 1995.

Journal of the U.S. Senate, March 2, 1865. Century of Lawmaking. www.memory.loc.gov.

K.A.H. "Mars in the Ascendancy." *L&N Magazine.* June 1939.

Kelly, R. M. "Holding Kentucky for the Union." In *Battles and Leaders of the Civil War: The Opening Battles.* Edited by Robert Underwood Johnson and Clarence Clough Buel. Edison, NJ: Castle Books, 1995.

Kerr, Kincaid A. *The Louisville and Nashville Railroad, 1850–1963.* Lexington: University Press of Kentucky, 2000.

Kleber, John E., ed. *The Encyclopedia of Louisville.* Lexington: University Press of Kentucky, 2001.

_____. *The Kentucky Encyclopedia.* Lexington: University Press of Kentucky, 1992.

Klein, Maury. *History of the Louisville and Nashville Railroad.* Lexington: University Press of Kentucky, 2003.

"The Last Hours of the Chicago Convention." *New York Times.* September 4, 1864.

Lee, Dan. *Kentuckian in Blue.* Jefferson, NC: McFarland, 2010.

Lincoln, Abraham. *The Collected Works of Abraham Lincoln, Vol. 5.* Edited by Roy P. Basler. New Brunswick, NJ: Rutgers University Press, 1953.

Livengood, James B. "Civil War Letters." *Hart County Historical Quarterly.* October 1988.

Longacre, Edward G. *A Soldier to the Last: Major General Joseph Wheeler in Blue and Gray.* Washington, D.C.: Potomac Books, 2007.

Lorant, Stefan. *The Presidency: A Pictorial History of Presidential Elections from Washington to Truman.* New York: Macmillan Company, 1952.

Louisville and Nashville Railroad Company Records. University of Louisville Archives and Records Center, Louisville, Kentucky.

Louisville Anzeiger. November 5, 1861.

Magruder, Henry C. *Three Years in the Saddle: The Life and Confession of*

Henry C. Magruder. Utica, KY: McDowell Publications, n.d.

Mallock, Daniel L. "For Want of a Primer. *North and South.* September 2008.

Matthews, William E. "Guerrillas of the Civil War." *Kentucky's Civil War, 1861–1865.* Edited by Jerlene Rose. Clay City: Back Home in Kentucky, 2005.

McBride, W. Stephen. *The Union Occupation of Munfordville, Kentucky, 1861–1865: A Narrative Summary.* Munfordville, KY: Hart County Historical Society, 1999.

McCague, James. *The Cumberland.* New York: Holt, Rinehart and Winston, 1973.

McClure, Alexander K. *Recollections of Half a Century.* Salem, MA: Salem Press, 1902.

McClure, Daniel E. *Two Centuries in Elizabethtown and Hardin County, Kentucky, 1776–1976.* Elizabethtown, KY: Hardin County Historical Society, 1979.

McCook, Alexander McDowell, letter to Gov. William P. Dennison, Nov. 15, 1861. Collection of the Ohio Historical Society, Columbus, Ohio.

McDonough, James Lee. *War in Kentucky: From Shiloh to Perryville.* Knoxville: University of Tennessee Press, 1994.

McDowell, Robert E. *City of Conflict: Louisville in the Civil War, 1861–1865.* Louisville, KY: Louisville Civil War Roundtable, 1962.

McMurtry, R. Gerald. "Funeral of Stephen Alexander Bridwell." Enclosure in a letter to the author, February 1, 1980.

Mears, Hazel. "Bacon Creek and Bonnieville." Bonnieville File. Hart County Historical Society, Munfordville, Kentucky.

"Morgan's Lines Extended a Mile Out From Lebanon." *Lebanon Enterprise.* June 27, 1963.

Morse, Bliss. *The Civil War Diary of Bliss Morse.* Edited by Loren J. Morse. Pittsburg, KS: Pittcraft, 1964.

Myers, Marshall. "The Big Bull is Dead." *Kentucky's Civil War, 1861–1865.* Edited by Jerlene Rose. Clay City: Back Home in Kentucky, 2005.

_____. "Union General Stephen Gano Burbridge: The Most Hated Man in Kentucky." In *Kentucky's Civil War, 1861–1865.* Edited by Jerlene Rose. Clay City: Back Home in Kentucky, 2005.

"Nashville." *Harper's Weekly.* March 8, 1862.

Noe, Kenneth W. *Perryville: This Grand Havoc of Battle.* Lexington: University Press of Kentucky, 2001.

"Our Army in Nashville." *New York Times.* March 1, 1862.

Peake, Michael A. *Indiana's German Sons: A History of the 1st German 32nd Regiment, Indiana Volunteer Infantry.* Indianapolis: Max Kade German-American Center, Indiana University-Purdue University at Indianapolis and Indiana German Heritage Society, 1999.

Pennsylvania Infantry, 78th Regiment. *History of the Seventy-Eighth Pennsylvania Volunteer Infantry.* Pittsburg, PA: Press of the Pittsburgh Printing Company, 1905.

Perret, Geoffrey. *Lincoln's War.* New York: Random House, 2004.

Pontiac. "Affairs in Kentucky." *New York Times.* July 12, 1861.

_____. "The Campaign in Kentucky." *New York Times.* December 27, 1861.

_____. "James Guthrie Speaks Out Again." *New York Times.* December 5, 1861.

Ramage, James A. *Rebel Raider: The Life*

of General John Hunt Morgan. Lexington: University of Kentucky Press, 1986.

_____. "Basil W. Duke: A Military Genius and Tactician Ahead of His Time." In *Kentucky's Civil War, 1861–1865*. Edited by Jerlene Rose. Clay City: Back Home in Kentucky, 2005.

"The Rebels in Kentucky: Defeat of the Guerrillas Under John Morgan." *New York Times*. December 30, 1862.

"Redstick." "Army Correspondence." *Fremont Journal*, November 22, 1861. Ohio Historical Society, Columbus, Ohio.

Robinson, William C. Letter of October 13, 1861. Abraham Lincoln Presidential Library. Springfield, Illinois.

Roland, Charles P. "Albert Sidney Johnston." In *Kentucky's Civil War, 1861–1865*. Edited by Jerlene Rose. Clay City: Back Home in Kentucky, 2005.

Sandberg, Carl. *Abraham Lincoln: The War Years, Volumes I and III*. New York: Charles Scribner's Sons, 1948.

Second Kentucky Cavalry Files. Kentucky Military History Museum, Frankfort, Kentucky.

Sherman, William T. *Memoirs of General W. T. Sherman*. New York: Library of America, 1990.

Sickles, John. *The Legends of Sue Mundy and One Armed Berry: Confederate Guerrillas*. Merrillville, IN: Heritage Press, 1999.

Speed, Thomas. *The Union Regiments of Kentucky*. Louisville, KY: Courier-Journal Job Printing Company, 1897.

Speed Family Papers — Farmington Collection. Filson Historical Society, Louisville, Kentucky.

Spiegel, Anna Ruth. "Public Career of James Guthrie (1792–1869)." M.A. diss., University of Louisville, 1940. http://digitallibrary.louisville.edu/u?/etd,448.

Stephens, Tom. "The Helms of Hardin County: John LaRue Helm." *News-Enterprise* (Elizabethtown, KY), July 19, 1993.

Stickles, Arndt M. *Simon Boliver Buckner: Borderland Knight*. Chapel Hill: University of North Carolina Press, 1940.

Stone, Henry. "Repelling Hood's Invasion of Tennessee." In *Battles and Leaders of the Civil War: Retreat With Honor*. Edited by Robert Underwood Johnson and Clarence Clough Buel. Edison, NJ: Castle Books, 1995.

Tarrant, Sergeant E. *The Wild Riders of the First Kentucky Cavalry*. Lexington, KY: Henry Clay Press, 1969.

Thirty-Third Kentucky Infantry Files. Kentucky Military History Museum, Frankfort, Kentucky.

Tilford, John E. "The Delicate Track — The L&N's Role in the Civil War." *Filson Club Historical Quarterly*. July 1962.

_____. "The Three Railroad Careers of Albert Fink." *Filson Club Historical Quarterly*. October 1959.

Trapasso, L. Michael. "Defenses Around the Confederate Capital: The Civil War in Bowling Green, Kentucky." In *Kentucky's Civil War, 1861–1865*. Edited by Jerlene Rose. Clay City, KY: Back Home in Kentucky, 2005.

Trefousse, Hans L. *Andrew Johnson: A Biography*. New York: W.W. Norton, 1989.

Twenty-Seventh Kentucky Infantry Files. Kentucky Military History Museum, Frankfort, Kentucky.

Twenty-Sixth Kentucky Infantry Files. Kentucky Military History Museum, Frankfort, Kentucky.

Underwood, Josie. *Josie Underwood's Civil War Diary*. Edited by Nancy Disher Baird. Lexington: University Press of Kentucky, 2009.

"The Union Banquet." *Louisville Daily Journal.* January 25, 1860.

"Unionism in Tennessee." *New York Times.* June 9, 1862.

U.S. War Department. *The War of the Rebellion: A Compilation of the Official Records of the Union and Confederate Armies.* 129 Volumes. Washington, D.C.: Government Printing Office, 1880–1901.

Waldo, James. "A Civil War Soldier's Letter." *Hart County Historical Quarterly.* January 1975.

"The War in Kentucky." *Harper's Weekly*, October 12, 1861.

Warner, Ezra J. *Generals in Blue.* Baton Rouge: Louisiana State University Press, 1992.

Watkins, Sam. *Company Aytch.* New York: Plume, 1999.

Weber, Thomas. *The Northern Railroads in the Civil War, 1861–1865.* Bloomington: University of Indiana Press, 1999.

West, Dean. "We Will Have to Whip These Fellows Sure Enough." *North and South.* September 2008.

Wheeler, Joseph. "Bragg's Invasion of Kentucky." In *Battles and Leaders of the Civil War: The Opening Battles.* Edited by Robert Underwood Johnson and Clarence Clough Buel. Edison, NJ: Castle Books, 1995.

Widney, Lyman S. *Campaigning With Uncle Billy.* Edited by Robert I. Girandi. Victoria, BC: Trafford Publishing, 2008.

_____. Diary. Diary Accounts File. Hart County Historical Society, Munfordville, Kentucky.

Wiley, Bell Irwin. *Embattled Confederates.* New York: Bonanza Books, 1964.

_____. *The Life of Billy Yank.* Baton Rouge: Louisiana State University Press, 1971.

Wilkins, David Matthew. "'The Parents of Progressive Improvement': Railroads and Public Policy in Kentucky, 1829–1900." M.A. thesis, University of Louisville, 2004. http://digitallibrary.louisville.edu/u?/479.

Wills, Brian Steel. *A Battle from the Start: The Life of Nathan Bedford Forrest.* New York: HarperCollins, 1992.

Wimp, Carolyn, ed. *Hardin County Kentucky Newspaper Abstracts, 1905 to 1907.* Vine Grove, KY: Ancestral Trails Historical Society, 2002.

Winn-Cook Family Papers. Filson Historical Society, Louisville, Kentucky.

Winstead, Guy. "The Civil War through the Eyes of Samuel Haycraft." *Hardin County Independent.* April 13, 1988.

_____. "James Montgomery wrote eyewitness account of Morgan's attack." *Hardin County Independent.* October 3, 1991.

Works Progress Administration. *Military History of Kentucky.* Edited by F. Kevin Simon. Frankfort: Adjutant General of Kentucky, 1939.

Wright, Steven L., ed. *Kentucky Soldiers and Their Regiments in the Civil War: Abstracted from the Pages of Contemporary Kentucky Newspapers.* 5 volumes. Published by the editor, 2009.

Wyeth, John Allan. *With Sabre and Scalpel: The Autobiography of a Soldier and Surgeon.* New York: Harper and Bros., 1914.

Young, Bennett. *Confederate Wizards of the Saddle.* Nashville, TN: J.S. Sanders and Company, 1999.

Index

Acworth, Georgia 168
Adair, John 19
Adams, Silas 95–96
Adams Express Company 6, 53
Albany, Kentucky 129
Alexandria, Tennessee 111, 129
Allatoona, Georgia 168
Allen, Robert 163
Allensville, Kentucky 186
American Colonization Society 20
Ammen, Jacob 82, 146
Anderson, John B. 142, 163
Anderson, Robert 26, 30, 31, 33
Anderson, William ("Bloody Bill") 12
Apache Indians 39
Appalachian Mountains 8, 23, 36, 138
Appomattox, Virginia 186
Arkansas Post, Arkansas 146
Army of Northern Virginia (CSA) 166
Army of Tennessee (CSA) 164, 167, 172, 179
Army of the Cumberland (USA) 5, 7, 34, 35, 107, 141
Army of the Mississippi (CSA) 76, 77, 82, 85, 89, 91, 97, 102
Army of the Ohio (USA) 5, 48, 56, 60, 68, 69, 77, 78, 79, 90, 91, 94, 97, 98, 99, 100, 101, 107, 169, 175, 176, 177
Army of the Potomac (USA) 6, 142, 161
Army of the Tennessee (USA) 175
Athens, Alabama 69
Atkinson, H.N. 73
Atlanta, Georgia 11, 12, 18, 154, 159, 163, 164, 165, 167, 174, 180
Auburn, Kentucky 158

Bacon Creek, Kentucky 28, 30, 34, 35, 44, 50, 94, 107, 112, 113, 118, 125
Ballard Rifles 184
Baltimore and Ohio RR 7, 12, 15,
Baltimore, Maryland 21

Bank of Tennessee 59
Barbourville, Kentucky 76
Bardstown Branch 14, 19, 101, 131, 145
Bardstown Junction 132, 133, 182
Bardstown, Kentucky 14, 17, 94, 95, 97, 102, 105, 119, 127, 131, 145, 157, 182, 183
Barren County, Kentucky 49
Barren River 49, 51, 57
Barren River Bridge (Bowling Green) 52, 53
Bear Wallow, Kentucky 93
Beatty, John 51
Beauregard, P.G.T. 60, 76–77
Beckwith, Amos 163
Bell, John 22, 23
Benjamin, Judah P. 37, 48
Benneson, William H. 119
Benwood, West Virginia 7
Berry, Samuel O. "One-Armed" 181
Big Creek Gap, Tennessee 76
Big Shanty, Georgia 168
Big South Tunnel, Tennessee 15, 71, 72, 107, 108. 109, 110, 111, 117, 138, 165, 176
Big Spring, Kentucky 134
Black Hawk War 36
Bladon Springs, Alabama 77
Blair, Montgomery 122
Bloomfield, Indiana 33
Boone, William P. 71
Booth, John Wilkes 186
Boston, Kentucky 117, 119, 157, 182
Bowling Green, Kentucky 11, 12, 13, 14, 15, 19, 26, 27, 28, 29, 35, 36, 39, 41, 43, 46, 47, 48, 49, 51, 52, 53, 54, 55, 56, 57, 62, 72, 82, 83, 84, 87. 90, 91, 100, 104, 106, 107, 108, 109, 110, 111, 112, 116, 117, 124, 125, 126, 128, 133, 134, 144, 145, 156, 158, 160, 181, 187, 189
Bowman, Ben F. 130
Boyle, Jeremiah 6, 25, 65–66, 67, 68, 98,

207

99, 100, 101, 104, 111, 113, 125, 128, 132, 133, 139, 144, 145, 146, 147
Boyle County, Kentucky 102
Brady and Davis v. the Louisville and Nashville Railroad 24
Bragg, Braxton 5, 7, 76, 77, 78, 82, 84, 85, 86, 88, 89, 91, 92, 93, 94, 95, 97, 98, 100, 103, 106, 111, 121, 125, 127, 128, 141, 142, 160
Bramlette, Thomas E. 147, 148, 152, 160, 180
Brandenburg, Kentucky 133, 134, 181
Breckinridge, John C. 21, 22
Breckinridge, W.C.P. 114, 117, 118
Breckinridge County, Kentucky 134, 172, 184
Brents, J.A. 58
Brice's Crossroads, Mississippi 171
Bridgeport, Alabama 7
Bridwell, Stephen A. 113
Brown, William 28
Brownsville, Kentucky 92
Bruce, Sanders D. 108
Buckner, Henry 48
Buckner, Simon Bolivar 11, 12, 26, 27, 28, 29, 30, 31, 34, 35, 44, 48, 49, 54, 89, 181
Buell, Don Carlos 3, 41, 43, 44, 46, 48, 49, 50, 51, 52, 55, 56, 58, 59, 60, 61, 66, 68, 69, 70, 71, 72, 77, 78, 79, 82, 83, 84, 87, 90, 91, 92, 93, 94, 95, 97, 98, 99, 100, 101, 102, 103, 105, 106, 107, 108, 110
Buell Commission 77, 79, 90
Buena Vista, Mexico 33, 77
Buffington Island, Ohio 135
Bull Run, Virginia 39
Bullitt, Joshua Fry 156, 159, 160, 161
Bullitt County, Kentucky 172, 181, 188
Bullock, Robert 117, 118
Bullock, William F. 16
Burbick, James 136. 137
Burbridge, Stephen G. 146, 147, 148, 152, 153, 154, 155, 157, 160, 166, 180, 185
Burkesville, Kentucky 129
Burnside, Ambrose 5, 129, 132, 137

Cadiz, Kentucky 171
Cairo, Illinois 26
Cairo, Tennessee 75
Caldwell, William B. 190
Calvary, Kentucky 14,
Cameron, Simon 42
Camp Boone, Tennessee 26
Camp Joe Holt, Indiana 25, 31, 34
Camp Muldraugh, Kentucky 32
Camp Nevin, Kentucky 34, 35, 38, 39, 41, 43, 45, 46, 50, 60, 74, 94, 172
Camp Sixth Ward, Kentucky 41
Camp Trousdale, Tennessee 48
Campbellsville, Kentucky 120, 182
Canton, Kentucky 183
Capitol Hill (Nashville) 79

Carpenter, John 191–192
Carthage, Tennessee 82
Cave City, Kentucky 29, 44, 45, 46, 57, 62, 65, 83, 86, 88, 93, 125, 157, 166, 181
Chalmers, James 83, 86, 87, 88
Chancellorsville, Virginia 140
Charleston, South Carolina 21
Chase, Salmon P. 5, 6
Chattahoochee River 164, 167
Chattanooga, Tennessee 5, 6, 7, 18, 67, 69, 72, 76, 78, 142, 163, 164, 171, 175, 180
Cheatham, B.F. 177
Chenault, D.W. 117, 119
Chenoweth, J.Q. 171
Chicago, Illinois 18, 21, 161
Chickamauga, Georgia 5, 142, 167
Chickasaw Bayou, Mississippi 146
Christian County, Kentucky 171
Churchill, Samuel B. 139–140
Churchill Downs (Louisville) 98
Cincinnati, Ohio 18, 66, 100, 104, 110, 111, 132, 134, 135
Clark, Jerome 3, 181, 183, 184, 185, 186
Clarksville, Tennessee 14, 19, 143, 171
Clay, Henry 22
Clear Creek Valley, Kentucky 31
Cleburne, Patrick 170
Cloverport, Kentucky 183
Cofer, Martin 29
Colesburg, Kentucky 117, 124, 172, 183
Columbia, Kentucky 48, 120, 125
Columbia, Tennessee 143
Columbus, Kentucky 26, 36
Comanche Indians 74
Confederate Congress 55
Constitutional Union Party 22
Cooper, Samuel 36, 93
Cooper, Wickliffe 126
Copperheads 161
Corinth, Mississippi 58, 60, 65, 76, 78, 106, 107, 170, 171, 175, 181
Corse, John 168
Corydon, Indiana 133, 134
Couch, Darius 177
Covington, Kentucky 158
Cox, Jacob D. 60
Crab Orchard, Kentucky 67
Craddock, A.G. 90
Crawford, Martin J. 95–96
Crittenden, John J. 22, 41
Crittenden, Thomas L. 65, 82, 91, 97, 100, 101, 102, 103, 107
Crittenden, Thomas T. 41
Cumberland Gap 37, 76
Cumberland River 13, 54, 55, 56, 71, 75, 80, 82, 106, 108, 109, 111, 120, 127, 142, 170, 171, 174, 176, 182
Cundiff, "Old Reverend" Jim 181
Curtis, Samuel 140

Index

"Curtius" 97, 101–102
"C.V.S." 80
Cynthiana, Kentucky 66–67, 182

Dallas, Georgia 168
Dalton, Georgia 168
Dana, Charles A. 5, 6, 141
Danville, Kentucky 100, 102, 104, 138
Davidson County, Tennessee 13,
Davis, Garrett 25, 26, 42
Davis, Jefferson 36, 55, 77, 164, 167
Davis, Jefferson C. 100
Davison, Bill 183, 184
Decatur, Alabama 55
Decherd, Tennessee 78
Democratic Party 20, 21, 22, 139, 155, 161–162, 190
Department of Louisville 99
Department of Missouri 140
Department of Nashville 158
Department of Ohio 43, 99, 106, 154, 158
Department of the Cumberland 26, 33
District of Kentucky 6, 65, 146, 158, 185
District of Middle Tennessee 185
District of Tennessee 143
District of Western Kentucky 14, 158
Doctor's Creek, Kentucky 102
Donaldson, J.L. 163
Douglas, Stephen A. 21, 22, 23
Dripping Springs, Kentucky 91, 145
Driskell, Turney G. 157
Duck River 143
Duke, Basil 31, 74, 112, 113, 114, 118, 119, 135
Duke, Charlton 147
Duke, John 147
Dumont, Ebenezer 58
Dunham, Cyrus 88, 89

Eagle Mill, Kentucky 94
Eddyville, Kentucky 170, 171
Edgefield, Tennessee 13, 15, 54, 56, 73, 107, 108, 109, 174, 189
Edwards, Alec 49
Edwards, Durenda 49
Elizabethtown, Kentucky 14, 28, 29, 31, 34, 35, 94, 95, 96, 97, 102, 105, 107, 113, 114–115, 117, 120, 124, 132, 133, 134, 157, 172, 181, 185
Ellsworth, George A. "Lightning" 63–64, 67, 71, 113, 116, 132
Emancipation Proclamation 151, 152
Enfield Rifles 37, 74, 82, 84, 93, 101, 116
Ewing, Hugh 158
Ezra Church, Georgia 164

Fairleigh, Thomas B. 144–145, 156, 157
Federal Hill Plantation, Kentucky 19
Ferguson, Champ 57, 127
Fink, Albert 15, 44, 45, 50, 72, 107, 189

Finnell, John W. 64
Florence, Alabama 168
Floyd, John B. 49, 54, 55
Foote, Andrew 49
Forrest, Nathan Bedford 55, 64, 69, 70, 77, 108, 165, 169, 171
Fort Allen, Kentucky 117
Fort Boyle, Kentucky 158, 172
Fort Craig, Kentucky 86, 87, 89, 93
Fort DeWolff, Kentucky 158
Fort Donelson, Tennessee 49, 50, 54, 55, 57, 143, 171
Fort Henry, Tennessee 49, 55
Fort Jones, Kentucky 183
Fort Negley, Tennessee 79, 173, 176
Fort Sands, Kentucky 126, 158, 172
Fort Sumter, South Carolina 23, 34
Fort Terrill, Kentucky 158
Fort Underwood, Kentucky 27, 28
Fort Willich, Kentucky 158
Foster, John G. 153
Fountainhead, Tennessee 158
Frankfort, Kentucky 64, 76, 146, 184
Franklin, Kentucky 15, 49, 52, 83, 126, 185
Franklin, Tennessee 169–170, 173, 177
French, Samuel G. 168
Fry, James B. 63, 153

Gainsboro, Tennessee 82
Gallagher Rifles 66
Gallatin, Tennessee 13, 15, 48, 61, 64, 69, 70–72, 73, 74–75, 81, 107, 108, 109, 110, 111, 112, 116, 117, 123, 124, 128, 152, 153, 157, 165, 166
Galt House (Louisville) 30, 98, 100, 107
Georgetown, Kentucky 64, 66, 146
Georgia troops: 3rd Cavalry 95
Germans 45, 46, 51
Gettysburg, Pennsylvania 6, 134, 167
Gilbert, Charles C. 100–101, 103, 107
Gilmer, J.F. 47, 54
Glasgow, Kentucky 48, 63, 82, 83, 84, 91, 112, 116, 120, 185
Glendale, Kentucky 14, 158, 172
Granger, Gordon 126
Granger, Robert S. 108, 113, 150
Grant, Ulysses S. 11, 12, 26, 47, 49, 50, 51, 56, 60, 140, 142, 174–175, 176
Grayson County, Kentucky 157
Great Hog Swindle 180
Green County, Kentucky 50, 132
Green River 14, 15, 28, 33, 35, 44, 86, 89, 92, 93, 120, 130, 171
Green River Bridge (Munfordville) 18, 44, 45, 50, 53, 85, 87, 93
Guild, Joseph C. 61
Guston, Kentucky 184
Guthrie, James: appearance 21; complaints against 68, 121–122, 141, 164; death 192;

early life and education 19; as L&N RR president 1–2, 20, 22–23, 24, 29–30, 42, 43, 53, 54, 62, 68, 69, 104, 106, 109–110, 121–122, 124, 138, 139, 140, 141–142, 143, 159, 160, 163, 164, 166, 189, 190–191, 192; personality 2–3, 20–21 23, 43, 53–54, 109–110, 121–122, 139–140, 141, 159, 164; political career 19, 20, 21–22, 43, 161–162, 185, 189; public services 19, 20, 22, 99
Guthrie, Kentucky 14, 19, 158

Halleck, Henry W. 5, 64, 68, 98, 104, 106, 174, 175
Hambright, Henry A. 108
Hamilton, William D. 150
Hamilton's Ford, Kentucky 116, 117, 118
Hancock, Winfield Scott 36
Hancock County, Kentucky 184
Hanson, Charles S. 130, 131
Hardee, William J. 35, 46, 47, 48, 77, 83, 89
Hardin County, Kentucky 13, 14, 32, 50, 94, 97, 134, 172, 181, 183
Harlan, John 116–117, 118, 119, 120
Harper, Ellis 3, 157, 165, 166, 185
Harper's Weekly 15
Harpeth River 169, 170
Harris, Isham 24, 37, 47, 54
Harrodsburg, Kentucky 64, 103, 182
Hart County, Kentucky 13, 14, 49, 88, 93
Hartford, Kentucky 171–172
Hartsville, Tennessee 72, 111
Hawes, J.M. 28
Hawesville, Kentucky 184
Hayes, Thomas 30
Heffren, Horace H. 73
Helm, John LaRue 14, 15, 19, 20
Henry County, Kentucky 157, 158
Henry Rifles 159
Hickory Flat, Kentucky 128
Hill, Aunt Beck 115
Hindman, Thomas C. 44, 45, 46, 85
Hobson, E.H. 112, 117, 131, 133, 134, 135, 137, 181
Hockensmith, Clark 187
Hodgenville, Kentucky 94, 102
Holt, Joseph 148
Home Guards (Militia) 25, 31, 64, 67, 70, 97, 100, 134, 135, 172, 181, 184
Hood, John Bell 164, 165, 166–170, 171, 172, 173, 174, 175, 176, 177, 178, 180
Hooker, Joseph 7, 140
Hopkinsville, Kentucky 105, 171
Horrall, Spillard 57, 107
Horse Cave, Kentucky 50, 52, 63–64, 83, 93, 181
Hoskins, William A. 116, 120, 121
Howard, Oliver O. 6
Huffman, J.W. 118
Huntsville, Alabama 66, 68

Hutcheson, J.B. 73
Hutchinson, John 112, 113

Illinois troops: 34th Infantry 38, 40, 50; 78th Infantry 116, 119; 91st Infantry 105, 112, 113, 114; 129th Infantry 126, 127
Indiana Legislature 20, 33
Indiana troops: 13th Artillery 85, 165, 166; 22nd Artillery 131; 2nd Cavalry 95, 96; 6th Infantry 35, 41; 17th Infantry 85; 30th Infantry 35; 32nd Infantry 39, 44–46; 38th Infantry 35; 39th Infantry 35, 40, 46; 42nd Infantry 57, 107; 50th Infantry 73; 67th Infantry 85, 86; 71st Infantry 115; 74th Infantry 85; 89th Infantry 85, 86
Indianapolis, Indiana 7, 134
Irish 14

Jackson, Andrew 84
Jackson, Mississippi 12
James, J.A. 113
Jefferson County, Kentucky 25, 172
Jeffersonville, Indiana 34, 133, 163, 164
Jeffersonville, Madison, & Indianapolis Railroad 7
Jessee, George M. 157–158
John (African American scout) 40–41
Johnson, Adam R. 112, 113
Johnson, Andrew 2, 58–59, 77–79, 82–83, 84, 91, 142, 143, 149, 150, 174
Johnson, George W. 47
Johnson, Richard W. 44, 74–75
Johnson's Island, Ohio 171
Johnsonville, Tennessee 143
Johnston, Albert Sidney 35, 36–37, 46, 47, 48, 49, 54, 55, 74, 76, 77, 94, 181
Johnston, Joseph E. 160, 164, 167
Jones, Lewis H. 40
Judah, Henry 128, 131, 132, 134, 135
Justin, Edsall, and Hawley 14

Kennesaw Mountain, Georgia 164, 168
Kennett, John 95, 96
Kentucky Institution for the Education of the Blind 104–105
Kentucky Legislature 12, 20, 25, 34, 153, 185
Kentucky Military Institute 146
Kentucky Troops (CSA): 1st Brigade (The Orphan Brigade) 29, 48; 2nd Cavalry 62; 2nd Infantry 30; 6th Infantry 29
Kentucky Troops (USA): 1st Artillery 35, 44; 1st Cavalry 57, 58, 95, 96; 2nd Cavalry 35, 40, 66; 3rd Cavalry 131, 153; 7th Cavalry 67; 8th Cavalry 131; 9th Cavalry 131; 12th Cavalry 117, 131; 13th Cavalry 157; 5th Infantry 34; 6th Infantry 35, 41; 13th Infantry 117; 18th Infantry 67; 20th Infantry 130; 26th Infantry 144, 146, 184;

27th Infantry 132, 153; 28th Infantry 71; 33rd Infantry 85; 48th Mtd. Infantry 157
Key, Alex 44
Know-Nothing Party 34
Knoxville, Tennessee 5, 63, 67, 75

LaFayette, Georgia 168
LaRue County, Kentucky 132
Lawrence, Kansas 183
Lebanon, Kentucky 14, 17, 47, 63, 64, 104, 106, 107, 116, 120, 121, 124, 127, 130, 131, 133, 157, 182, 185, 186
Lebanon Branch 19, 63, 95, 122, 138, 143, 145, 182, 183, 190
Lebanon Junction, Kentucky 13, 14, 30, 31, 64, 119, 172, 182, 183
Lebanon, Tennessee 127
Lee, Phillip Lightfoot 30, 34
Lee, Robert E. 6, 11, 12, 36, 74, 140, 174, 175, 186
Lee, Stephen D. 177, 178, 179
Leitchfield, Kentucky 105, 134, 172
Lewis, Joseph H. 29
Lewis, J.P. 184, 186
Lexington, Kentucky 38, 76, 92, 105, 154
Lincoln, Abraham 5, 6, 21, 22, 23, 29, 42–43, 58, 59, 64, 66, 98–99, 105, 106, 107, 122, 139, 140, 141, 152, 154–155, 161, 165, 180, 186
Lincoln County, Kentucky 33
Little South Tunnel, Tennessee 15, 71
Liverpool, England 37,
Livingston, Tennessee 67
Logan County, Kentucky 14, 146
London, Kentucky 76, 106
Longstreet, James 166, 167
Lookout Mountain, Tennessee 5, 7
Loomis, Cyrus 51
Louisville and Nashville Turnpike 34, 50, 51, 56, 85, 86, 93, 94, 102, 114
The *Louisville Anzeiger* 41
The *Louisville Courier-Journal* 192
The *Louisville Daily Democrat* 187
The *Louisville Daily Journal* 16, 35, 65, 67, 109, 128, 135, 145, 155, 180, 182, 184, 186, 187, 188
Louisville, Kentucky 7, 13, 14, 15, 16, 17, 18, 19 20, 21, 23, 25, 26, 30, 31, 32, 33, 34, 35, 39, 41, 43, 48, 58, 59, 62, 63, 65, 66, 68, 78, 83, 85, 88, 89, 91, 92, 94, 95, 96, 97–98, 100, 101, 104, 105, 107, 109, 110, 111, 113, 115, 122, 124, 129, 132, 133, 135, 138, 140, 141, 145, 148, 149, 150, 151, 153, 155, 156, 157, 162, 163, 164, 167, 172, 174, 180, 182, 184, 185, 186, 189, 190, 192
Louisville Military Prison 185, 187
Louisville Provost Guard 85
Lovejoy, George E. 40
Lyon, Hylan B. 170–173, 183

MacFeely, Robert 68
Madisonville, Kentucky 171
Magoffin, Beriah 25, 29
Magruder, Henry C. 3, 130, 181–185, 186, 187–188
Mallory, Robert 154–155
Mammoth Cave, Kentucky 18, 93
Manson, Mahlon 112
Marion, Bill 181, 185, 186
Marion County, Kentucky 14
Matson, Courtland 116
Matthews, Stanley 58
Mattingly, Ignatius 144
Maxwell, Cicero 144
McAlester, Miles D. 128
McClellan, George B. 46, 48, 56, 91, 107, 155, 161–162
McCook, Alexander McDowell 35, 38, 39, 41, 43, 44, 46, 49, 50, 51, 56, 57, 79, 82, 85, 86, 95, 100, 101, 102, 103, 107, 108
McCook, Edward M. 95, 96, 97, 171
McDowell, Belle 115
McLellan, George W. 122
McMinnville, Tennessee 69, 77, 143
McNeill, John H. 12
Meade, George G. 6
Meade County, Kentucky 133, 134, 172, 183, 186
Meigs, Montgomery 190
Memphis & Charleston Railroad 5, 68, 69
Memphis & Ohio Railroad 19, 23
Memphis Branch 26, 51, 105, 110, 122, 158, 185, 186
Memphis, Tennessee 15, 19, 20, 161
Metcalf, Henry 183, 184, 186
Mexican War 33, 36, 77
Michigan troops: 11th Artillery 130; 2nd Cavalry 112; 8th Cavalry 130; 9th Cavalry 130, 157; 25th Infantry 130
Midway, Kentucky 64
Mill Springs, Kentucky 48
Miller, J.F. 58, 70, 71, 72, 73, 77, 79
Miller, Washington 90
The *Minnetonka* 56
Missionary Ridge, Tennessee 5
Mississippi River 19, 26
Missouri troops: 1st Infantry 47, 55
Mitchel, Ormsby M. 50, 51, 52, 56
Mitchell, Robert B. 128
Mitchellville, Tennessee 15, 81, 108, 127, 157
Mobile, Alabama 77
Mobile & Ohio Railroad 23
Monterrey, Mexico 36
Montgomery, James 115
Montgomery, Alabama 12
Monticello, Kentucky 67
Moody, Granville 82–83
Moore, Orlando H. 130
Morgan, Calvin 130

Morgan, Charelton H. 131, 135
Morgan, John Hunt 31, 38, 44, 55, 56, 59, 60–65, 66–67, 68, 70, 71–72, 73, 74, 75, 76, 77, 84, 85, 93, 105, 108, 111, 111–116, 117–119, 120, 121, 123, 125, 128, 129–137, 138, 143, 154, 181, 182
Morgan, Richard 135
Morgan, Thomas 130, 131
Morgan, Thomas J. 177
Morgantown, Kentucky 92
Morrow, Tom 187
Morton, James St. Clair 70, 79
Morton, Oliver P. 41, 116, 134
Morton, Seymour, and Co. 13, 14
Mosby, John S. 12
Mt. Air Plantation, Kentucky 24, 47, 49
Mt. Washington, Kentucky 101
Muir, P.B. 24
Muldraugh Hill, Kentucky 14, 18, 31, 32, 34, 111, 115–116, 121, 124, 126, 133, 156, 172
Mundy, Sue *see* Clark, Jerome
Munfordville, Kentucky 14, 15, 28, 35, 44, 47, 48, 49, 53, 70, 84–89, 90, 91, 92, 93, 100, 106, 107, 111, 112, 113, 117, 121, 124, 125, 126, 132, 133, 158
Murfreesboro, Tennessee 55, 61, 64, 69, 77, 82, 121, 125
Murrell, John 40

Nashville & Chattanooga Railroad 7, 55, 68, 69, 70, 141, 142, 143
Nashville & Decatur Railroad 68, 70, 143
Nashville & Northwestern Railroad 143, 151
The *Nashville Daily Union* 182
Nashville, Tennessee 6, 7, 13, 15, 16, 17, 23, 25, 36, 37, 41, 48, 49, 51, 53, 54, 55, 56, 57, 58, 59, 62, 63, 68, 69, 70, 71, 72, 73, 77, 78–82, 83, 84, 91, 97, 106, 107, 108, 109, 110, 117, 119, 121, 124, 126, 127, 128, 132, 143, 149, 150, 151, 152, 156, 163, 164, 165, 167, 169, 170, 172, 173, 174, 175, 176–179, 180, 185, 186, 190
Negley, James 84, 108, 109
Nelson, William ("Bull") 25, 56, 82, 99, 100
Nelson County, Kentucky 14, 19, 101, 102, 118, 157, 183
Nevin, David 34, 35, 44
New Albany, Indiana 133
New Haven, Kentucky 95–96, 117, 119, 145, 158, 182, 183
New Hope Church, Georgia 168
New Hope, Kentucky 64, 145, 157, 182
New Market, Kentucky 120
New Orleans, Louisiana 19
The *New York Times* 17, 24, 41, 59, 75, 80, 93, 97, 101, 109, 162
The *New York Tribune* 23, 30

New York troops: 150th Infantry 7
Newport, Kentucky 158
Nicklin, Benjamin S. 165, 166
Nolin, Kentucky 30, 33, 34, 94, 112, 113, 125, 145, 172
Nolin River 34, 35, 38, 44, 74, 172
Northern Missouri Railroad 12

Oakland Race Track (Louisville) 98
Ohio River 7, 13, 17, 20, 25, 26, 34, 50, 58, 92, 97, 129, 133, 134, 135, 138, 143, 148, 164, 168, 174, 176, 181
Ohio State Penitentiary 137
Ohio troops: 9th Cavalry 150; 15th Infantry 35; 49th Infantry 35, 40, 46
Orphan Brigade *see* Kentucky Troops (CSA), 1st Brigade
Overton's Hill (Nashville) 178
Owen County, Kentucky 157
Owensboro, Kentucky 146

Paducah, Kentucky 26, 47
Paine, Eleazer A. 108, 126, 127, 128, 152
Palmer, John M. 109, 180, 187
Paris, Kentucky 67
Paris, Tennessee 183
Patterson, James 40–41
Peace Conference, 1861 22
Peachtree Creek, Georgia 164
Peddicord, _____ (guerrilla) 125
Pendleton, George H. 162
Pendleton, Virgil 118
Pennebaker, Charles D. 132
Pennsylvania troops: 9th Cavalry 66, 157; 78th Infantry 40; 79th Infantry 39, 40, 41
Perryville, Kentucky 97, 102, 103, 104, 105, 106, 109, 123, 125
Petersburg, Virginia 12, 175
Peyton, Samuel O. 172
Pierce, Franklin 20
Pietzuch, Joseph 44
Pillow, Gideon 49, 54
Pilot Knob Bridge, Tennessee 71, 72
Pilot Knob, Tennessee 73
Pittman, Capt. _____ 94
Poe, O.M. 158
Polk, James K. 58
Polk, Leonidas 25, 37, 77, 83, 89
Polk, Sarah Childress 58
Pope, John 140, 141
Portsmouth, Ohio 135
Powell, Lazarus W. 139, 154–155, 185
Prentice, George D. 35, 65, 67, 181, 184
Prewitt's Knob, Kentucky 91, 92
Price, Sterling 12
Prime, Frederick E. 33, 34
Princeton, Kentucky 171
Pulaski, Tennessee 169

Quantrill, William C. 183, 187
Quirk, Tom 112, 114, 118

Red Mill, Kentucky 94
"Redstick" 40
Remington Army Revolvers 187
Republican Party 21, 22
Resaca, Georgia 168
Reynolds, Joseph J. 120
Rich, Lucius L. 27–28, 47, 49, 55
Richardson, Littleton 145
Richland, Tennessee 123, 126–127
Richmond, Kentucky 25, 67, 76, 104, 105
Richmond, Virginia 36, 37, 47, 93, 167
Rifle and Light Infantry Tactics 35
Robertson County, Tennessee 13,
Robinson, James F. 99
Robinson, William C. 38
Rocky Hill, Kentucky 144, 145, 156, 166
Rolling Fork Bridge (Lebanon) 64
Rolling Fork Bridge (New Haven) 117, 119
Rolling Fork River 14, 30, 95, 116, 117, 118, 120
Rosecrans, William S. 3, 5, 6, 107, 108, 109, 110, 111, 116, 121, 125, 126, 128, 130, 140, 141, 142
Rough River 172
Rousseau, Lovell H. 12, 25, 31, 33–34, 35, 41, 44, 50, 77, 82, 83, 90, 103, 143, 149, 150, 154, 158, 165, 185
Rowan, John 19
Rowlett's Station, Kentucky 46, 88
Russellville, Kentucky 47, 48, 51, 109, 185

St. Cloud Hotel (Nashville) 176
St. Cloud's Hill (Nashville) 79
St. Ignatius Catholic Church 14
St. Joseph's College (Bardstown) 102
St. Louis, Missouri 139, 140, 141
Salem, Indiana 134
Salt Creek, Kentucky 31
Salt River 57, 95, 102
Sandersville, Tennessee 73
Savannah, Georgia 11
Schofield, John M. 154, 169–170, 175, 176, 177, 178
Scott, John 42, 86, 87, 88, 93
Scott, Thomas A. 2, 6, 42, 110
Scott County, Kentucky 146
Scottsville, Kentucky 48, 64
Severns Valley, Kentucky 14
Seward, William H. 5, 6, 43
Shackelford, James M. 131, 134, 135, 136–137
Shanks, Quintus Cincinnatus 117
Shelby County, Kentucky 157
Shepherdsville, Kentucky 101, 107, 119, 133, 158
Sheridan, Philip H. 103

Sherman, Ellen 42
Sherman, William T. 3, 5, 11, 30, 31, 32, 33, 39, 41, 42, 43, 142, 146, 159–161, 163, 164, 167, 168, 169, 174
Shiloh, Tennessee 56, 60, 62, 76, 125, 175, 181
Shreve, Leven L. 14
Simpson, J.H. 110, 128
Simpson County, Kentucky 13, 49, 144
Simpsonville, Kentucky 13
Slaughter, Joseph 131
Slocum, Henry W. 6
Smith, A.J. 176, 177, 178
Smith, Edmund Kirby 62, 76, 86, 88, 92, 93, 94, 98, 103, 104, 105, 106, 111, 121
Smith, H.S. 114, 115
Smith, Nat 181
Smoky Row (Nashville) 150
Somerset, Kentucky 67, 138
Sonora, Kentucky 41, 94
Sons of Liberty 145, 156, 157, 159
Sparta, Tennessee 63, 77
Speed, James 42, 98–99
Speed, Joshua 25, 42, 99
Spencer County, Kentucky 187
Spring Hill, Tennessee 169
Springfield, Kentucky 64, 131
Springfield Rifles 71
Staggerwall, George 40
Stanton, Edwin M. 5, 6, 7, 59, 99, 104, 106, 122, 140, 148
Steedman, James B. 176, 177, 178, 179
Stephensburg, Kentucky 157
Stevens, George L. 152
Stevenson, Alabama 69, 72
Stewart, Alexander P. 177
Stewart, Robert R. 96
Stidger, Felix 156
Stones River 121, 125, 180
Sullivan, Thomas W. 131
Sumner County, Tennessee 13
Sunman, Indiana 134
Swords, Thomas 68

Tarrant, Sergeant E. 57, 96
Tebb's Bend, Kentucky 130
Tennessee & Alabama Railroad 55
Tennessee Legislature 13, 54
Tennessee River 37, 49, 60, 68, 106, 143, 170
Tennessee troops: 1st Infantry (CSA) 83, 173; 1st Mtd. Infantry 165
Terry, Benjamin 45, 46
Texas Revolution (1836) 36
Texas troops: 8th Cavalry (CSA) 45–46
Thomas, George H. 3, 26, 47, 48, 56, 57, 79, 82, 84, 95, 102, 107, 108, 142, 169, 170, 172, 173, 174–176, 178, 179, 180
Thompson, Charles R. 178
Three Years in the Saddle 188

Tillson, Davis 158
Tompkinsville, Kentucky 63
Tomppart, Philip, Sr. 186
Tullahoma, Tennessee 129, 140
Turchin, Basil 51
Turner, J.J. 171

Umber, ____ (guerrilla) 144
Underwood, Henry 47
Underwood, Josie 26, 27, 28, 47
Underwood, Lewis 47
Underwood, Warner 27–28, 47, 49
United States Colored troops: 12th Artillery 183; 1st Brigade 177, 178; 2nd Brigade 178; 40th Infantry 165; 101st Infantry 166; 125th Infantry 188
United States House of Representatives 22
United States Marine Hospital (Louisville) 104
United States Military Railroads, Division of the Mississippi 151
United States Senate 22, 185, 192
United States troops: 2nd Cavalry 74; 15th Infantry 35; 16th Infantry 35; 18th Infantry 85
Upton, Kentucky 40, 51, 57, 112–113

Vallandigham, Clement 161–162
Van Dorn, Earl 93, 107
Vernon, Indiana 134
Versailles, Indiana 134
Vicksburg, Mississippi 12, 134, 140, 142, 146, 171
Villard, Henry 30
Vinegar Hill, Kentucky 94
Von Treba, Henry 45

Walker's Station, Kentucky 14
Wampler, J.M. 94

Ward, John H. 153–154
Ward, William T. 154
Warren County, Kentucky 11, 12, 13, 29, 144
Washington, George 23
Washington, D.C. 5, 6, 7, 22, 25, 42, 43, 58, 64, 106, 121, 122, 154, 155, 180, 186
Watkins, Sam 83, 88, 173, 178
Weatherford, J.W. 157
West Point, Kentucky 14, 50, 95
West Point, New York (U.S. Military Academy) 11, 36, 107, 108, 166, 170
West Point, Ohio 136
Western & Atlantic RR 164
Western Freedman's Association 149
Wharton, John 102
Wheeler, Joseph 82, 92, 93, 94, 103, 127, 129, 165
Whig Party 33
Widney, Lyman S. 40, 50
Wilder, John T. 84, 85, 86–89, 90, 91, 92, 93
Willard Hotel (Washington, D.C.) 22
Williams, Press 181
Willich, August 39, 45, 46, 85
Wilson, Cyrus J. 184, 187–188
Wilson, James H. 174, 176, 177, 178
Winchester, Kentucky 67
Winn, Robert 153
Wisconsin troops: 1st Infantry 50; 30th Infantry 184
Wolford, Frank 131, 154–155
Wood, Thomas J. 50, 79, 82, 91, 176, 177, 178, 179
Woodburn, Kentucky 126, 166
Woodson, Anthony L. 50, 86
Wright, Horatio G. 99, 100, 104, 106, 111
Wyeth, John Allen 112, 116

Zollicoffer, Felix 37, 48

www.ingramcontent.com/pod-product-compliance
Ingram Content Group UK Ltd.
Pitfield, Milton Keynes, MK11 3LW, UK
UKHW021833140426
52171PUK00021B/1428